D1583536

90710 000 446 560

GEORGE AND ROBERT STEPHENSON

GEORGE AND ROBERT STEPHENSON

PIONEER INVENTORS AND ENGINEERS

ANTHONY BURTON

PEN & SWORD
TRANSPORT
AN IMPRINT OF PEN & SWORD BOOKS LTD.
YORKSHIRE – PHILADELPHIA

First published in Great Britain in 2020 by
Pen and Sword Transport
An imprint of
Pen & Sword Books Ltd.
Yorkshire - Philadelphia

Copyright © Anthony Burton, 2020

ISBN 978 1 52675 498 1

The right of Anthony Burton to be identified as Author of this work has been
asserted by him in accordance with the Copyright, Designs and Patents Act 1988.

A CIP catalogue record for this book is available from the British Library.

All rights reserved. No part of this book may be reproduced or transmitted in
any form or by any means, electronic or mechanical including photocopying,
recording or by any information storage and retrieval system, without
permission from the Publisher in writing.

Typeset in 10.5/13.5 pt Palatino
Typeset by SJmagic DESIGN SERVICES, India.
Printed and bound in the UK by TJ International Ltd.

Pen & Sword Books Ltd incorporates the Imprints of Pen & Sword Books
Archaeology, Atlas, Aviation, Battleground, Discovery, Family History, History,
Maritime, Military, Naval, Politics, Railways, Select, Transport, True Crime,
Fiction, Frontline Books, Leo Cooper, Praetorian Press, Seaforth Publishing,
Wharncliffe and White Owl.

For a complete list of Pen & Sword titles please contact

PEN & SWORD BOOKS LIMITED
47 Church Street, Barnsley, South Yorkshire, S70 2AS, England
E-mail: enquiries@pen-and-sword.co.uk
Website: www.pen-and-sword.co.uk

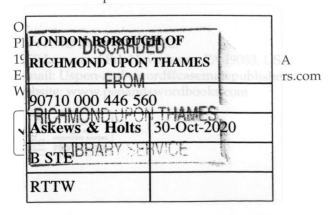
LONDON BOROUGH OF
DISCARDED
RICHMOND UPON THAMES
FROM

90710 000 446 560

RICHMOND UPON THAMES

Askews & Holts	30-Oct-2020
B STE LIBRARY SERVICE	
RTTW	

CONTENTS

PREFACE

My interest in the Stephensons goes back to my childhood years. My mother's family were from Stockton-on-Tees and there was a family tradition that forebears had assisted George Stephenson in constructing the locomotives for the Stockton & Darlington Railway (S & DR). Sadly, like so many family stories, this turned out to be totally wrong: at the time the engines were being constructed the family were living in Leeds and my ancestor was working at Kirkstall Forge. But once my interest had been aroused it never died away, and when I was older I was enthralled by L. T. C. Rolt's masterly biography. I was therefore delighted to accept an invitation to present the BBC TV documentary *The Rainhill Story* that was to follow the construction of the replicas of the three locomotives that took part in the famous trial. It brought new insights into the nature and construction of these early engines and the ingenuity and skill of those who had designed and built the originals. Subsequent research for books on a variety of railway topics, including a biography of Joseph Locke, seemed to indicate that there were new things to say on these two great engineers, George and Robert Stephenson. I hope readers will agree.

Anthony Burton
Stroud
July 2020

Chapter 1

THE COLLIERIES OF THE TYNE

Tyneside in the eighteenth century was dominated by the coal trade. The miners toiled away underground, hacking out the raw material, while ships waited in the river at Newcastle, ready to carry it away, mostly to the most important customer, the City of London. It had been so for centuries. The name Sacoles Lane {Sea Coal Lane} is recorded in a London document of 1228, suggesting that even at this early date ships were bringing coal by sea to the capital from the north-east. But the eighteenth century was a time of change for many industries, and particularly for mining.

In the early days, coal could be got from seams close to the surface, but as these were worked out it became necessary to go ever deeper underground, and that was where a major problem occurred. The miners inevitably reached water and could only carry on working by pumping it out. For a time, this could be done by using pumps powered by waterwheels, but as the mines got deeper, ever more effort was needed to keep them from flooding. A new technology was required, and the man who supplied it was a Dartmouth blacksmith, Thomas Newcomen. A great deal of his trade came from supplying iron tools to the tin and copper miners of south-west England. He inevitably became aware that these miners were facing exactly the same problem as the colliers in other parts of Britain, so he set about creating a new type of pumping engine. It is often referred to as the first successful steam engine, but it is more accurately known as an atmospheric engine. The idea behind its operation is comparatively simple.

The main working part consists of an open-topped cylinder, inside which is a snugly fitting piston. If steam is forced into the cylinder below the piston and then sprayed with cold water, the steam will condense, creating a partial vacuum. Air pressure will then force the piston down. In order to make this useful, the piston is attached by a chain to one end of a massive overhead beam. The pump rods that are actually going to do the work of lifting the water to the surface are hung from the opposite end of the beam. So, when the piston at one end is pushed down, the pump rods at the opposite end are lifted up. Then, pressure in the cylinder being equalised, the weight of the rods will pull them down again. So, the beam rocks to and fro like a giant

The Newcomen engine: the first successful steam pumping engine that made deep mining possible.

seesaw and the pump rods rise and fall. It was a robust, practical machine that was first put to work at a colliery at Dudley in the Black Country in 1712.

It did not take long for news of this powerful machine to spread through all the mining districts of the land. It worked well in that it did the job it was supposed to do. It was, however, extremely inefficient in the sense that the amount of work done was only a tiny fraction of the amount of energy that had to be put into making steam. This, however, was not a major problem on Tyneside. The one commodity they had in plenty was coal, and the furnace used to heat the boiler could be fed with poorest quality fuel that would only fetch a low price in the marketplace. In a report of 1769, quoted in Robert L. Galloway *Annals of Coal Mining and the Coal Trade* (1898) there were then fifty-seven of these engines at work in the collieries around the Tyne. They were listed according to the diameter of the steam cylinder, the smallest being just 20 inches in diameter, but the largest was a massive 73 inches. Providing steam for the smaller engines was not too difficult. The primitive boilers were little better than overgrown kettles and in these cases the boilers were placed right under the cylinder. But the big engines might require two or even three boilers to keep them fed with steam. The fireman who had to keep these engines going had a hard and busy working day.

If the fireman had a tough job, that of the miners below ground was far worse. The mines were dark, gloomy places, for only the feeblest of lights could be used as there was always the danger of an explosion of what was known as 'fire damp' – methane gas. This was particularly prevalent in the deeper pits, yet the only means of light seemed to be the naked flame of the candle. In 1733 a new, allegedly safer, device was introduced, the steel mill: the miner turned a handle to run a flint across the steel to create sparks. Quite why this was considered safe is unknown. There are remarkable stories of miners using the luminescence from putrefying fish as a source of light. Even without the dangers inherent in trying to light the deep mine, there were plenty of other sources of danger. The coal could be loosened by drilling holes into the rock, then packing them with gunpowder and ramming it home – the use of metal rods could actually create sparks that would set off the powder, with fatal results for the miners. Once a seam was opened up, the work was down to muscle power, working with pickaxes to cut the material loose, then shovelling it in carts to be taken from the coal face to the shaft. This was arduous work but the movement of the coal was made far easier when in 1776 a mining engineer, John Curr introduced a system of iron rails, also known as plates, to take four-wheeled wagons or corves. This made such a huge difference that a Tyneside poet Thomas Wilson sang his praises in a dialect poem.

> God bless the man wi' peace and plenty
> That first invented metal plates
> Draw out his years te five tines twenty
> Then slide him though the heavenly gates.

The life of an underground worker was hard and perilous. In the early years few statistics were collected, but records for the north-east covering the period from 1790 to 1840 show 1,480 miners killed in accidents. The figures, however, have nothing to say about the premature deaths from lung disease caused by inhaling coal dust. The sense in the mining community that the underground workers were unique and had to be self-reliant was based on shared dangers and the absolute need to trust those who worked alongside you. The other side of this coin was a wariness and even distrust of those who did not belong to this very tight-knit community.

Once the coal had been taken to the foot of the shaft, there was still the job of raising it to the surface. Until the end of the eighteenth century, the most efficient way of achieving this was with the horse gin. Basically, this consisted of a rotating shaft, with a drum above it. At the top of the shaft was a pivot from which a long beam extended. A horse was harnessed to the other end of the beam and it walked round a circular track. A rope wound round the drum passed out to a pulley. As the horse plodded round its track, the drum turned, and the rope either wound or unwound, pulling up or lowering down the load in the shaft. There were attempts to use steam power, but these were ineffective until James Watt made the great breakthrough. He had recognised the great weakness in the Newcomen engine, that heat was being wasted because the cylinder was being cooled down at every stroke and had to be reheated. His brilliant idea was still to condense the steam, but in a separate vessel. He realised that this would still not be entirely satisfactory if heat could escape from an open-topped cylinder. But if he closed the cylinder off, air pressure would not be available to force the piston down – so he used steam pressure instead. The atmospheric engine was now a true steam engine, and steam could be used to push the piston either up or down in the cylinder – and if he could do that the engine could be adapted to turn a wheel. The steam winding engine was a reality by the end of the century.

As the eighteenth century progressed so the demand for coal became ever greater. The second half of the century saw the start of what we now call the Industrial Revolution. The iron industry was moving from ore smelted in charcoal-fired furnaces to ones using coke as a fuel. The growth of mills and factories saw families moving from the countryside to the towns. The world was changing and the changes depended increasingly on coal. To meet this demand, the coal had to be moved by water: first down the Tyne and then out round the coast. The roads of the eighteenth century were notoriously bad, but the same period saw the development of railed tracks,

George Stephenson's birthplace may look like a substantial, comfortable home, but the family only occupied a small part of it.

known as tramways. The earliest version used wooden rails, later improved by adding a strip of wrought iron along the top to stop the timber being worn away. By 1767, the first iron rails were being cast at the Darby works in Coalbrookdale, Shropshire. The tramways did not look much like the railways we see today. The chaldrons, the specially designed coal wagons, had to be pulled by horses. This meant that the space between the rails had to be kept clear. So instead of the familiar sleepers of today, the tracks were laid with a series of square stone blocks. Each block had a hole drilled into the centre that was fitted with a wooden plug, into which the rails could be spiked. Even the iron rails were themselves different. They were L-shaped in cross section, the upright parts keeping the plain wheels in a straight line. A complex network of these tramways ran from the individual collieries to the river. There they ended in the staithes, wooden platforms from which the coal could be tipped into waiting barges to be taken down river to the sailing ships that would set off round the coast.

Various elements distinguish the mining community at this time, and all had an effect in some way or other on the life of George Stephenson and, to a lesser extent, his son Robert. The obvious ones are the development of railed tracks and steam engines, but the sense of a community that held together in the face of outside forces, which could all too often be hostile to outsiders, was no less important. A useful starting point is to look at just one of those many tramways, the one built in 1748 linking Wylam Colliery to the Tyne at Lemington, close to what is now the western outskirts of Newcastle. In its working days in the eighteenth century, it would have been an exceptionally busy route. Wylam was then sending out 8,500 tons of coal a year and that meant a total of 14,000 chaldrons a year being hauled up and down this line. The rails have long since gone, but the track bed remains as a pleasant public footpath. If you walk this way coming from the direction of the city, you will find as you near Wylam itself a rather ordinary, double-fronted stone cottage right next to the track. This was the birthplace of George Stephenson on 9 June 1781. First impressions suggest that they must have had quite a comfortable home and a pleasant lifestyle, but appearances are deceptive. The Stephensons shared the house with three other families.

The father, Robert Stephenson and his wife, Mabel already had one child – and would go on to have four more, which must have made the apartment on the ground floor almost impossibly crowded. Little is known of their early life. It was said that Robert's father was Scottish and had come down to England as a servant. Robert was certainly in Northumberland when he met his wife, the daughter of a dyer at Ovingham. He originally worked at Walbottle Colliery, but later moved to Wylam as a fireman, responsible for keeping the boiler going on one of the two old pumping engines. His pay was a miserly 12 shillings a week – approximately £100 a week at today's prices, not an income on which many would try and raise a family of six children. Samuel Smiles in his biography of the Stephensons, originally published in 1862 had the opportunity to talk to an old Wylam collier, who knew 'Old Bob' and described him in his strong local accent: 'Geordie's fayther was like a peer o' deals nailed together, an' a bit o' flesh I' th' inside. Mabel was a delicat' boddie, an' very flighty.' He described them as an honest couple, but 'sair hadden doon I' th' world'. It suggests that Robert was once better off, but there is no indication of why the family were now so poor.

Anecdotal evidence suggests that Robert Stephenson had an attractive personality and was particularly fond of birds. It was said that robins always gathered round him when he paused to take a break to eat his meagre lunch, because they knew there would always be crumbs available. This love of nature was one trait he passed on to his son George. They lived beside the rumbling wagonway until George was 8 years old, at which point the coal was worked out and the now very aged engine was simply so much scrap metal. Robert was at once given a new job as fireman at nearby Dewley Burn Colliery and the family moved to a cottage close to the mine. It was only a short distance away but this time they had the luxury of a cottage all to themselves, even if it still consisted of just one room. Inevitably, given the family's finances there was no money available for education – and probably the idea wasn't even seriously considered. If you lived in a mining community it was more or less taken as a matter of course, that in time you would do as others of your family had done before you: become a miner, an occupation for which educational qualifications were considered of little or no importance. There was very little choice in the matter and there were often unwritten agreements between mine owners and other employers in the area that boys from mining families would not be taken on in other occupations. Amazingly, this practice lasted into the twentieth century: I was told by an old miner that his father was desperate to keep him out of the pit and he found a job in a local factory. He had been there for just a week, when the foreman came round and said, 'Your dad's a miner, isn't he?' When the boy agreed, he was handed his papers and told to go and join his father. In the case of young George Stephenson this was never a problem – he was fascinated by the workings of the great machines his father tended and his only wish was to join him. At 8 years old he was not going to find any sort of work at the pit, but he had reached an age where he was expected to make his contribution to the family economy. His working life was about to start.

Chapter 2

GEORGE STEPHENSON'S EARLY CAREER

Young George Stephenson's first job was to look after a small herd of cows belonging to a widow, Grace Aimlie of Dewley Farm. According to Smiles she used to graze them near the tramroad and the boy's job was to keep them clear of the regular traffic. This seems a little odd, since the farm, which still exists, is some 2 miles north of the Wylam track. However, he did certainly get employed to look after the beasts at a wage of 2*d* a day. From the scant information that we have, it seems likely that his main occupation was taking them to the fields and bringing them back, an occupation that left him with some time on his hands. He and a friend Bill Thirlwall seem to have become interested in the new engines that had started to appear. These were the whim engines that were used to wind the coal up from the pit bottom: the very latest technology on view in the coalfields. They set about making their own model out of clay and reeds – a first hint that George had a natural aptitude for things mechanical. The playtime period was short lived. Soon he was given more responsibility on the farm, leading the plough horses and various tasks including the strenuous job of hoeing the turnip field. This was all very tough work for a boy who today would still be at primary school, but to George it was what he expected and he had the satisfaction of having his wages doubled to 4*d* a day. He was making a genuine contribution to the family now and it seems he was quite capable of making a little extra on his own initiative. Smiles has an anecdote of his going into Newcastle's Bigg Market with his sister Nell, who had set her heart on a new bonnet, but she lacked the money, being short by 15*d*. Seeing her disappointment, George told her to wait and disappeared for the rest of the day. By the time he got back, he had the money which he had earned 'for holding the gentlemen's horses'. It does make you wonder why, if he could make 15*d* just holding horses for a day, he was slaving away with a hoe for the rest of the week for just 4*d* a day. But Smiles liked a good tale.

George was no enthusiast for farm work and as soon as he was old enough, he joined his elder brother James as a picker. Inevitably, the coal that came up from the shaft was mixed with a certain amount of stone and dross, and the picker's job was just what the name suggests – to pick out the rubbish. He may not have been an enthusiast for farming, but his time leading horses at the plough proved to have been useful. When a job became available leading the horses at the horse gin he got the post. This was obviously one pit that had not yet converted to the steam winding engine. His wage rose steadily, eventually reaching 8*d* a day. It was tedious work, but he soon accepted a job working the horse gin at Black Callerton. The colliery was 2 miles from the cottage at Dewley Burn, so George had a good long walk to get to work, would spend the day working with the horses, then have the trek home again at the end of the day. But by all accounts he was a strong boy – 'a grit, growing lad', as one who knew him in those days remarked, and keen on sports. He was apparently well known for hammer throwing, which by an odd coincidence was something for which that other famous pioneer of the railway age, Richard Trevithick, had also gained a great reputation. Later he would turn to weight lifting and Smiles records him lifting 840lbs, which seems greatly exaggerated – he would be a modern world champion.

A lot of what we know about George suggests a strong, resourceful personality, perhaps a little stern and even forbidding. Yet there was a sensitive side to him as well. He had inherited a love of natural history from his father. He was particularly fond of blackbirds, and though his behaviour would certainly not be approved of today, his interest was so great that he used to take young birds home with him and allow them to fly around the cottage. One bird, at least, seemed to enjoy the experience, for it returned regularly to take up residence in the cottage. He also kept rabbits, though this was not uncommon in mining families – where they were liable to end up on the table. But George seems to have valued them merely as pets.

The Dewley Burn colliery, like the Wylam, now ran out of profitable coal seams to work, so the family were on the move again, this time to a spot called Jolly's Close near Newburn. There was no improvement in their living conditions, still crowded into a one-room cottage, which must have been increasingly uncomfortable as the children grew older. Robert was now fireman at one of the Duke of Northumberland's pits, while the two older boys, James and George, had been promoted to new jobs as assistant firemen. It was something of a chaotic time in the region, with old pits closing and new ones being opened up, but all happening within a comparatively small area. One could comfortably walk to all three of the Stephenson homes in a day. George was now 15 years old and was promoted as fireman in his own right at the nearby Mid Mill mine. He shared the responsibility with another fireman and as the pumps needed to be kept going day and night, each of the boys had to work a 12-hour shift. George continued to move around the collieries of the region, gradually gaining experience and, more importantly, enjoying a steady rise in salary – on reaching the princely sum of 14 shillings a week, he declared himself 'a made man'. He was, in fact, still a teenager.

Once again, the family found themselves moving from pit to pit, this time to Water Row, close to the Wylam tramway at Newburn, where Robert was taken on in his usual job as fireman, but this time with his 17-year-old son George as plugman. He now had a more responsible job than his father, for he had a vital role to play in ensuring the smooth working of the engine. It was essential that the machinery continued running smoothly without any sudden alterations, which would need correction. One common problem was caused when water levels dropped due to the pumping action. Holes in the pump barrel would then draw in air instead of water. The plugman had to go down to the bottom of the shaft and insert plugs in the holes that were exposed – hence the name. The new job gave George ample opportunity to study the working of the engine and its various parts. He was gaining a practical knowledge of mechanical engineering but was becoming aware that there was more to be learned than he could find out by simply working with one engine on one site. The trouble was that the extra information was written down and he was still illiterate. He might have received help from a more experienced engineer, but that was apparently not an option at the colliery. Later in life he would claim that the Duke of Northumberland's engineer, Robert Hawthorn, had been his been his 'enemy' during his time at Water Row. No details have ever been given as to why George made this statement. It is difficult to believe that Hawthorn, an established engineer with a sound reputation would have given much thought to the teenage boy. But what we do know about George Stephenson, from his later life, is that he was quick to take offence and slow to forgive. The letter in question is quoted in full in Chapter Five.

George began taking lessons from a school teacher who ran a night school at Walbottle. He paid 3*d* a week for rudimentary lessons in reading and writing. In the winter of 1799, a new night school opened at Newburn near the family home. It cost George an extra penny a week, but it was a price well worth paying, for the new teacher Andrew Robertson was also able to teach his class arithmetic. Robert Gray, who attended the same class, said of George that 'he took figures wonderful'. The young scholar made steady

A Boulton and Watt steam engine of a type with which George Stephenson would have been very familiar during his early working life at collieries.

progress and was so keen to learn that he asked the schoolmaster to set him problems that he could work on in his spare time, such as it was. As soon as he had solved one set of problems, he asked for more. When George moved yet again, this time to Black Callerton, the schoolmaster closed the school and followed his star pupil to open a new establishment. It seems to be clear by now as George's teenage years came to an end, that he was unusually hard working and ambitious to learn. There is, however, a question mark over just how much he really had absorbed, as we shall find later. Although eventually he became reasonably literate, he was never completely confident as a letter writer and in his later successful years was more than happy to have a secretary who had a better command of spelling and grammar than he had achieved. But he had acquired the skill he needed to make progress in the world: he could read what others had written and learn from them. He also continued to learn as much as he could about the practical side of running and maintaining a steam engine.

While George was still at the Water Row Pit at Black Callerton, a new whim engine was installed to bring the coal up from the bottom of the pit. Controlling this engine required a different set of skills from those needed for the pumping engine. Once the latter had been started it would keep going automatically until such time as it required adjustments, for example to allow for differences in the water level. The whim engine required constant attention. The corve had to be lowered down the shaft, then after it was filled, the engine would be reversed to bring it to the surface. The man in charge had to rely on an indicator in the engine house to show him where the corve was and his job was to brake the movement on the way down to ensure a safe landing and brake again on the way up to bring the corve to the right level so that it could be wheeled out. Getting everything quite right involved coordination: using hand-operated steam valves to control the speed of the ascent, and a foot pedal to operate a wooden brake on the rim of the flywheel. This was the job of the brakeman, and George's old fireman colleague Bill Coe had been given the job but was prepared to instruct George in the system.

Readers will by now have gathered that Samuel Smiles loved a good story, and especially a story that showed his hero overcoming obstacles and he had just such a story here. In this version, the overseer at the pit, William Locke, objected to these unauthorised lessons. When Coe handed the working to George, Locke stopped the engine and refused to allow work to go on. When the manager demanded to know why, Locke replied, 'Young Stephenson couldn't brake, and, what was more, never would brake, he was so clumsy'. Needless to say, our hero proved Locke wrong. Apart from the invented dialogue, the story seems most unlikely to be true. George continued to bear a grudge against Robert Hawthorn long after he had ceased to have any sort of dealings with him. Yet after Locke had left Northumberland and settled in Barnsley, Stephenson went out of his way to visit him and do him an immense favour by giving his son Joseph a job, as we shall see later.

When George went to Black Callerton in 1801 he was appointed brakeman at the Dolly Pit. With new responsibilities and better pay, he was able to take lodgings of his own at a nearby farm. A local farmer's daughter, Frances (Fanny) Henderson, was employed there as a servant. She was then 31 years old and had probably resigned herself to life as a spinster, but the new lodger was soon showing more than a passingly friendly interest in her. She was described as 'comely' and sweetly spoken, with a gentle character. She was also described as being very sensible, a quality that certainly appealed to the younger man. George was earning what was considered a reasonable pay of up to £1 a week but took in extra work in what little spare time he had, in repairing shoes, and when he had mastered that art began making them as well. One particular job gave him special pleasure – he was asked to mend Fanny's shoes, and when he had finished the job, instead of handing them over straight away he carried them around all day. George was clearly in love. He began putting money away, and when he was confident that his future was bright, he proposed, was accepted and they were married in Newburn Church on 2 November 1802.

George had established a reputation as a good workman and had shown skill in handling the complexity of a whim engine. It was mentioned earlier that George bore a serious grudge against Robert Hawthorn, yet it was Hawthorn who put his name forward for a new job, working as the brakeman at Willington Quay on the north bank of the navigable section of the Tyne, beyond Wallsend and almost opposite Jarrow. Perhaps there really was some antagonism between the established engineer and the young man, and Hawthorn, rather than sacking him, decided to help get him removed to a job several miles away. It was probably the furthest George had ever travelled from home in his life. The ships that carried the coals away from Newcastle rarely had any form of cargo for the return journey, so they had to carry ballast. When they reached the quay, it was emptied out and the ships could proceed up the river to take on their next load of coal. A steam engine had been installed to move the ballast from the holds, after which it was carted off and dumped, forming what would eventually become a sizeable man made hill. It was in front of this mound that George rented a room in a cottage and arrived with his bride. There was no bridal chariot: they came on a farm carthorse, with George in front and Fanny riding pillion behind him.

George soon found he had a young admirer, a teenage apprentice engineer who was working nearby, William Fairbairn, who was to have a highly successful career, becoming president of the Institute of Mechanical Engineers and later to be knighted in recognition of his work. He will appear again in this story, but at this point in the narrative he has an

The small cottage at Willington Quay where George Stephenson set up house with his new wife, Fanny.

importance in being able to give us some account of George's life at this stage in his career. As always, he was keen to take every opportunity to make extra money, often helping in the manual work of shifting ballast from the ship's hold. At times Fairbairn was entrusted with the engine, while George made his extra pennies. In his spare time, he tinkered with making a variety of mechanical models and even believed for a time that he might be able to devise a perpetual motion machine. His version involved attaching tubes of mercury to the outside of a wheel, so that as the wheel turned, the mercury tipped into a lower tube, and so forth. It was doomed, as all such ventures must be that try and defy the basic laws of physics.

But it shows that he had an inquisitive and inventive mind. He was soon to learn a more practical and useful skill.

One day, while George was at work, a chimney caught fire in the cottage. There was no shortage of enthusiastic neighbours to help put out the fire, but in the process everything in the room was soaked and covered in soot. Commentators of the time who bothered to enquire into the living conditions of working-class people were apt to speak rather scornfully of the 'ostentation' of miners' houses and rooms, with rather showy furniture and, in pride of place, a magnificent clock. It was as if it was somehow immoral for poor people to squander their money on such luxuries. But for the families, who had little enough in the way of comforts, these were treasured objects, symbols of success in preserving a decent standard of living. The Stephenson household was no different, but now the splendid eight-day clock appeared to be ruined forever. But George decided that it was after all a mechanical object, that he was familiar with such things and saw no reason why he could not mend the clock himself. His first task was carefully to take it to pieces, then thoroughly to clean all the working parts, before reassembling them exactly as they had been before the accident. The experiment was a success, and the clock ticked again – while George Stephenson had acquired a new skill. He could add to his income as a part-time cobbler by also offering his services mending clocks and watches.

On 16 October 1803 Fanny gave birth to a son, named Robert after his grandfather. In 1804, George was offered a post at Killingworth as brakeman at the West Moor pit. It was here on 11 July 1805 that Fanny gave birth to a daughter, also named Frances, who only survived for three weeks. Fanny herself was suffering from poor health and died in May the following year. Mother and daughter were buried side by side in Long Benton churchyard. Shortly afterwards, George was offered a job as an engine man to look after a Boulton & Watt engine at a textile mill at Melrose in the Scottish borders. The area was developing as an important centre for the woollen industry, but it seems odd that they should bring a man who had worked mainly in collieries all the way to Scotland. George Stephenson did, however, have one connection with the area. His young friend William Fairbairn came from a family in nearby Kelso and it is possible that aware that George was anxious to get away from the scene of two tragedies, he made the suggestion. Whatever the reason for the offer, it was accepted. Young Robert was left in the care of a reliable housekeeper, and the young widower set off for a new phase of his life, north of the border.

Chapter 3

KILLINGWORTH

George Stephenson spent just one year in Scotland, and the only event of any note comes from an anecdote later related by his son. Apparently, water for the works and for the engine's boiler was drawn from a well in sandy ground. The result was that sand was constantly causing a problem, clogging the pumps. It was George who came up with the simple solution of surrounding the bottom of the pump with a tall wooden box, so that the sand only accumulated on the outside and clear water could be drawn from inside the container. He had, in many ways, a successful career in Melrose and managed to save £28, which was a considerable sum of money at that time. But he was not happy, gave in his notice and began the long walk back to Northumberland. En route he arrived, worn out, at a small farm and asked if he could be put up for the night. He was told there was no room and he then asked if he might just be allowed to lie down on the straw of a barn. The farmer and his wife relented and let him into the house. Many years later, when he was famous and wealthy, he found himself in the same area and made a special point of calling back to see the now elderly pair. They had asked for no payment when he had arrived as a foot-weary stranger, but they were more than compensated years later.

Arriving back among his family, he was delighted to see his son again, but horrified to discover that his father had suffered a serious accident. While working on an engine, a workmate had accidentally allowed steam to escape through a valve and Robert had taken the full force right in his face. He was badly burnt and his eyesight was ruined. He was no longer able to work, and in those days there was no question of compensation being paid. The unhappy man was reduced to extreme poverty and had run up debts of around £15. George no doubt had different plans for the money he had saved in Scotland, but now he used more than half of it to pay off his father's debts. He did, however, have enough left to take on a cottage where he could look after his son and his stricken father. The building at West Moor stood beside the Killingworth tramway and when he first moved in it consisted of a single room and a garret. As he grew more prosperous, George was able to extend

GEORGE STEPHENSON, ENGINEER, INVENTOR OF THE LOCOMOTIVE ENGINE
LIVED IN THIS COTTAGE FROM 1805 TO 1823;
HIS FIRST LOCOMOTIVE (BLÜCHER) WAS BUILT AT THE ADJACENT
COLLIERY WAGON SHOPS, AND ON JULY 25TH 1814 WAS PLACED ON THE
WAGONWAY WHICH CROSSES THE ROAD AT THE EAST END OF THIS COTTAGE.

The sundial that George Stephenson attached to his cottage near Killingworth, giving it the name Dial Cottage. It was here his son Robert was born.

the building to create a four-roomed house. He added a sundial at the front that he made himself, and the cottage that still stands and is now known as Dial Cottage has a plaque over the door, describing Stephenson as 'inventor of the locomotive engine', which he most certainly was not. If young Robert was to live with his father, then a new housekeeper would have to be employed. A woman was appointed, but proved unsatisfactory, and George's unmarried sister, Eleanor (Aunt Nelly) agreed to move in and take the job. She proved to be the ideal choice, treating the boy as if he were her own son.

Stephenson was able to work again as brakeman at West Moor colliery, but times were hard. Trade was slack due to the war with France and there was little spare cash around – there was less demand for those skills that the part time cobbler and clock maker had once relied on for extra income. The war brought even worse news: he was called up to join the militia. He certainly did not want to go into the army and the only way out was to pay someone else to go in his place. That ate up the rest of his savings. When he heard that his sister Anne had married and was heading off to America he thought very seriously about joining her. In the event he decided to stay where he was and fortune smiled on him.

The Watt engine and its successors were now installed at many pits, but West Moor still had an atmospheric pumping engine – a later version of the Newcomen, built by John Smeaton. It was not, however, performing at all well. The engine was not George's responsibility but he decided to look it over anyway and quite soon identified the fundamental problem: not enough water was being sprayed into the cylinder to effectively condense all the steam. He realised that the solution was to change the nozzle on the water jet and to raise the water tank to create a greater pressure. But, rather than pass on his findings to anyone, he merely told one of the workmen, Kit Heppel, that he thought that given the chance he could fix the problem inside a week. Heppel passed the information to the head viewer, Ralph Dodds. As the engine was almost useless in its present condition, Dodds agreed to let George have a go – and even agreed that George should select his own team to help with the work.

He put his ideas into practise, doubling the size of the nozzle and raising the injection water tank by a further 10ft. He also arranged to increase the steam pressure from 5lbs per square inch (psi) to 10psi. In effect, this would increase the pressure on the piston and help raise it more efficiently as the pump rods pulled down on the far side of the beam. When it was started up it certainly moved with far more energy than it ever had before, so much so that it seemed in danger of demolishing itself and the engine house. In George's own words it 'came bounce into the house'. The only person who was not alarmed was George himself, for he knew that when it started up there was no load being applied, but as water began to be raised, the motion slowed to a steady beat. Within hours, water levels in the pit were lower than they had ever been and within two days the pit was clear and the men could go to work. Dodd was quite rightly impressed and George was awarded £10 for his efforts. The money was very welcome, but even more important was the recognition by his employers that they had in their midst a man of considerable talents.

The following year 1812, the Killingworth enginewright was killed in an accident and there can be little doubt that the appointment of

Bruce's School in Newcastle where Robert Stephenson received his early education.

George Stephenson to take over the post was a direct result of the good impression he had made in dealing with the atmospheric engine. In fact, he was now so highly thought of that he was appointed to supervise all the engines owned by the Grand Allies. This was a consortium of wealthy colliery owners, whose mines dominated the coalfields of the north-east, so this was work of the first importance. He was paid a salary of £100 a year, but the agreement stipulated that he could also do work for other concerns, provided he fulfilled all his obligations to the Grand Allies. It represented the biggest leap in his fortunes and also opened up opportunities for him to exercise his mechanical inventiveness. He set about increasing the network

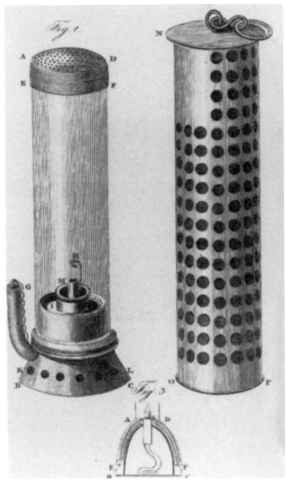

The 'Geordie' safety lamp invented by George Stephenson.

of tramways at the surface and also a system of rope haulage for use underground at Killingworth, worked by three engines, named Geordie, Jimmy and Bobby after members of his family. He was now one of the most respected engineers in the region, and as befitted his new status, he had been presented with a horse to carry him between the different mines under his care.

Now that the family was together again, George was determined his son would have the education that he himself had been denied. Robert was sent first to the village school at Long Benton, over a mile away. As a baby, Robert had been thought a sickly child, but his father considered him quite strong enough to walk there and back every day. As he got stronger, he was called on to help with the work of the pit. A vital tool in use down the pit was the iron pick that became blunted with regular use. As soon as he grew strong enough, the little boy was given picks to take to the blacksmith for sharpening and collected them again on his way home. At the age of 12 he had probably learned all he could at the local school, so George decided the time had come for him to go to Dr Bruce's school in Newcastle, which had a reputation as one of the best academies in the area. He was certainly not expected to walk 10 miles a day to school and the same to come home again in the evening, so George bought him a donkey. It must have been a difficult time for the boy. School children are notorious for unthinking cruelty towards anyone who doesn't conform and Robert was undeniably different. The majority were from what we would now call middle-class families, well dressed and well spoken. Robert was from a mining family, roughly dressed and with a strong local accent. Nevertheless, he was a good scholar and the experience changed him, most notably in that, unlike his father, he lost the Geordie accent.

When he came home from school it seems the father became the pupil and the son the teacher. Here we have conflicting accounts of just how educated George ever became. As we have seen earlier, Smiles recalls talking to those who knew him when he went to night school, who described him as being particularly good at arithmetic. On the other hand, an associate of George's called Summerside recalled being at the cottage and seeing the father's 'cypher book' and noting that he had made very little progress in the subject. It is impossible at this time to say which version is nearer the truth, but it is to some extent irrelevant. George was essentially a practical engineer with very little if any interest in theory. It has to be remembered that engineering in those days made very little use of mathematical and theoretical considerations when building even the most complex structures. A very good example is Thomas Telford's famous suspension bridge over the Menai Straits. There was a beautiful book produced at the time and at the back were equations expressing the stresses and strains and describing the curves of the suspension cables. But these calculations were made after it was completed – they had no part in its planning. Telford worked out the curves and construction details by building a model, not by using equations. George Stephenson was no different – and was, if anything, inclined to dismiss theorists and experts out of hand. For him, practical experience outweighed theory every time and he was dismissive of any theoreticians who disagreed with his own views, even if – one could almost say especially if – the former were right and he was wrong.

One aspect of working in the mines had not changed: the danger from explosions was an ever-present threat. At 11.30am on 25 May 1812, the area round Felling colliery was shaken by a huge explosion, described by a local clergyman, Rev John Hodgson.

A slight trembling, as from an earthquake, was felt for about half a mile around the workings, and the noise of the explosion, though dull, was heard to three or four miles distance, and much resembled an unsteady fire of infantry. Immense quantities of dust and small coal accompanied these blasts and rose high into the air, in the form of an inverted cone.

The heaviest part of the ejected matter, such as corves, pieces of wood, and small coal, fell near the pit but the dust, borne away by a strong west wind, fell in a continuous shower from the pit to a distance of a mile and a half. In the village of Heworth, it caused a darkness like that of early twilight.

The explosion happened just as the shifts were changing and as a result some colliers, near the bottom of the shaft, were able to get out, though three of them later died. But altogether eighty-seven men and boys were known to be underground. Rescue teams were sent down but were unable to reach them because of devastation and gas and tragically all that could be done was to abandon them. How many died instantly in the explosion and how many lingered with injuries but unable to escape will never be known. It was a shocking incident and it resulted in a committee being set up to promote the idea of finding some means of avoiding such tragedies in the future. It was all too obvious what the problem was: gas ignited by a naked flame. One man who came up with a solution is famous for his invention – Sir Humphry Davy, whose safety lamp remained in use as long as deep mines were worked, at first merely to light the work and later when electric lights became used, as an indicator for the presence of gas. What is less well known is that George Stephenson also set to work to try and devise a safety lamp.

While Davy was conducting experiments in his lab, George took an altogether riskier route in his experiments. He held a candle flame up to a 'blower' – a jet of escaping gas. He observed the way in which the flame burned, and designed a lamp where air was only admitted into the bottom of a glass cylinder through a single tube. When methane came into the tube, it forced out the air, depriving the flame of oxygen, so that it was extinguished. This gave an instant warning to the miners that gas was present and they had to evacuate the area. It worked on an entirely different principle from that of the Davy lamp. He received some help from the Killingworth head viewer, Nicholas Wood. Once a lamp had been constructed it had to be tested. Stephenson, Wood and John Moody went down the pit to make the experiment. Moody wrote his own account of what happened.

I accompany'd Mr. Stephenson and Mr. Wood down the A pit at Killingworth on purpose to try Mr. Stephenson's first safety lamp at a blower. But when we came near the blower it was making so much more gas than usual that I told Mr. Stephenson and Mr. Wood if the lamp should deceive him we should be severely burnt, but Mr. Stephenson would insist upon the tryal which was very much against my desire. So Mr. Wood and I went out of the way at a distance and left Mr. Stephenson to himself, but we soon heard that the lamp had answer'd his expectations with safety.

Whether this action was brave, foolhardy or merely the mark of a man with complete confidence in his idea, is open to debate. Later he modified his lamp and in its final version it was similar to the Davy lamp, except that where the latter surrounded the flame with a metal gauze, the Stephenson lamp used a perforated metal cylinder.

Davy had been invited by the committee to make his experiments and when the results proved satisfactory, they awarded him £2,000. The men of the

An artist's impression of Stephenson testing his lamp in a gaseous mine.

north-east felt that their local hero should also receive a substantial award and began raising a subscription. Davy was incensed. To him it was inconceivable that a mere mine engineer could compete with a professional scientist. He wrote to the body raising the money in the north-east deriding the address of thanks to Stephenson 'which every Man of Science in the Kingdom knows to be as false in substance as it is absurd in expression'. Not surprisingly, Stephenson was disgusted and it became the first of what would be a long list of occasions when he found himself up against London experts, a group of men whom he soon came to regard with ever stronger distaste and distrust. When the scientific establishment then went on to suggest that all he had done was make a copy of the Davy lamp, he wrote a thorough and reasoned reply – with more than a little help from his more literate son.

> I observe you have thought proper to insert in the last number of the Philosophical Magazine your opinion that my attempts at safety Tubes and apertures were borrowed from what I have heard of Sir Humphry Davy's researches. You cannot have read the Statement I considered myself called upon to lay before the public, or you would not have questioned my veracity without producing the Evidence that induced you to do so. If the Fire damp was admitted to the flame of a Lamp through a small tube, that it would be consumed by combustion, and that explosion would not pass and communicate with the external Gas, was the Idea I had embraced, as the principle upon which a safety Lamp might be constructed, and which I stated to several persons long before Sir Humphry Davy came into this part of the Country, the plan of such a Lamp was seen by several, and the Lamp itself was in the hands of the manufacturers during the Time he was here, at which period it is not pretended he had formed any correct idea upon which he intended to act. With any *subsequent* private communication between him and Mr. Hodgson, I was not acquainted, nor can it in the slightest degree affect my claim. That I pursued the principle thus discovered and applied, and constructed a Lamp with three Tubes and one with small perforations without knowing that Sir Humphry had adopted the same Idea and without receiving any hint of his experiments is what I solemnly assert. To my statement (which may be procured at Mr. Baldwins) you are bound to give credit unless by the evidence of facts and dates you are able to disprove it. If you are in possession of any, I call upon you to lay them before the public, if not, as editor of a journal, professing to be independent, I trust you will acknowledge that *you* have hastily committed an act of great injustice.

The letter was signed, rather surprisingly 'George Stevenson'. In 1818, George received £1,000 and a suitably engraved silver tankard at a ceremony in Newcastle. For many years his safety lamp, usually known as the Geordie lamp, was preferred in northern collieries to the Davy lamp. It must have been a great satisfaction to have achievements recognised by the men best placed to judge its merits – but it did little to change his mind that he had been the victim of southern prejudices.

There was one other important change in the Killingworth days. Aunt Nelly got married. George decided that he needed a female presence in the house and determined to get married again. Even before he had met Fanny, he had courted Elizabeth Hindmarsh, the daughter of a wealthy farmer at Black Callerton. There was no shortage of encouragement on her side, but her father absolutely forbade the match. His daughter was far too good to marry a common pitman. She declared that if she couldn't marry George then she would remain single and was true to her word. George made no such vow as we know. But now he sought her out again, not as a poor man but with as high a reputation as any in the district. This time the father made no objection and they were married in March 1820. The house at West Moor was once more a family home.

Chapter 4

THE STEAM LOCOMOTIVE

The first attempt to design a vehicle moved by steam power was made by a French former army officer Nicolas Cugnot in 1769. His idea was that it could be used in warfare as a tractor to haul artillery but it was not a great success. It has no real bearing on future developments as the idea was not followed up in France and it is doubtful if any British engineer even heard of the experiment. In Britain, development in the eighteenth century was hampered to a large extent by James Watt's all-embracing patent and he was adamant that there was no future for the use of high pressure steam. The Boulton and Watt agent, William Murdoch, who took responsibility for their engines in Cornwall, built a model steam carriage. However, when news of his experiment reached his employers he was given a clear choice – continue working for us or carry on

The Middleton Colliery Railway, the first commercially successful steam railway: it was here that Stephenson saw his first locomotive.

with your experiments. He opted for the former course and although he played only a minor role in the development of steam power he did earn himself a place in history by developing gas lighting. So now there was just one man showing an interest in the subject, the Cornish engineer, Richard Trevithick.

In the 1790s Trevithick had been able to work out, with the help of a scientific friend, Davies Gilbert, that a steam engine did not have to rely on condensing the steam to create a partial vacuum below the piston, so that steam pressure on the opposite side of the piston could force it to move. If steam pressure was high enough, it alone could do the job of forcing the piston along the cylinder in either direction. He then realised that although in the past the only way to get more work from an engine was to make it bigger, this was no longer essential: you could increase the pressure instead. The engines he designed became known as 'puffers' because they allowed the exhaust steam to puff out into the air instead of being condensed. There was now a logical progression. You could, in fact, make engines small enough and light enough to be moved around from place to place, a job that was made easier by mounting them on wheels. But then a new idea was born: once you put a puffer on wheels, why not use the engine to move itself? Trevithick set about making a road locomotive.

His first experimental model was driven up Camborne Hill in Cornwall on Christmas Eve 1801. It was successful but short lived. On 28 December the engine was given its second outing but ran into a ditch. Trevithick and his friend abandoned it in favour of the local hostelry, but left the fire burning. As they drank, the engine became hotter and hotter until eventually it burst into flames. This was only ever intended as a prototype to see if the system worked and Trevithick next built what can best be described as a steam-powered stagecoach that he took to London in the hope of attracting customers. It was an extraordinary looking device, with a single wheel with tiller steering at the front and an immense pair of drive wheels. The carriage itself sat above the horizontal engine. A replica built by Tom Brogden of Macclesfield was brought down to London to mark the bicentenary. I had the good fortune to travel in it for a trip round Regent's Park and it was a surprisingly smooth and comfortable ride. The nineteenth-century Londoners, however, were less impressed and no orders were ever received. One of the problems was the difficulty in steering the machine, and that was shortly to be solved. The next steam vehicle would run on rails.

The sequence of events is not altogether clear. There is strong evidence that a railway locomotive was built and ran at the famous Darby works at

Coalbrookdale in 1803, but there are no details. We are on much surer ground when we come to the next engine. The South Wales ironmaster Samuel Homfray of Merthyr Tydfil approached Trevithick and asked him to develop a locomotive that was to be capable of carrying out two quite different tasks. It must be able to work as a stationary engine, powering machinery, and also act as a locomotive on the Penydarren tramway. The track had been built to join Homfray's works to the Glamorganshire Canal at Abercynon. It was a success, in that it did what it was designed to do as Trevithick wrote to a friend on 20 February 1804:

> The Tram Waggon have been at work several times. It works exceeding well, and is much more manageable than horses. We have not try to draw but ten tons at a time yet, but I doubt not but we cou'd draw forty tons at a time very well for ten tons stands no chance at all with it.

We know a great deal about this engine. Steam was raised by a return flue boiler. The outer case containing the water was constructed from cast iron. Inside this was a wrought-iron tube bent into a U-shape. The actual firebox was at one end of the tube and from there the hot gases passed to the chimney, situated at the same end. By doubling up the flue, a far greater heating area was presented to the water than with the single flue version. The 8¼-inch diameter cylinder with a 54-inch stroke was placed horizontally above the flue and drove a pair of wheels on one side of the engine through a crosshead and gearing. In motion it is all rather alarming as the crosshead shoots backwards and forwards like a giant trombone slide. On the opposite side of the engine was a large flywheel, an essential element for stationary working. An important feature of the various Trevithick engines was the blast exhaust. The exhaust steam was sent up the chimney, as in the original puffers, which had the effect of increasing the draught to the fire and improving steaming. The effect, however, could not have been very great, given the comparatively crude boiler. Nonetheless, the idea was to prove essential to later developments. In many respects it was a success and the engine's ultimate failure was not due to any design flaws. It was simply too heavy for the brittle cast-iron plates of the tramway. After being used for some time, it was decided that it was uneconomical to keep repairing the track and the engine was taken off its wheels and simply used at the foundry.

Trevithick was convinced, probably quite incorrectly, that if his invention was to get the funds it needed, he would have to interest the money men of London. He set up a circular track near the present site of Euston station and ran a locomotive that he called *Catch-me-who-can*, more or less turning it into a fairground attraction. He did receive one order from the north-east from Christopher Blackett of the Wylam colliery. It was built using Trevithick's design for the Penydarren engine at the Whinfield ironworks at Gateshead. When it was completed, Blackett at once realised that it was far too heavy for the rails of the Wylam tramway and this engine too was destined to be demoted to a stationary role. One result of this series of mishaps was the general downplaying of Trevithick's importance, particularly by engineers of the north of England. Obituaries generally try to say something positive about their subject, but the one in the *Civil Engineers' and Architects' Journal* was scathing, ending with this comment on the Wylam engine that 'like most other things in which he had a hand was so wretchedly made that it was put to other uses'. The writer was clearly not aware that it was not Trevithick who made it. In fact, Blackett seems to have found no fault in the locomotive. He realised there was a problem with the track, had it re-laid with metal rails and in 1808 invited Trevithick to build another locomotive. By this time Trevithick had become disenchanted with locomotives, on which he had spent much time and a deal of money for very little reward, so declined. Shortly afterwards he received an invitation to supply high pressure engines for a silver mine in Peru and set off for South America, for what was intended to be a comparatively short visit. Things turned out very differently as we shall discover later.

It is important to look at Trevithick's role in some detail, because it has real bearing on our assessment of Stephenson's accomplishments. There were many voices raised to praise the latter at the expense of the former and even suggestions that Trevithick had not been responsible for the Wylam engine and that his Penydarren locomotive was a copy. The main evidence came from John Turnbull, who had been an apprentice at Whitfield's and wrote that the engine had actually been built by an engineer called John Steel. He was correct in that Steel was in charge of the construction, but he had been sent to Gateshead from Penydarren, where he had worked on the earlier engine. The design was all Trevithick's.

After this flurry of locomotive building there was a long pause that was only ended due to circumstances brought on by the wars with France. The price of fodder had been steadily rising. John Blenkinsop of the Middleton colliery just outside Leeds was faced with the problem that he needed to send the coal via his tramway to the Aire & Calder Navigation for transport to his customers. Like all the other tramways it relied on horses to do the work and the feed bill was eating away his profits. He knew of the earlier work done

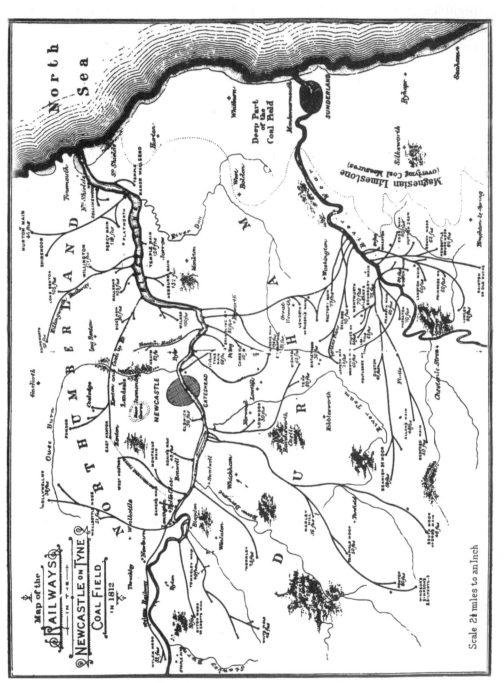

A map showing the network of tramways, connecting collieries to the rivers Tyne and Wear.

by Trevithick and was aware that the problem was not so much with the locomotives as with the track. There were two possible solutions other than re-laying the track: build a lighter engine, but the problem was it might not be powerful enough to do the job, or build an engine with better traction. Blenkinsop opted for the latter course. He realised that one solution would be a rack and pinion system, in which a cog on the engine would engage with a toothed rail – a system that is now familiar from mountain railways. To help with designing the locomotive itself he turned to another Leeds man, the engineer Matthew Murray of Fenton, Murray and Wood, who already had experience building steam engines.

Ideally for a rack and pinion system, the rack rail would be set between the running rails, but at Middleton, the tramway was still being used by horses, so this was impossible. The other option to obtain balanced running would have been to have two rack rails, one to each side, but this was thought to be too expensive, so a single rack was laid. Blenkinsop paid for use of the Trevithick patent but Murray introduced a number of changes. *Catch-me-who-can* had been built with a single, vertical steam cylinder, but Murray used two cylinders, both set vertically in the boiler, with two connecting rods geared to a central shaft to which the rack wheel was attached. This was an improvement in terms of smooth running over the single cylinder version, but in other respects the Blenkinsop-Murray engine fell short of Trevithick's design. For a start, instead of the return flue, there was just a single straight flue that had a much smaller heating surface, and the exhaust steam instead of being turned up the chimney simply blew away into the air. Nevertheless, two engines were built: *Prince Regent* and *Salamanca* that began work in August 1812. They were said to be able to haul a load of 94 tons at a speed of just over 5 mph.

Blenkinsop was keen to capitalise on his success and provided details to interested parties, showing just how economical steam could be. He wrote to the manager of Oxbridge colliery with the following details. Previously haulage had cost £9,653 13s per annum, of which the major expense was feed for eighty-one horses at £50 each. The men needed to look after the horses came somewhat cheaper at just £40 a year. By using locomotives the running cost was reduced to £1,468 4s. Re-laying the track for rack and pinion working had cost £6,247 but that was partly offset by selling off seventy-seven horses for £4,465. Not surprisingly, a lot of colliery managers and others took an interest in this new railway. The most illustrious visitor was a grand duke from Russia, soon to become Czar Nicholas I. He was obviously very impressed, which goes some way to explaining why Russia was one of the first countries to follow Britain's lead in developing a railway system. Another visitor who took detailed notes was the engineer from Killingworth, George Stephenson.

The flurry of interest surrounding the successful running of the Middleton railway produced some orders for the Blenkinsop-Murray system, but other engineers felt that this might be a dead end and began to explore alternatives. George Stephenson was not the first in the fray. Some strange alternatives were tried. William and Edward Chapman patented a system in which the engine hauled itself along a chain, by means of a grooved wheel under the locomotive. It seems the Chapmans mainly intended this system for use on steep slopes. A second locomotive was built in 1814 that dispensed with the chain and reduced the risk of damaging the track by spreading the load over two four-wheeled bogies. All eight wheels were driven through gearing, which would surely have lost a lot of power through friction. A far more extravagant idea was tried by William Brunton, who decided the problem was basically having a locomotive on wheels. So, he built an engine that was moved along by steam-powered legs. Even if it could have been made to work, its fate was sealed at the trials when it exploded, killing the crew.

The most important advance was made by the Wylam colliery engineer, William Hedley. He too had seen the Middleton engine, was impressed by some aspects of its performance but was unconvinced of the need for the rack rail. What he did not have, however, was any information on traction with smooth wheels on a track, so he set about providing them himself. He built a light truck, which could be moved along by men turning a crank. He then steadily increased the load to get an idea of how much power would be needed, and then extrapolated the results to design his first steam locomotive. His first attempt of 1813 was not a great success, with a single flue boiler, just one cylinder and a flywheel. He soon made improvements. The next version had a return flue boiler and two cylinders, this time placed vertically to either side of the boiler. The system he used for transferring the drive from the piston to the wheels was complex. The pistons drove upwards and each was connected to one end of a pivoted beam – a system not unlike that of the familiar beam pumping engines. The far end of the beam was attached to a vertical support by the chimney. Connecting rods from the centres of the two beams drove a central shaft. That was connected to the wheels through gearing. It was an improvement over the Middleton engine in many ways: having the two pistons driving the same shaft, instead of working independently, made for far smoother running, and the return flue boiler was far more efficient. Unfortunately, the old problem at once appeared: the engine was too heavy for the Wylam tramway track. Hedley then borrowed an idea from the Chapmans and mounted the engine on two four-wheeled bogies. The design was sufficiently successful that a total of four locomotives were constructed, two of which survive, *Wylam Dilly* and *Puffing Billy* – though they were later converted to the original four-wheel configuration. The actual construction work was largely carried out with the help of the Wylam blacksmith, Timothy Hackworth, who will play a major role in this story.

The Hedley locomotives puffed their way past Stephenson's birthplace at about the same time as George was beginning work on his own design. With so much activity going on in the north-east it was inevitable that the Grand Allies, the powerful forces that ran Killingworth, would not want to be left behind, and George Stephenson was invited to build a locomotive for the local tramway. His first engine obviously owed a great deal to the notes he had taken on his visit to the Middleton colliery. The engine that was first steamed in 1814 and was later named *Blucher* after the Prussian General Blücher who had led his forces in successful campaigns against Napoleon. It too had cylinders in line and exhausted steam straight into the air. It was carried on six wheels, with the drive transmitted through gearing to the front and rear pair. It does not seem to have been an entirely satisfactory arrangement and according to Nicholas Wood in his *Treatise on Railroads*

An early Killingworth locomotive: the chain drive had replaced the gears of the first engine on the line.

'the communication of the pressure upon the cogwheels produced great noise, and in some parts of the stroke considerable jerks, and when the teeth became all worn created a rattling noise.' The original driver of the engine was George's brother James. It was obviously a troublesome engine and on one trip, hauling a load of 36 tons, it completely gave up and came to a standstill in the most inconvenient spot imaginable, just at the point where the tracks crossed the main turnpike road, completely blocking the way. It was, however, close to James' cottage and he called for his wife to lend them a hand. She was clearly a brawny woman as with her help the engine was moved and sent on its way. In many respects it represented no sort of advance on its predecessors, but it did have one railway first to its credit. All previous locomotives had run on tramway plates, with smooth wheels kept in place by vertical flanges. The Killingworth route was laid with edge rails, so *Blucher* had to be fitted with flanged wheels. In that respect at least it was the forerunner of the modern locomotive.

George was fortunate in that he had the full backing of one of the wealthiest organisations in the region, so when he began experimenting with ways of improving engine performance he had no need to invest his own money in the enterprise. One idea that he did try was to send the exhaust steam up the chimney in the hopes that it would improve the performance, but with his rather primitive boiler the effect was negligible. He then turned attention to the problem caused by those noisy gears and he worked out his ideas with the Head Viewer at Killingworth, Ralph Dodds. The solution was described in two patents of 1815, both starting with the same basic idea. A connecting rod from the piston was to be attached directly to a crank pin cast into the wheel. There remained the problem that each cylinder was now driving one set of wheels quite independently of the other, but they needed to have the motion set at 90° to keep the momentum going. The first impractical solution involved a complex system of cranks. The second had the wheels connected by something quite new, what Wood described as a 'peculiar sort of endless chain'. It is, of course, something with which we are all familiar on modern bicycles, but this was its first practical application in any form of transport. This was the system that was used in the second engine, *Wellington*.

In 1815, William Losh, a partner in the ironworks of Losh, Wilson & Bell in Newcastle, who had been one of his most enthusiastic supporters in the safety lamp controversy, invited George to work for the Company for two days a week at a salary of £100. When the Grand Allies had agreed that Stephenson could work for other interest, they had not perhaps been prepared for such a formal arrangement. They gave their consent, perhaps thinking, quite wisely,

Hetton Colliery with Stephenson locomotives.

that the extra experience could turn out to everyone's advantage, and so it was to prove. Stephenson and Losh were to have a fruitful relationship, for a time at least.

The first problem that they tackled was the one that plagued all early locomotive builders, the damage done to the track by the heavy engines. Chapman had come up with his solution of the bogie, which he had patented. George Stephenson decided to look for an alternative, and the answer he came up with was the so-called 'steam spring'. The axles were held in bearings attached to piston rods from cylinders set right inside the boiler. As steam pressure rose it had a cushioning effect. In the days when the only way to keep a cylinder steam-tight was to pack it with hemp, this must have resulted in a lot of steam escaping, but the system did work and remained in use until the time when technology had advanced to the point when practical metal springs could be manufactured. These early locomotives were all four-wheeled, but in 1817 he supplied a six-wheeled version for the Kilmarnock & Troon plateway, in which all six wheels were connected by chain in a 0-6-0 arrangement.

The next problem they dealt with also involved looking at ways of improving the smooth running of the trains. At this stage, tracks whether of plates or edge rails, were still attached to stone-block sleepers. The general practice was to have the cast-iron rails simply butting on to each other. As the stone blocks were not always stable, they were liable to tilt, which in turn caused the rails to turn so that they were no longer properly aligned. The Stephenson and Losh solution was to create a new type of rail, in which the ends met in lap joints – seen in elevation, the joint looked like the letter S laid on its side. The rails were held in chairs with a slight curve, so that even if the block slipped, the rails could slide along the curve and remain attached and level. It was a considerable improvement, and the whole Killingworth system was re-laid with the new track.

In spite of leading a very hectic engineering life, Stephenson did find time for other activities. Although he was happy to pay someone else to go into the militia in his place, now that the country was at peace he was happy to join up, but clearly did not take his duties very seriously. In December 1819 he described his experiences to an old friend, Joseph Cabery.

> I am sorry to inform you I have become a Soldier – We send a Dozen every day to Mr. Brandling's to learn exercise – & I do assure you we can handle the sword pretty well – Mr. Wood makes & excellent soldier – But I hope we shall never be called to action as I think if any of us be wounded it will be on the <u>Back.</u>
>
> We have about 3 hours drill every day & then plenty to eat & drink at Gosforth house – The Reformed have also been learning these exercise – I do assure you they have alarmed the Gents in our country especially our worthy maters – Lord Strathmore's Cavalry having marched through Winlaton lately, the day following the Reformers of that place marched their Cavalry through in imitation of their Noble Lords – It consisted of 72 Asses with hardy Nailers for their Riders – I think upon the whole Reformers are now diminishing in numbers – We are afraid your books have been miss-carried as it is a Month since they were sent from here accompanied by a letter from your Wife with directions as you requested – Your family are all well & send Their Kind Love to you – Give my Kind respects to Mr. Ashurst – Mr. Jones

The letter is also a reminder that this was a period of considerable upheaval with the Chartists demanding that all men get the vote. The movement was bitterly opposed by the powers that be – an opposition that saw its climax in the infamous massacre of Peterloo in the same year the letter was written. Stephenson seems more amused than worried by the sight of the reformers parodying the upper-class militia.

Earlier in the same letter, George mentioned that they had been having a great problem dealing with fires. This referred to a system George had devised for ventilating mines by allowing flues to pass right down to the lowest level. There was a danger, however, that gases rising up the flues might catch fire in passing through hot coal measures. This is exactly what happened. Soot accumulated in the flues caught alight and that in turn started a fire in the coal seam. Robert added his own footnote to the letter:

> My father has almost wrought me to Death in the Flues but he himself has been two or three times dropt with the choak damp but I took care not to go so far as that – But where I was I think I would not have been in making a joint of Meat Ready.

'Choak' or choke damp is the carbon dioxide released from the burning coal that could prove fatal. It was typical of George Stephenson that he was prepared to risk his life in doing what he felt to be his duty. After experiences such as that, playing at soldiers must have seemed rather good fun.

Stephenson may not have led the way in inventing the steam locomotive, but he was now right at the forefront of development. And, thanks to his secondment to Losh, Wilson & Bell, he was now equally concerned with improving the permanent way. Stephenson was unique in seeing the railways as a whole. This combination of experience in both the civil and mechanical development of the system set him apart.

Although development in the nineteenth century was very much concentrated in the northern coalfields, there was an enthusiastic promoter of railways living in Henley-in-Arden. William James was a land agent and a visionary who saw railways becoming a national transport system, carrying both goods and passengers. At the height of the Napoleonic Wars, he wrote to the Prince Regent suggesting the value of a tramway connecting the two great naval dockyards of Chatham and Portsmouth. He also proposed the construction of a line from Stratford-upon-Avon to London, which would have been a notable achievement, but there was little interest in his ideas. Undeterred, he travelled to the north, where he met Stephenson and Losh. He was hugely impressed by the Stephenson locomotives that he saw in action and was astute enough to see the value of the Stephenson-Losh rail, which he undertook to market in territories south of the Humber, renaming it, rather cheekily, the 'land agent rail'. He was to play an important but ultimately, rather sad part in the next stages of railway development.

Chapter 5

THE STOCKTON AND DARLINGTON RAILWAY

The story of the Stockton & Darlington Railway is one that got off to a notably lethargic start. The Durham coalfield, like its northern neighbour, had developed a system of tramways, mostly running northwards to the River Wear. There was a lack of similar systems running south to Stockton and the River Tees. The facilities at Stockton had recently been improved and it was essential to attract trade to the port. On 18 September 1810 the Recorder Leonard Rainsbeck called a meeting at Stockton Town Hall to discuss what might be done. At this stage there were two alternatives to be considered, building either a canal or a tramway. A committee was duly formed, discussed the issue at length and eventually in 1812 they decided to go for the tramway option and invited the distinguished engineer John Rennie to carry out a survey. Rennie was even more dilatory than the committee and eventually reported back to them three years later. The timing could hardly have been worse: the country was gripped in a financial crisis and several local banks had failed. There was no money available: the report was shelved to gather dust.

In 1818, the financial situation had improved and it was decided to return to the plan for building a railway. They wrote again to Rennie, this time suggesting he worked in collaboration with another engineer, Robert Stevenson, one of the distinguished family famous for building lighthouses all around the Scottish coast – and also notable for an even more famous grandson, Robert Louis Stevenson. Rennie regarded the suggestion as being intolerably insulting. 'I have been accustomed', he wrote scathingly, 'to think for myself in the numerous Publick Works in which I have been engaged, many of them of infinitely greater magnitude and importance than the Darlington railway'. And that was the end of that. Now a brand new problem arose. Where once there had been one committee, now there were two: one representing Stockton-on-Tees, the other Darlington. The former wanted the most direct line from the coalfields to Stockton, and rather than a railway they

A Stockton & Darlington share certificate.

were back again with the canal proposal. A local worthy Christopher Tennant raised the money for a survey in 1818, carried out by George Leather, who had recently worked on improvements to the Aire & Calder Navigation. He came up with a route, which unfortunately meant that the proposed line would by-pass Darlington. The latter group, not surprisingly would have none of that. The Darlington men led by, among others, a notable local business man and Quaker, Edward Pease, now came up with an alternative railway proposal that would indeed connect with Darlington.

The whole subject was debated at some length, and it was agreed eventually that the canal proposal was to be scrapped and the railway was to go ahead, with a compromise being reached on the possible route. So, a new engineer had to be called in, George Overton, who had been responsible for building an extensive network of tramways in South Wales, notably connecting local mines and ironworks to the Brecon & Abergavenny Canal, the remains of many of which can still be traced today. He was also responsible for the Penydarren tramway, on which the pioneering Trevithick locomotive had run. This was far more difficult country for rail building than Durham, with steep hills requiring elaborate systems of inclines worked by stationary engines and a tunnel of considerable length. He was an experienced and also a true railway enthusiast but was also very aware that the Penydarren experiment had ultimately failed and he was far from convinced of the necessity for locomotives. He proceeded to do a sound demolition job on any surviving doubts of the canal faction, with the very telling argument that in serving the industries of South Wales his railway was carrying more goods than the canal and returning a dividend of 7 per cent while the canal owners were making a measly 1 per cent. This was just the argument most likely to appeal to businessmen and he was authorised to start the survey. He brought with him his assistant David Davies. Having accepted the post in August 1818 the two men wasted no time and by March the following year their report was ready and the committee could apply to Parliament for an Act to authorise construction.

A problem now appeared that had plagued many a canal engineer in the past: local landowners who wanted nothing as vulgar as a transport system anywhere near their hallowed land. In this case the opponents were two noble lords – Eldon and Darlington. The principal objection appears to have been that the proposed line ran through a fox covert and would have interfered with the hunting. In the still unreformed Parliament such men still wielded considerable power and the Bill was rejected. The committee were undeterred by this setback. They asked Overton to resurvey the line to try and overcome the objection. He was reluctant, largely because he was unused to such ideas. In South Wales where he had worked before, it was mostly the wealthy landowners who also owned the mines and factories, and simply saw improved transport as a way of increasing their already considerable incomes. But when Robert Stevenson declared himself far too busy to take over the task, Overton was persuaded back to Durham, where he completed his work as quickly and efficiently as before. The new plans were now ready to take back to Parliament. The proposal was for a main line of 26½ miles with five branch lines, making a total of almost 37 miles. Although it was unusually long for a tramway it was still intended as a plateway to be worked for horses. This first Act contained no references to steam engines, though it was envisaged there would be one stationary engine for haulage on an incline.

The opposition remained as implacable as ever. Francis Mewburn, solicitor for the railway company, tells an amusing story that gives us a good idea of just what that meant.

> On approaching the second reading, Lord Darlington received a letter from his Solicitors informing his Lordship the Quakers were much stronger than had been anticipated, and entreating him instantly to post to town. His servant was despatched from Newton House 'cross country with the letter marked 'immediate'. He found his Lord in full chase with a beautiful scent! On receiving the letter his Lordship read it in great vexation, called off the hounds, and all the way home abused the Quakers, whom he never forgave, in the fashionable language of the time. He then swallowed an early dinner, and posted up to town, where he arrived on the morning of the second reading of the Bill.

From the account it is difficult to work out which annoyed him most: having to deal with the railway or losing his fox.

The second reading of the Bill was one of two events that took place in April 1821, one of which was recorded in strictly official and dryly factual form; the other was shrouded in dubious mythology. The first was the Passing of 'An Act for making and maintaining a Railway or Tram-road, from the River Tees, at Stockton, to Wilton Park Colliery'. The Stockton & Darlington Railway Company was authorised to raise £82,000 in £100 shares, with provision to raise a further £90,000 if needed. There were several clauses laying down the charges the Company could make for those using the line and carrying various commodities. At this stage it was envisaged that the line would be run much as the canals were, in which all kinds of carriers would be using it, rather than everything being moved by the Company's own vehicles. There was also a slightly odd provision that allowed any landowners within 5 miles of the railway to lay down their own branch lines. It was all to be very different from the railway system we know today. The more obvious point was that in spite of its name, this was not a line from Stockton to Darlington – they were simply the two largest towns on the route.

At just the time the Act was being approved, a meeting was taking place at Pease's home in Darlington with George Stephenson and Nicholas Wood. The stories surrounding this historic meeting are numerous, but most of them centre round the idea that Wood and Stephenson were mere humble workers facing this important man. One version has them taking off their boots and appearing barefoot to show respect; another has them actually walking barefoot from Newcastle, and the least likely of all is Smiles' account that has Stephenson arriving unannounced as a 'humble pitman' and being shown into the kitchen. George Stephenson has been called many things over the years but rarely if ever described as humble. He had no need to be, for he now had a considerable reputation throughout the north-east and had acquired more experience in laying out railways and building locomotives than any of his contemporaries. The one reliable source is Nicholas Wood himself, who recounted exactly what had happened.

> The fact is, we rode on horseback from Killingworth to Newcastle, a distance of five miles, travelling from thence by coach, thirty-two miles, to Stockton, then walked along the proposed line of railway, twelve miles, from Stockton to Darlington. We had then the interview with Mr. Pease, by appointment, afterwards walked eighteen long miles to Durham, within three miles of which I broke down, but was obliged to proceed, the beds all engaged at the 'Traveller's Rest'.

This all makes a great deal of sense. The two men were well able to afford coach fares, but felt it was necessary to get a good idea of the possible route for the railway before beginning to discuss it with Pease. As the discussion must have gone well they decided to continue to inspect the northern part of the route on foot – a decision that Wood obviously came to regret, as he was almost totally exhausted by the end – a fact that amused the more robust Stephenson. The whole point of the meeting was to persuade Pease that the tramway concept was now outmoded, and that the future lay with steam locomotives running on tracks laid with edge rails. At this stage it has to be remembered Overton was the engineer who had carried out all the early surveys and could reasonably have expected to be taken on as chief engineer in constructing the line. Yet Pease seems to have realised that while he might have had just the right experience for constructing a tramway for horse traffic, he was not the man for a line to be worked by steam locomotives. In any case he wrote to Stephenson and, although the letter has not survived, the latter's reply dated 28 April indicates quite clearly that he was being offered the job.

I have been favoured with your letter of the 20 Inst & am glad to learn that the Bill has passed for the Darlington Rail Way.

I am much obliged by the favourable sentiments you express towards me: & shall be happy if I can be of service in carrying into execution your plans.

From the nature of my engagement here and in the neighbourhood, I could not devote the whole of my time to your Rail Way, but I am willing to undertake a survey & mark out the best line of Way within the limits prescribed by the Act of Parliament and also, to assist the Committee with plans & estimates, and in letting to the different Contractors such work as they might judge it advisable to do by Contract and also to superintend the execution of the Work. And I am induced to recommend the whole being done by Contract under the superintendence of competent persons appointed by the Committee.

Were I to contract for the whole line of Road it would be necessary for me to do so at an advanced price upon the Sub Contractors, and it would also be necessary for the Committee to have some persons to superintend my undertaking. This would be attended by an extra expense, and the Committee would derive no advantage to compensate for it.

If you wish it I will wait upon you at Darlington at an early opportunity when I can enter more particulars as to remuneration &c &c.

Stephenson was indeed very busy at that time. Apart from his work for the Grand Allies and Losh, he was much in demand from other collieries. One of the most important new ventures began in 1819, when the Hetton Coal Company was formed with the idea of opening a new mine near Hetton-le-Hole in Durham. They realised that they would need to export the coal from Sunderland and that they would need a transport system to link the pits to the River Wear. They approached George Stephenson and he set to work to devise a route. The main difficulty came in the shape of a long line of low hills that lay between the mines and the river at Warden Law, near Houghton-Le-Spring. It was decided to overcome the slopes by inclined planes, that involved the erection of two steam engines for haulage up to the summit of Warden Law, over 600ft above sea level. As the route was only used to transport coal to the Wear, the slope on the far side could be worked by self-acting inclines, in which the weight of the loaded wagons could be used to haul the empties to the top. The remainder of the route was to be worked by locomotives. Altogether, five Killingworth type locomotives were supplied by Stephenson in 1822, four of which were named – *Hetton, Tallyho,*

The replica of *Locomotion* at the Beamish Museum.

Star and *David*. Although George laid out the route, the actual construction was begun in March 1821 under the supervision of his brother Robert. It was a single-track line, laid with the new Losh-Stephenson rails. Almost no trace of this line has survived, though one of the original Stephenson-Wood engines that remained in use until the early twentieth century is now in the permanent collection of the National Railway Museum. This almost-forgotten line is actually of considerable historic interest as it was the very first railway to be worked entirely with steam and on which no horses were used.

During this period, George's son Robert had finished with school and had been apprenticed to Nicholas Wood at Killingworth to gain practical experience in the workings of the mine and its transport system. It could very easily have ended disastrously. On one occasion he had accompanied Wood and the Under Viewer, Moodie, to inspect a rock fall in part of the mine. When they reached the spot, Wood clambered up on the stones to assess the damage, using a naked flame, which was by this time usually quite strictly forbidden, as the arrival of the Geordie and Davy lamps had made it unnecessary. Gas had accumulated above the rock fall and there was a sudden, violent explosion. Robert and Moodie at once began to run back towards the shaft but realised that Wood was not following. They turned back to find him stunned but unhurt apart from burnt hands. It was fortunate for all concerned that the explosion was limited to the confined space above the rock fall or the career of Robert Stephenson could have ended there and then. As it was he ended his apprenticeship, was employed for a time at West Moor Colliery but by 1821 was available to help his father with his important project yet, the Stockton & Darlington Railway.

It is not known whether George Overton was told his services were no longer required or whether, on being informed that the committee were opting for a different system, he resigned. We do know he returned to South Wales and continued developing tramroads there including the extensive Rhymney Railway which, ironically, would later be converted to a standard gauge steam railway. Whatever the circumstances, the way was now clear for George Stephenson to take up the post of chief engineer. He had another meeting with Pease in May and spent three days looking over the ground the railway was to traverse before beginning on the actual survey, which was authorised by Pease on 28 July 1821.

In the previous month, however, interesting news had reached George of a new type of rail, invented by John Birkinshaw, an engineer at Michael Longridge's ironworks at Bedlington. He had developed a system for rolling wrought-iron rails. The initial version was I-shaped, roughly 1in wide and

5in deep, but later versions were fish-bellied, available in lengths up to 20ft and weighing 80lbs per yard. They represented a direct challenge to the cast-iron rails patented by Losh and Stephenson, but as the letter to Pease of 28 July 1821 makes clear, they were not being dismissed on that account.

> After carefully examining your favour, I find it impossible to form an accurate idea of what such a survey would cost, as not only the old line must be gone over, but all the other deviating parts, which will be equal to a double survey, and, indeed it must be done in a very different manner from your former one, so as to enable me to make a correct measurement of all the cuts and batteries on the whole one. It would, I think, occupy me at least five weeks. My charge shall include all necessary assistance for the accomplishment of the survey, estimates of the expense of cuts and batteries [embankments] on the different projected lines, together with all remarks, reports, &c., of the same. Also the comparative cost of malleable iron and cast-iron rails, winning and preparing the blocks of stone, and all materials wanted to complete the line. I could not do this for less than £140, allowing me to be moderately paid. I assure you, in completing the undertaking, I will act with that economy which would influence me if the whole of the work was my own.

George Stephenson asked Pease to recommend an assistant who knew the country: there were still landowners whose grounds would need to be either appropriated or by-passed along the route. John Dixon was appointed as that assistant. His connection with the area went right back to the 1760s when his father, George Dixon, had been involved in surveying the same country for a possible canal – a scheme that never materialised. Shortly afterwards, George's son Robert was added to the team as an assistant surveyor. He had not yet ended his three-year apprenticeship, but Nicholas Wood was persuaded to let him go. Possibly the father had been alarmed by the narrow escape from the explosion down the pit or was worried about the young man's health. He was not robust and working underground was hardly going to benefit his wellbeing. Whatever the reason, it marked a turning point in his career.

Surveying at this time had to depend entirely on work on the ground, for there were no useful maps to refer to. The Ordnance Survey had begun mapping the whole country at the end of the eighteenth century but had not yet reached the north of England. One of the essentials was an accurate measurement of heights along the line, using a theodolite since, as Stephenson explained in a letter to William James, there were limits to the slopes that a locomotive could cope with.

> I would not recommend my Locomotive Engines to travel on a line that ascends or descends more than 3/16 when there is a load both ways, but if the load is always passing on a descending line the Engines would return with the empty wagons up an ascent of ½ inch per yard, or in a short distance from 5/8 to 6/8 per yard. The above is within the limits at which my Engines will work, but it is my wish to state it below its powers.

It was also found to be necessary to smooth out some of the more extravagant curves that appeared in the original Overton plan. The actual survey began on 14 October 1821 when the crops had all been gathered in, and the survey team could cross the fields without causing damage. The weather was fine, the team enthusiastic and by the end of the month the work was completed. The job of surveying the 4½-mile long Haggars Leases branch was entrusted to the young Robert Stephenson, and the printed plans were the very first to bear the acknowledgement to 'Robert Stephenson Engineer'.

The Stockton & Darlington is rightly hailed as the first public railway to be worked by steam locomotives. But at this stage although its public status was written into the Act of Parliament, that same Act made no mention of locomotives. In many ways, it remained a colliery line, mostly distinguished by its length, and in other respects it also had more in common with the early lines than with later railways. The rails were still laid on sleeper blocks, mainly familiar stone blocks from a nearby quarry and partly wooden, using seasoned timber from a ship-breaking yard. Stephenson, however, had by this time been convinced of the superiority of the wrought-iron rails and recommended their use. When eventually the committee came to consider the question, they looked at tenders for both types of rail. Michael Longridge offered wrought-iron Birkinshaw rails at a price of £15 per ton. The tender for cast iron was £6 15s per ton, but as the weight of the wrought-iron rails was more or less half that of the cast iron of the same length, price was not the deciding factor. Initially it was decided to lay two-thirds of the track with wrought iron and the rest with cast iron, but that was rapidly changed and the whole track, apart from passing loops, was to be laid with wrought iron. Losh was furious at the loss of such valuable business and blamed his old partner for recommending the rival system. From his point of view, it was treacherous behaviour, but Stephenson was looking to the future and his choice was entirely rational. Losh it seems was so disgusted that he did not even bother to tender for the cast-iron sections and the work went to an ironworks in South Wales.

Although the line was far longer than the Hetton Colliery railway, Stephenson faced a similar problem: hills running right across the proposed line. And he went for precisely the same solution: inclined planes, partly worked by stationary steam engines, partly self-acting. There were four inclines altogether, climbing either side of the ridges at Brusselton and Etherley. The former were the more impressive – the western incline was 1,960 yards long with a total rise of 150ft; the eastern, 880 yards long with a 90ft rise. As originally built each was worked by a pair of 30-horsepower steam engines driving a single winding drum, which was soon found to cause needless delays, and a second drum was later added. The remains at Brusselton, with many of the original sleeper blocks still in place, can still be seen, roughly half way between Bishop Auckland and the A68 road.

The route was carefully thought through. Overton's original had required material to be brought in to construct embankments. Stephenson followed the long-established practice of the canal builders of using the spoil from cuttings to build up the banks – the process known as 'cut and fill'. He also devised the line south of Darlington to be either level or sloping down towards the Tees: the direction in which loaded wagons would be travelling. Engineers at this period always provided estimates that were literally costed down to the last penny. This gave a comforting impression of great accuracy – but only rarely bore much of a resemblance to the actual final costs. However, the Stephenson estimate was £60,987 13s 3d against Overton's of £77,541 18s 8d. This clearly delighted the committee, who at once ordered work to get under way and confirmed George Stephenson as chief engineer at a salary of £600 per annum, with two assistant engineers, John Dixon and Thomas Storey. Stephenson had already made it clear that he could not be available all the time because of other commitments, but he agreed to put in at least one week a month on site. The committee also agreed his suggestion that contracts should be let out in lots of just 1 mile each. This now seems an extraordinary decision. Over the previous sixty years and more of canal construction, a system had been developed in which major contractors took over large sections, bringing to the job both expertise and a body of experienced, tough navvies. The Stockton & Darlington was being handed over to small concerns with no experience and, as it turned out all too frequently, very little aptitude. Perhaps it suited Stephenson to have complete personal control and not to have to compete with powerful contractors, who might have their own ideas on how things should be done. Inevitably, some sub-contractors took responsibility for larger works and this gave rise to another problem, equally common in canal work. The contractors were paid by the amount of work carried out, consequently the quicker they got it done, the less they had to pay out in wages and the greater their profit. Speed tended to take precedence over thoroughness and regulations that might slow things down could be ignored. Thomas Storey wrote a letter full of complaints to Edward Pease:

> When I arrived at home on Friday last I found J. Hastings has been making another break up of the wagons and carrying away walls by running them <u>amain</u> which might as easily been homes. The destruction of the Co's property by their sub-contractor had not been less than 50 or 60£. He refuses to carry on the work any way but that of his own, deposits the earth where and how he pleases, and runs the risk of lives and Property by wilfully running the wagons at improper speed both down the inclines and across the turnpike at Auckland. John Stephenson wishes to be clear of him and has therefore for that purpose given the cut up.

Occasional letters from George Stephenson give some idea of his overall satisfaction with progress. He noted in April 1822 that the quarries were producing plenty of stone blocks and he was arranging for the pins to hold the rails to be made in Stockton. By January the following year he could report that work in the cuttings was proceeding smoothly, was costing rather less than he had expected and that the men involved were making an average of 30 shillings a week. No detail was too small: he deliberated on the relative advantages of hedges and fences to mark the boundary – and decided on the latter as there would be delays waiting for the hedges to grow. The most interesting features were probably the bridges. A conventional three -arched stone bridge, designed by Ignatius Bonomi carried the lines across the River Skerne at Darlington. The one across the River Gaunless was designed by Stephenson himself. It had a total span of 50ft, made up of four wrought-iron girders, each 12½ft long, resting on cast-iron supports. The idea had been criticised by ironmasters at Yorkshire, but Stephenson would have none of it, as he explained in a letter of 19 October 1824;

> The remarks that the Rotherham people have made of the liability of the Cast Iron breaking when cast round the Wrought Iron is very erroneous,

for it is well understood at Newcastle upon Tyne not to have that effect, if a certain allowance is made for the bulk of metal in forming those junctions – I am well aware that none of these people will give themselves the trouble to erect such a Bridge, so long as they have more orders than they can execute, which is the case I suppose with every Ironmaster in the kingdom.

The combination of cast and wrought iron would not always work so perfectly as his son would later find out. The Gaunless Bridge is often referred to as the oldest iron railway bridge in the world, but this is only true if one discounts tramway bridges. A very fine example of a wrought-iron tramway bridge survives at Robertstown in South Wales, built in 1811 to a design by none other than the first surveyor of the S & DR – George Overton. The Gaunless Bridge, however, is certainly the first iron bridge to be crossed by a locomotive.

With the survey completed and work getting under way, George decided that Robert should get another bout of education and paid for him to attend Edinburgh University. At this period the old English universities offered little that would be of any use to Robert, concentrating almost entirely on the Classics and arts, suitable for a career in law or the church but not for a would-be engineer. The great civil engineer John Rennie even went so far as to declare that attending Oxford or Cambridge completely ruined a man for any practical work. The Scottish universities were very different – it was, after all, while working as an instrument maker at Glasgow University that James Watt developed his steam engine. According to Smiles, Robert took the trouble to learn shorthand before attending the university so that he could take down lectures verbatim, probably using the system developed by Samuel Taylor in 1786, the forerunner of the modern Pitman shorthand. He attended lectures in chemistry and 'natural philosophy' – what we would now simply call 'science'. He also became interested in what was then the very new and exciting study of geology, which was changing the way scientists perceived the world. The highlight of his time at Edinburgh was a geological field trip down the Great Glen, which included a journey on the newly opened Caledonian Canal. But his time at Edinburgh was short, just six months. Smiles suggests that he was worried about the amount it was costing his father to keep him there, but it is more likely that he had come to the conclusion that though the lectures might be intrinsically interesting, nothing he was learning was likely to be much help in furthering his career as an engineer.

Train of Waggons crossing the Turnpike Road near Darlington.

The opening of the Stockton & Darlington Railway: most of the guests are travelling in adapted coal wagons.

On the construction front, things were progressing well, and it was decided that a new branch line was needed, which would run for just over 3 miles to Croft Bridge, near Hurworth south of Darlington. There were also several alterations planned to improve the main route, reducing it in length by 2 miles. This would require a new Act of Parliament, but before that took place, Stephenson invited Edward Pease to Killingworth to see his locomotives in action. Pease brought with him his cousin Thomas Richardson, co-founder of the powerful London bankers Richardson, Overend, Gurney & Co. in 1800. The engineer was very keen to impress his visitors with the performance of the engines for he had in mind another addition to the Bill for the changes to the line – he wanted to include a clause that would specifically allow the use of locomotives. He needed the active support of men of influence such as Richardson and he obviously considered the whole matter to be so important that he went personally to Westminster to present the new estimates and explain what was needed. As a result, the Bill was passed with virtually no opposition, though one wonders how many of the Members were aware that this was to be an historic document: the very first Act of Parliament to authorise the construction of a railway to be used by steam locomotives. The relevant clause covered all possibilities:

> That it shall and may be lawful to and for the said Company of proprietors or any person or persons authorised or permitted by them, from and after the passing of this Act, to make and erect such and so many loco-motives or moveable engines as the said company or proprietors shall from time to time think proper and expedient and to use and employ the same in or upon the said railways or tramroads or any of them, by the said Act, and this Act, directed or authorised to be made, for the purpose of facilitating the transport, conveyance and carriage of goods, merchandise and other articles and things upon and along the same roads, and for the conveyance of passengers upon and along the same road.

The sentence about conveying passengers is interesting, given later developments.

It seemed clear that, apart, from George Stephenson, no one else appeared to have much of an interest in building locomotives. It seemed equally clear that if the Stockton & Darlington was the success that its promoters hoped and were convinced it would be, the future demand for engines would be considerable. The logical step was to set up a manufacturing company. It was to be called Robert Stephenson & Co. The initial capital of £4,000 was raised by issuing ten shares, four of which went to Pease, the others to Michael Longridge and the two Stephensons. Robert, of course, did not have the money to pay such a sum and Pease lent him £500, but it turned out to be a very sound investment on his part, bringing him substantial dividends for years to come. It perhaps seems a little odd to give the Company the name of the young man who was very much the junior partner in the enterprise, but there might have been awkward questions asked if engineer George Stephenson had been seen to give contracts for locomotives to George Stephenson manufacturer. The terms of the agreement made young Robert the Managing Partner at a salary of £200. The title was impressive, but other clauses made clear the reality of the situation: he had the job 'on condition that his Father George Stephenson furnish all the Plans, &c, which may be required, and take the general charge of the Manufactory as long as required by the Partners.' Nevertheless, with George busy on so many other projects, it was clear that the day to day running of the new factory would be Robert's responsibility.

The works at Forth Street, Newcastle were opened in 1823 with the 19-year-old Robert in charge. On 31 March that year George wrote to his old colleague William Locke, who was now settled in Barnsley. As mentioned earlier, he clearly had no bad memories of working with Locke, addressing him in very friendly terms, but at the same time, rather typically, went over old grievances.

From the great elapse of time since I saw you, you will hardly know that such a man is in the land of the living.

I fully expected to have seen you about two years ago, as I passed through Barnsley on my way to South Wales; but being informed you were not at home, I did not call. I expect to be in London in the course of a fortnight or three weeks, when I shall do myself the pleasure of calling, either in going or coming. This will be handed to you by Mr. Wilson, a friend of mine, who is by profession an attorney-at-law, and intends to settle in your neighbourhood. You will greatly oblige me by throwing any business in his way you conveniently can. I think you will find him an active man in his profession.

There have been many ups and downs in this neighbourhood since you left. You will no doubt have heard that Charles Nixon was thrown out of Wall-Bottle Colliery by his partners some years ago. He has little to depend on now but the profits of the ballast-machine at Wellington Quay which I daresay are very small. Many of his family have turned out very badly; he has been very unfortunate in family affairs,

If I should have the pleasure of seeing you, I shall give you a long list of occurrences since you and I worked together at Newburn. Hawthorn is still at Wall-Bottle. I dare say you will remember he was a great enemy to you but much more so after you left. I left Wall-Bottle Colliery soon after you and have been very prosperous in my concerns ever since. I am now far above Hawthorn's reach. I am now concerned as civil engineer in different parts of the kingdom. I have only one son whom I have brought up in my own profession. He is now nearly twenty years of age. I have had him educated in the first schools, and he is now at college in Edinboro'. I have found a great want of education myself, but fortune has made me amends for that want.

Locke would have read this letter with very mixed feelings. His own path had been far from smooth and his son Joseph was proving to be something of a family problem. He had been sent more than once to apprenticeships, but nothing had worked out and the father was in some despair over what to do with him. It seems, however, that when the two men did get together in Barnsley as promised, Stephenson offered the boy an apprenticeship, without asking for the usual premium from his father. He was soon to be taken on at the new works at Forth Street. He was slightly younger than Robert Stephenson, having been born on 9 August 1805. Although Robert was technically the boss and Joseph a humble apprentice, the two became good friends, and Joseph was to play an important part in the fortunes of the Stephenson family. By June 1825, he was no longer merely an apprentice, but an assistant with a salary of £80 a year and with a clause in his contract that stated that he would also be taught 'The business of an Engineer as now practised by the said George Stephenson'.

One of the first jobs required of the new Forth Street works was to build locomotives for the Stockton & Darlington. The first two were named *Locomotion* and *Hope* – the former has been preserved and is now in the Darlington Railway Museum but has been much altered over the years. The main difference between *Locomotion* and the earlier Killingworth engines was that the chains were dispensed with and replaced by more connecting rods, creating a conventional 0-4-0 wheel arrangement. The engine still had a single flue boiler, with the firebox at one end the flue bent up at the far end to create the chimney. The two cylinders were set in line and they had cross beams set above the piston rods, with the motion controlled by a parallel motion, similar to that used in beam engines, Indeed the whole arrangement is very similar to that of the 'grasshopper' type of beam engine, in that the beam instead of being pivoted at the centre is fixed at one end. The drive down to the wheels was attached to crank pins, set at a quarter turn from each other. There was no reversing gear as such, so when the engine wanted to change direction, the driver had to work from a platform at the side of the boiler, disconnect the valve motion and reset it for reverse travel. A replica was built for the 150th anniversary of the opening of the railway by Mike Satow's company, Locomotion Enterprises. Seeing the engine at work made one realise how complex operations were – and the driver seemed in real danger of losing a finger as he clipped and unclipped the moving parts. In practice the real danger of driving the engine was very different. The Killingworth engines only travelled short distances, but the new engines had to go much further and were always in danger of running out of steam, because of the primitive boilers. The frustrated drivers would apparently try to increase pressure by tampering with the safety valve. This, of course, was a risky business and in 1818, boiler explosions on both Killingworth engines killed their drivers. These locomotives were adequate for the job in hand: hauling their loaded wagons at little more than a brisk walking pace. As work was proceeding in the construction of the line, a maintenance works was established at Shildon, and Timothy Hackworth was given the job of looking after the Company's locomotives and rolling stock.

The Stockton & Darlington was far from being a modern railway. Although it was intended to carry passengers there would have been no takers for a steam system that would actually be slower than the conventional stagecoaches of the day. So it was decided to take advantage of the fact that the railway provided a better running surface than the roads of the day, by operating a coach of their own that would be pulled by horses and would only differ from the road coaches by having flanged wheels. Called the *Experiment* it was to run the journey between Stockton and Darlington in two hours, for which the passengers would pay a fare of 1s. As the average speed was even then only around 6mph. it was scarcely a great improvement on existing conditions.

The Stockton & Darlington originally used a number of inclines with rope haulage. This illustration of the winding engine at the top of the Brusselton incline was made long after the system had fallen into disuse.

An official notice was posted on 14 September 1825, announcing that the railway would be officially opened on Tuesday, 27 September. The proprietors were to meet at the Brusselton engine house at 8 that morning and after inspecting the inclines would join a train at 9am hauled by 'a superior locomotive engine, of the most improved construction' – this was *Locomotion* – and they were expected at Stockton at 1pm where a dinner would be laid on for 'the neighbouring nobility and gentry'. A later handbill gave more details. There was to be quite a grand procession, with the locomotive and tender, six wagon loads of coal, the coach *Experiment* for the proprietors and six wagons with seats for the gentry and fourteen wagons, standing room only, for everyone else. The workmen who had built the line would be hauled on more wagons, pulled by horses. Tickets were issued to the shareholders who got one each, with an extra ticket for those with 10 shares or more; a total of 400 were issued and everything made ready for the great day.

In the event, huge crowds turned out to watch the spectacle and those who had tickets had to fight for their places as more and more people simply jumped into the wagons or clung to the outside. The train set off with George Stephenson driving, joined by his brothers James and Ralph, while Timothy Hackworth acted as guard. A horseman carrying a banner led the way and the train set off, cheered all along the route by the waiting crowd. The start was described in the *Courant* newspaper:

> The signal being given, the engine started off with this immense train of carriages; and here the scene became most interesting, the horsemen galloping across the fields to accompany the engine and the people on foot running on each side of the road, endeavouring in vain to keep up with the cavalcade. The railway descending with a gentle inclination towards Darlington, though not uniform, the rate of speed was consequently variable. On the part of the railway it was intended to ascertain at what rate of speed the engine could travel with safety. In some parts the speed was frequently 12 miles per hour, and in one place, for short distance, near Darlington, 15 miles per hour; and at that time the number of passengers was counted to 450, which, together with the coals, merchandise, and carriages, would amount to near 90 tons.

The scene was also described in *The Scotsman*.

> Nothing could exceed the beauty and grandeur of the scene. Throughout the whole distance the fields and lanes were covered with elegantly dressed

females and all descriptions of spectators. The bridge, under which the process in some places darted through with astonishing rapidity, lined with spectators cheering and waving their hats had a grand effect ... At one time the passengers by the engine had the pleasure of accompanying and seeing their brother passengers by the stage coach which passed alongside and observing the striking contrast exhibited by the power of the engine and the horse – the engine with her 600 passengers and load and the coach with four horses and only 16 passengers.

It was a great occasion and the train arrived at Stockton to be greeted by a seven-gun salute and a band playing the National Anthem. After that the invited guests processed to the town hall for their banquet, which ended with twenty-three official toasts, the last one of which was to George Stephenson. It was a day of triumph for him to see all his plans coming to fruition, but already by this time the world of railways was beginning to move on.

Chapter 6

THE LIVERPOOL AND MANCHESTER RAILWAY

While Stephenson was busy in the north of England, developing his lines, William James was equally busy promoting the whole idea of a national rail network. His plan for a line from Stratford-upon-Avon to London had resulted merely in Stratford being joined to Moreton-in-the-Marsh by a horse-drawn tramway, a small part of which survives in the shape of the original bridge across the Avon at Stratford. But the more fertile ground for developing his ideas was once again in the north of England. The impetus for change came from the burgeoning cotton industry. Ever since Richard Arkwright had established his mill for spinning cotton in the 1770s, the industry had developed at an extraordinary rate: £1 million a year in the 1780s, £6 million in 1800 and £20 million by 1820. The commercial heart of the cotton industry was Manchester, where the merchants and agents had their offices and warehouses, and mills were developing all round them. Originally the raw material had come in from India and the Near East, but by the early nineteenth century the main suppliers were the cotton plantations of the Southern States of America. And the principal port through which the supplies came was Liverpool. Commerce between Liverpool and Manchester was a vital part of the whole process, and it was far from satisfactory.

The main connection was the Bridgewater Canal, opened between Manchester and the Mersey in 1762, but grumbles about the inadequacy of the system were becoming ever louder. The promoters of the idea of constructing a railway to join the two cities were making a special case, but even allowing for a degree of exaggeration, their arguments are still cogent and the facts they quote astounding.

It will be shown that it has taken longer to pass goods from Liverpool to Manchester than to bring them from America to Liverpool. It will be shown, that what is stated, takes place not once occasionally, but often; that goods have taken twenty-one days in coming from America to Liverpool, and that they have staid upon the wharfs before they could get the conveyance to Manchester for more than six weeks.

It has been suggested that the first proposal for a tramway was made in the 1790s with a survey conducted by William Jessop, but Charles Hadfield in his biography of the engineer had diligently searched the records and could find no trace of any such work. We do know, however, that Thomas Gray advocated a line using the Blenkinsop system in his pamphlet *Observations on a General Iron Railway* published in 1820, but nothing came of that suggestion. So it was William James who was the first to be taken seriously. He approached Joseph Sandars, a wealthy Liverpool corn merchant, a man heavily involved in Whig politics and a supporter of many ideas that seemed very radical at the time. He was also highly critical of the companies who monopolised the canal trade. He was, therefore more than ready to take James seriously. He was, in fact, so convinced by the arguments for a railway that he personally put up the money for a survey. He was also able to get Parliamentary support from two local MPs, George Canning and William Huskisson.

James agreed to make the survey of a possible line between Liverpool and Manchester and was joined in the enterprise by his brother-in-law Paul Padley as the main surveyor and Robert Stephenson was added to the team. They started on the task in 1822, but by this time James was already busy with

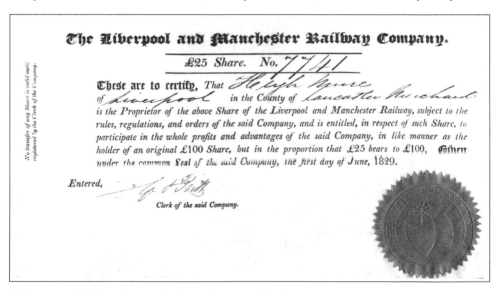

A Liverpool & Manchester Railway share certificate.

new ideas. He carried out a survey for a line from Canterbury to Whitstable, a difficult route for, although the two towns are only 9 miles apart, they are separated by a line of hills rising to a height of 200ft. James put forward plans for a direct route, involving inclines and a tunnel, together with a proposal for major works to improve Whitstable harbour. This was not the only line he was pursuing at the time. He was actively supporting the use of locomotives on the Surrey Iron Railway and was promoting an ambitious line to join London and Cambridge.

Meanwhile, the Liverpool-Manchester survey was not going well. There were real physical obstacles in the way, notably the black, oozing peat bog of Chat Moss. Rather more seriously, there were problems with local landowners, many of whom had shares in the existing canal and river navigation system. Without the backing of an Act of Parliament, the surveyors could not demand access to private land, and they were frequently turned away and if the local villagers showed their dislike of the intruders by hurling abuse and occasionally more solid matter at them, then the landlords who were also the local magistrates were going to do nothing to stop them. It was all time consuming, and James was kept busy travelling between his various projects. Unfortunately, he was so carried away by his enthusiasm for railways that he neglected his main business as a land agent. He was taken to court, declared bankrupt and sent to the King's Bench prison in Southwark as a debtor. As a result, someone else had to be found to take over those of his projects that looked most likely to succeed. The promoters of the Liverpool & Manchester (L & MR) and the Canterbury & Whitstable both turned to the most obvious candidate, George Stephenson.

In 1824, the Liverpool & Manchester Committee wrote to Edward Pease to inform him that they intended to appoint Stephenson to the post of chief engineer to carry out a survey of the line. They also wrote to James to tell him of the decision.

I think it right to inform you that the Committee have engaged your friend Mr. G. Stephenson. We expect him in a few days.

The subscription list for £30,000 is filled, and the Manchester gentlemen have conceded us the entire management. I very much regret that by delay and promises you have forfeited the confidence of the subscribers. I cannot help it. I fear now that you will only have the fame of being connected with the commencement of this undertaking. If you will send me down your plans and estimates I will everything for you I can, and I believe I possess as much influence as any person. I am quite sure that the appointment of Stephenson will, under all circumstance, be agreeable to you.

If Sandars really believed that James would find the appointment 'agreeable' he was very much mistaken. James regarded it as very disagreeable indeed and spoke openly of Stephenson's 'duplicity'. It is difficult not to feel sympathy for James who had worked so hard to set this great project in motion only to see the honour of carrying it forward go to another. When he was finally released from prison, he moved to Cornwall to manage the important estate of Lanhydrock, but old habits resurfaced. Soon he was trying to develop plans for a railway to unite the county's two coasts, running from Fowey in the south to Padstow in the north. He also produced schemes for improving local ports. Sadly, none of his Cornish ideas were ever realised, and he died in 1837, after contracting pneumonia. He is a sad figure and, it seems, one of those men who enthusiastically start great schemes but seem to lack the staying power to see them through. In those troubled days James did a least have one loyal supporter, the young man who had worked beside him, Robert Stephenson.

It gives rise to feelings of true regret when I reflect on your situation; but yet a consolation springs up when I consider your persevering spirit will forever bear you up in the arms of triumph, instances of which I have witnessed of too forcible a character to be easily effaced from my memory. It is these thoughts and these alone, that could banish from my soul feelings of despair for one; the respect I have for him can be easier conceived than described. Can I ever forget the advice you have afforded me in your last letters? And what a heavenly inducement you pointed before me at the close, when you said that attention and obedience to my dear father would afford me music at midnight.

Both the Stephensons were extremely busy as the father was being asked to consult on a wide range of railway projects in many parts of the country including Ireland. Robert was equally busy managing the Newcastle works and into this hectic life there came a new proposal from one of the Forth Street partners, Richardson. As well as his banking business he also had extensive interests in several mining operations in South America. He was keen for someone from the Stephenson family to go to Mexico to give an opinion on how the mines in that country might be developed and to look at the possibility of building a line from the mining area to the coast. At first it was agreed that George's brother Robert would make the journey, but apparently his wife was so firmly set against any such idea that he declined the offer. George was clearly far too busy with his current arrangements so an offer was made to Robert.

There has been a great deal of speculation as to why he agreed to go. There were suggestions that he had fallen out with his father over the treatment of William James, but that scarcely seems likely. It was not George's fault that the Liverpool & Manchester Committee sacked him. It has also been suggested that it would be good for his health. He was apparently already in a position as head of a major engineering concern, but when one looks at the terms of his position it is very clear that all the really important decisions were still to be taken by the father. Now he was being offered the opportunity to strike out on his own and, not only that, but to travel to what must have seemed an almost impossibly exotic part of the world. It would be a very timid sort of young man who would not see this as the adventure of a lifetime. The obvious difficulty was persuading both his father and the partners in the engineering works that this was acceptable, given that he would be leaving his position at Forth Street for a long period of time. In his letter, his enthusiasm for the whole project shines through.

> There are some new prospects here in agitation, which I look forward to with great satisfaction. It is the making of a road in Colombia. What a place London is for prospects! This new scheme of a road or railway is also connected with four silver mines in Marquita. The road is projected between La Guayra and the city of Caraccas. You may find La Guayra on the coast, I believe, of the Gulf of Mexico. The climate, from Humboldt, is not quite so salubrious as that of Mexico. Mr. Powles is the head of the concern, and he assures me there is no one to meddle with us. We are to have all the machinery to make, and we are to construct the road in the most advisable away we may think, after making surveys and levellings.

George clearly did not share his enthusiasm for the project, and Robert was soon having to write again, pointing out that he would 'only be away for a time' and there were competent people to run the Newcastle business in his absence. He had clearly made up his mind to go, and had bought so many necessary instruments that if he was prevented from going he would look 'extremely foolish'. In the event, he set off as head of an important expedition at a handsome salary of £500 and sailed from Liverpool in June 1824. His one regret seems to have been that he could not be a part of setting up what was destined to be an historic railway venture, the proposed line from Manchester to Liverpool.

The first task that George Stephenson had to take in hand was a survey in order to draw up plans for that railway. With his increasingly busy life this was a job that largely had to be left to his assistants, and the difficulties that James had faced in coping with intractable landowners had certainly not disappeared in the interim. Peter Lecount described the difficulties in *A Practical Treatise on Railways* (1839).

> We have sad work with Lord Derby, Lord Sefton and Bradshaw the great Canal Proprietors whose ground we go through with the projected railway. Their Ground is blockaded on every side to prevent us getting on with the Survey – Bradshaw fires guns through the ground in the course of the night to prevent the surveyors coming on in the dark – We are to have a grand field-day next week, the Liverpool Railway Company are determined to force a survey through if possible – Lord Sefton says he will have a hundred men against us – the company thinks these great men have no right to stop a survey.

The survey team came up with their own strategy.

> But one midnight a survey was obtained by the following ruse. Some men, under the orders of the surveying party, were set to fire off guns in a particular quarter, on which all the gamekeepers on the watch made off in that direction, and they were drawn away to such a distance in pursuit of the supposed poachers, as to enable a rapid survey to be made during their absence.

This was all very well, but rapid surveys carried out at midnight are not perhaps going to be notable for their accuracy or attention to detail. The committee were understandably worried and asked William Cubitt to carry out some spot checks on the levels. He did so, found numerous errors, but no one thought it necessary to do other than make a few corrections and hope that the rest would prove to be all right. The plans were drawn up, estimates prepared and the Bill sent to Parliament for investigation by a Select Committee of the House of Commons. They might just possibly have

The bleak waste of Chat Moss: crossing it was the greatest challenge faced by the engineers.

got away with it: parliament had grown weary of canal Bills over the last few decades and probably regarded railway Bills as no more interesting and not worth spending a huge amount of time on. But the canal companies had hired a very skilful lawyer: Edward Hall Alderson, later Baron Alderson.

At first things seemed to be going reasonably well until Stephenson was placed in the witness box and within minutes every single fault and flaw had been exposed, and the increasingly unhappy engineer was subjected to a humiliating ordeal of cross questioning. The question of the levels came up and Stephenson was forced to admit that he was not quite sure where the base line had been fixed on which all other measurements depended, other than somewhere near the Vauxhall Road – 'I think about 150 yards from it, but I am not quite sure'. Under questioning the engineer had to admit that the estimates he was submitting were based on levels he had not personally taken or supervised. Worse was to follow. The bridge over the Irwell was to be between 10 and 15ft high, which would have left the river scarcely navigable when water levels were high, and completely submerged in a flood. Alderson was merciless.

> Did any ignorance ever arrive at such a pitch as this? Was there ever any ignorance exhibited like it? Is Mr. Stephenson to be the person upon whose faith this Committee is to pass the bill, involving property to the extent of 400,000 *l* or 500,000 *l* when he is so ignorant of his profession, as to propose to build a bridge not sufficient to carry off the flood water of the river, or to permit any of the vessels to pass which of necessity must pass under it, and to leave his own Railroad to be several feet under water.

Alderson then went in for the killer punch:

> My learned friends almost endeavoured to stop my examination. They wished me to put in the plan, but I had rather have the exhibition of Mr. Stephenson in that box. I say he never had a plan – I believe he never had one – I do not believe he is capable of making one

His final cutting comment was: 'He is either ignorant or something else which I will not mention.' Not surprisingly, George Stephenson later remarked that when he was in that box he wished he could have found a hole to crawl away through. Inevitably the Bill was thrown out, and the engineer's reputation was in tatters.

Back in Newcastle, Joseph Locke wrote to his friend Robert Stephenson. It is very much the letter of one cheerful young man to a contemporary, and his account of what has been going on goes some way to explaining why George had been lax in overseeing the surveyn and gives at least an indication of just how badly things had gone wrong.

> Since writing to you I have been busily engaged levelling and surveying a proposed line of Railway from Leeds to Hull a distance of 50 miles. This plan is now finished and our directors have fixed not to apply to Parliament until the next sessions but one, about 38 miles is nearly a perfect level and the remaining 12 will require 3 permanent Engines. I have been 8 or 9 months engaged in this survey and have spent my time very comfortably.

Amid all the gay scenes which my Wildness led me into I still remember'd you and the happiness I should have felt to have been with you – but however whilst surveying what do you think I did? Only what others have done – fell in love! And (you may be sure) with one of the most enchanting creatures under Heaven. And my only regret is that we have finished surveying in that neighbourhood.

Since finishing that line I have been levelling one between Manchester and Bolton for which we are going to Parliament next sessions, and I trust the levels will be found to be correct. No doubt that you would hear of this inaccuracy of the Manchester & Liverpool levels which has affected the interest of your Father very much: we must endeavour by our future attention to regain that opinion which we have of late lost.

The manufactory here is quite metamorphosed into a place quite beyond your conception.

The opening of the Darlington Railway has made an impression on the Public which has gain'd your father much popularity.

Having been so much from home this year I cannot give you any home news therefore you must excuse me for not giving you any. Your father and I have been examining the country from here to Hexham for the Carlisle Railway. Hoping to hear from you at the first opportunity; believe me my Robert Your ever faithful Friend.

There are more than a few hints in the letter that Robert would be more use to the family business at home than in South America – a view that would later be expressed with ever-increasing insistence by other writers. Robert himself wrote to Longridge and remarked that although the loss of the Bill was a setback, it would almost certainly only be temporary, and then added: 'It is to be regretted that my father placed the conducting of the levelling under the care of young men without experience'. Indeed it was, but he must have been aware that things might have been very different if he had been available instead of thousands of miles away.

The Parliamentary debacle led inevitably to George being removed from the post of engineer. He was understandably bitter. It had all been a humiliating experience, as the Members made fun of his strong Geordie accent: 'One member asked me if I was a foreigner, and another hinted that I was mad.' It all tended to reinforce a prejudice against the wealthy, well-educated men of London – a feeling that had begun when Davy had called him a fraud and was now considerably strengthened. His discomfort could hardly have been improved by the knowledge that in many ways he had only himself to blame: the plans had been badly drawn up and too many mistakes had been made. But no one ever accused George Stephenson of being a weak character, the sort of man to give up in the face of adversity, and he was greatly buoyed up by the opening of the Stockton & Darlington just six months after his mauling in Parliament.

Meanwhile the Company had to gather itself together and arrange for a new survey and new plans to be made for a second attempt at gaining their Act. They went to George and John Rennie, sons of the famous John Rennie, builder of bridges and canals. Like their father, the two Rennies were experienced engineers and knew how to play the Parliamentary game. They needed a competent engineer to oversee the survey and they turned to Charles Vignoles. He was born into a military family, but both his parents died young and he was mainly brought up by his grandfather who was professor of mathematics at the Royal Military Academy in Woolwich. He was persuaded by his grandfather to train for a career in law, but that proved very unappealing to the young man, and he left to join the army. Like many young officers, when the Napoleonic wars came to an end he found himself pensioned off on half pay. He set off for America, originally with the notion of volunteering for Bolivar's army. In the event, he ended up first in South Carolina working as assistant to the State Civil Engineer and then in Florida, where he surveyed and mapped the state. On returning to England in 1823, he worked for James Walker in the construction of the Commercial Docks in London, then set up on his own with an office in Hatton Garden. Thus, when he was approached by the Rennies he seemed the ideal choice, not only as an experienced engineer, but with his early legal training he would be well able to cope with time in the witness box.

The survey work went ahead smoothly, with many alterations made to the first route suggested by Stephenson. The new Bill still used the old description of being for a 'Railway or Tramroad' and virtually the only mention of locomotives guaranteed that they would not be used in the town at Liverpool. As with the Stockton & Darlington, the Company set out a series of charges for carrying various types of goods – passengers were not mentioned. It made the scheme seem little more than another general carrier and this time the Bill was passed with scarcely a voice raised against it in 1826. The committee now naturally turned to the two Rennies and asked them to take over responsibility for constructing the line. After some deliberation, it was decided that George Rennie should be chief engineer at a salary of £600, but that he would need the assistance of an 'operative engineer'. Two engineers were proposed by the committee: John Urpeth Rastrick and George Stephenson. Rennie would have realised that working with Stephenson was never going to be possible – even if George had been prepared to work for him. They also rejected Rastrick, who although he had experience as a civil engineer – he had built a splendid cast-iron bridge across the Wye at Chepstow – was perhaps better known as a manufacturer at his ironworks. There was always more than a hint of pomposity about the Rennie family. The Minute Book recorded that George 'would not object to Mr Jessop, Mr Telford or any member of the Society of Engineers being consulted'. He could hardly object to Telford, then the most senior and most experienced in the land, nor Josias Jessop, son of the highly successful canal engineer, and experienced in his own right. The committee were beginning to get the impression that no one would be quite good enough for Mr Rennie. In the meantime, Vignoles was left temporarily in charge.

Given George Rennie's reluctance to agree terms, the committee now had to make other arrangements. They eventually appointed Josias Jessop as consultant engineer, Vignoles was still employed and George Stephenson was brought back into the fold as the 'working engineer' agreeing to spend nine months a year on the project at a salary of £800. On paper, it looked like a good arrangement: in practice, personality clashes were all but inevitable. From their very first meeting Jessop and Stephenson disagreed about the line to be taken. And although Jessop was nominally the senior figure, the committee generally agreed with George. This put Jessop in an intolerable position. George Stephenson, once disgraced, was now back in charge and brought Joseph Locke in as one of the resident engineers to take charge of the eastern end of the works. That only left Vignoles as a survivor from the previous regime. He got off to a bad start, offering George a letter of commendation from the professor of mathematics at Greenwich, not realising that recommendation from a 'London scientific expert' was a red rag to a bull. He was not destined to last long, but at least construction could now get under way.

Meanwhile, things at the Forth Street works were not going as well as they should have been. Michael Longridge had understood that he would only take charge on a temporary basis while Robert was away. As soon as he realised that he was in fact signing up for three years, Longridge was horrified and wrote to Robert as he was leaving England, to hope that he would be back by 1825 at the latest. It was now clear that with all that was happening on the Liverpool & Manchester he was badly needed back home. He was probably only too glad to be summoned back – South America had not turned out quite in the way he had expected.

Chapter 7

ROBERT IN SOUTH AMERICA

Robert Stephenson arrived in London on 27 April 1824. He had a frustrating time, haggling with the agents for the Colombian mining company, but he was able to use his time in the capital to his advantage. He visited the Royal Mint, and devised a machine for striking coins that he hoped would be used in the Colombian mint. He took lessons in mineralogical chemistry from Professor Robert Phillips, for which the Company paid the rather extravagant fee of 5 guineas a lesson and also put his mind to the design for a machine for drying paper. He and his father had spent time in London and Cork, where they were encouraged to devise an efficient method for paper mills manufacturing bank notes. Paper at this time was manufactured from rags, which were finely chopped and mixed with water: when the mixture was passed through a fine mesh, the fibres clung together to form the paper. In the simplest drying method, the individual sheets were placed within layers of a suitable fabric, such as felt, and then pressed to squeeze out the liquid. It was essential to keep them separate or they would simply have congealed into a pulp. The system had already been mechanised, but the Stephensons felt improvements could be made. Robert visited the *Times* printing house, house, which gave him a new idea:

> I was almost as much delighted as I was in the Mint. The facility with which they print is truly wonderful. They were working papers at the rate of 2,000 per hour, which they can hold for any length of time. The mode they have of conveying the sheet of paper from one part of the machine to the other is, I think, precisely what is wanted in the drying machine.

The resulting machine used a continuous band of felt to carry the paper over three drying cylinders, gradually increasing in heat from 80 to 120°F. Having devised the new machine, he had to leave London before a second example was installed at Albury Mill. He boarded his ship *Sir William Congreve* at Liverpool in June 1824. In his log he made it clear that he knew he was taking a risk: 'many will say that I am wrong but I will never admit that: I know the experience which I shall gain will be worth all the trouble.' He was just as busy during the voyage as he had been in London, keeping a log and taking a number of measurements, such as recording sea temperature. A month later he had arrived at what is now La Guairá in Venezuela but which was then part of the Federation of Gran Colombia, which also included present-day Ecuador. He disembarked, but his assistant Charles Empson and a small group of miners stayed on board to travel on to Cartagena to make their way to the mining region. His first impressions were definitely not favourable as he 'observed in silence the miserable appearance of the town'. Since the late sixteenth century the town had been the main port serving Caracas and Robert had been given two tasks: to see if the port facilities could be improved and to look at the possibility of building a railway of some sort from the port to Caracas.

When Robert arrived, the ship had to anchor in the bay and cargo was unloaded into lighters. He had been asked to consider building a breakwater to protect the anchorage, and although he decided that was impractical he thought a new pier could be constructed that ships could tie up alongside at a cost of £6,000. He would no doubt be pleased to know that today this is a thriving harbour though perhaps surprised to find it is regularly visited by cruise ships carrying tourists. As for the railway, his first sight of the town must have made it seem impossible. Even today the task would be daunting as it is overlooked by high, forested hills. He described those hills as 'six or eight times as high as Brusselton'. He actually underestimated the terrain, which rose steadily to Caracas at 3,000ft above sea level. It did not take him long to realise just how impossible the enterprise was: 'it is quite incredible the difficulties I have had to contend with' as he struggled to survey the land route to Caracas. In the event, he decided that the obstacles were simply too great and the cost too high – he estimated £160,000 – to make it profitable. He was surely right, but a line was eventually built but was only opened in 1883, by which time railway technology was far in advance of anything available to the young engineer. His next assignment was to assess the mines of Colombia, and he set out with an interpreter and a servant for Bogotá, the capital.

This was an arduous journey, climbing steadily on poor tracks, only suitable for mules, to the capital that stands 8,800ft above sea level. Robert took four months for the journey, looking at various potential mine sites along the way, but he was at least able to do a little prospecting on his own account, collecting mineral samples. In Bogotá he made contact with the Colombian Mining Association's local representative R. S. Illingworth.

Meanwhile Empson and the rest of the party had made their way up the Magdalena River to the head of navigation at Honda, where Robert joined them. The heavy mining equipment they had brought with them was still on the riverside wharf. The problem was that although the route to Maraquita lay across the plain, the final 12 miles to the Santa Ana silver mine was via a rough, narrow mule track climbing up the steep slope of the Andes. Robert reported the news back to London, but the message did not arrive before another shipment of more heavy machinery was on its way to South America and it too would be stuck on the riverbank. The only consolation was that the climate at Santa Ana was far more bearable than the stifling heat of the plain and Robert would eventually have a rough house of bamboo thatched with palm leaves from which he could enjoy both magnificent views and cooling mountain breezes

In spite of the problem with machinery, work went ahead under Empson's supervision, to prepare the silver mine for when the main work force arrived. Robert now set off on a second expedition, once again travelling by mule for over a thousand miles, looking for potential sites for development. It was a lonely existence and he wrote to his step-mother Elizabeth: 'you may easily conceive how often I think of an English fireside and all the joys that spring around it.' At the end of the journeys, he was back at Maraquita where the main work force of Cornish miners was arriving to start the serious business of extracting the valuable ore. The arrival of the miners should have been a signal to get down to serious work but instead marked the beginning of new troubles. The men had been recruited in Cornwall and offered high wages. Some may have seen it as an opportunity to save for the future, but for most of them it was money to spend, and almost the only thing they could find to spend it on was booze. As soon as they arrived at Honda they went on a spree to the despair of the young engineer.

I have no idea of letting linger out another week without some work being done. Indeed, some of them are anxious to get on with something. Many of them, however, are ungovernable. I dread the management of them. They have already commenced to drink in the most outrageous manner. Their behaviour in Honda has, I am afraid, incurred for ever the displeasure of the Governor, at all events as far as induces me to calculate upon his friendly co-operation in any of our future proceedings. I hope when they are once quietly settled at Santa Ana and the works regularly advancing, that some improvement may take place.

It appears remarkable that having been all my life accustomed to deal with miners, and having had a body of them under my control, and I may say in my employ, that I should now find it difficult to contribute to their comfort and welfare.

He had hoped that by the time they reached Santa Ana temptation would be removed, but inevitably the news of the arrival of a large body of single men with money to burn soon spread locally. There would soon be traders arriving to make sure they had something to spend it on, and that something would again be drink. Robert faced real problems in asserting his authority over the men, partly no doubt because being young and not from Cornwall, they did not give him the respect they would have shown to a mine captain back home. Drunkenness was by far the biggest problem, and he never managed to get all the men together to complete a full day's work. In fact, he estimated that the best he could expect was an average of half a day per man. Emerson was his only companion and at times the drunks even tried to pick a fight with him. Relations did gradually improve, but the mines were not, it seems, proving as profitable as the investors in England had hoped. The solicitor of the Stockton & Darlington wrote in his diary that he had read reports from Robert and in 1826 was noting that the whole venture was comparable to John Law's Mississippi Bubble – a venture that had seen as spectacular a financial crash as the better-known South Sea Bubble. However, as time went on Robert became altogether more optimistic about the prospects of mining in South America.

The mines in this country I believe will turn out very advantageous if carefully & skilfully conducted. Many of the Silver Mines are exceedingly rich, but they are much inferior to some Gold mines which are now in the possession of the Association: they have been examined carefully and the produce of them is enormous, and should they be followed up with attention & skill; they will produce to the satisfaction of the most avaricious.

He had also written an account of the works to his father, who had replied in February 1827, one of the few surviving letters in George's own handwriting, reproduced here with the original spellings.

My Dear Robert your very welcom letter dated Oct 26 1826 we duly received and was glad to hear such newes from Colombia respecting the mines – but at the same time greatly disappointed at you not getting home so soon as was expected however I hope all will be for the best, and I must waddle on as well as I can until you get to join me. There has been a florishing a count of your men in the English pappers and great credit is given to <u>Robert Stephenson</u> for his good management of them. I must now let you know how we are getting on in this quarter yore mother is getting her tea beside me while I am riting this and in good spirits, she has been in Liverpool a bout a fortnight. We have got a very comfortable home, and a Roume set a side for Robert and Chareles when they arrive in England.

Reports such as this would have reached the Association and they were now pressing Robert to extend his stay in South America. At the same time, he was also being pressed to return to England as soon as possible.

Nothing but the fullest consent of my partners could induce me to stay in this country and an assurance that an important necessity existed to call me home.

To remain in my present situation until the expiration of the term of my Engagement I cannot urge any reasonable objection since a legal agreement binds me.

He served out his term, handed over responsibility for the mines to Illingworth in Bogotá and he and Empson set off for Cartagena to join a ship to return to Britain. It was while he was there waiting for a suitable vessel that, by an extraordinary coincidence, he met the man who had first set a steam locomotive on rails, Richard Trevithick.

Trevithick had arrived in South America eleven years earlier. He had supplied high pressure engines for a silver mine in the Peruvian Andes, and when the men he had sent out to install them reported problems, had sailed off himself to sort things out. The arrangement was that he would be paid in bullion that would be worth a small fortune. Unfortunately, he had not paid attention to South American politics. Simon Bolivar's army marched into Peru, taking over not only the mines but also Trevithick's share of the bullion. He spent the next few years attempting to recoup his losses. Eventually he appeared to have some success, when he was able to help develop a successful gold mine in Costa Rica. He realised that in order to make the mine profitable, he would need to transport the gold to the coast, but there were no existing roads. He set off with three companions to try to find a satisfactory route to the sea. It was a desperate journey, beset with disasters, the last of which happened in the mouth of the Magdalena River, when Trevithick's boat was capsized and as he struggled in the water, a large alligator set off towards him. Fortunately, a British officer, Bruce Napier Hall was out pig shooting, shot the alligator and rescued the engineer, who was brought to Cartagena in a sorry condition. The expedition had been a failure, he had lost all his possessions and was stranded. It was there that he had the meeting with Robert Stephenson. There are various accounts of what happened. Francis Trevithick in his biography of his father, told the story as he heard it from James Fairbairn, who had the tale from a third party.

> Thus it was that he fell in with Mr. Stephenson, who, like most Englishmen, was reserved and took no notice of Mr. Trevithick, until the officer said to him, meeting Mr. Stephenson at the door, 'I suppose the old proverb of 'two of a trade cannot agree' is true, by the way you keep aloof from your brother chip. It is not thus your father would have treated that worthy man, and it is not creditable to your father's son that he and you should meet here day after day like two strange cats in a garret; it would not sound well at home.' 'Who is it?' said Mr. Stephenson. 'The inventor of the locomotive, your father's friend and fellow-worker; his name is Trevithick, you may have heard it,' the officer said; and then Mr. Stephenson went up to Trevithick. That Mr. Trevithick felt the previous neglect was clear.

In Hall's own account, when Trevithick met Stephenson, he said 'Is that Bobby?', adding 'I've nursed him many a time'. Now this is all very curious as there is no record of Trevithick ever having met George Stephenson. His only connection with the north-eastern collieries was when he received an order for a locomotive for Wylam Colliery and he sent one of his men from South Wales to oversee its construction at Gateshead. Even if he had gone himself there would have been no reason to see Stephenson who had yet to make his reputation. In any case, when Robert was at an age when he might have nursed him his father was away in Scotland. So, the sad fact is that we simply do not know very much at all about the meeting between the two engineers. We can be fairly sure they discussed the ways in which the rail system had developed in the Cornishman's absence and the even brighter future for the system – a system to which the younger man was about to make a major contribution. Hall wrote: 'I know not the cause, but they were not so cordial as I could have wished'. One can only speculate, but the older man might well have felt depressed by the news of developments in which he could have played a leading role, yet here he was without possessions or money after eleven years of what was ultimately fruitless endeavour. Robert Stephenson did, however, provide him with £50 with which he was able to pay for a passage back to England.

Robert decided to return via New York and Trevithick's partner James Gerard, who had travelled with Trevithick on the momentous journey, joined him. They had a horrific encounter in the West Indies, when they picked up survivors from a ship wrecked in a hurricane. They were in a pitiful condition and had only kept themselves alive by eating two of the company who had died during the ordeal. Then Robert's own ship was also caught in a fierce hurricane that drove them onto the rocks on the American coast. Almost all Robert's possessions and most of his money was lost as the ship broke up and sank. He and the other passengers managed to scramble ashore and Robert now found himself in the same predicament in which he had so recently found Trevithick. Fortunately, however, they were near to New York, where Robert was able by some means or other to get funds, not only for the rest of the journey but also to give himself the opportunity to explore North America.

He was not greatly impressed by the New Yorkers. At first, he considered them quite genteel, 'but on closer inspection we soon discovered the characteristic impudence of the people. In many cases it was nothing short of disgusting'. He then set out to travel up to Canada, and on the way the poor impression he'd had of Americans in the city was replaced by admiration for the generosity and hospitality of the rural communities. He stopped off, like all good tourists, to see Niagara Falls, then made his way up to Montreal. He found the Canadians to be quite backward and far less enterprising than the Americans – an opinion that was to be modified later in his life, when he was responsible for major engineering works in that country. After that he returned to New York for passage on the *Pacific* bound for Liverpool. He arrived in late November 1827 to be greeted by his father, who was busy with the Liverpool & Manchester Railway and had made his temporary home in the town.

Robert had been told by Joseph Locke that he would find his father 'much changed', and although at 46 he was still vigorous and healthy his hair had now turned snowy white. Robert too had changed, now having the self-confidence of a man who had been in charge of important enterprises in his own right. He was more than ready to resume his place in the rapidly developing world of the railways. He had a lot of catching up to do.

Chapter 8

BUILDING THE LINE

During Robert's absence, his father had been exceptionally busy with a whole range of different schemes. Apart from completing the Stockton & Darlington and overseeing – or perhaps not overseeing – the work on the Liverpool & Manchester, he had also been consulted in 1824 on the Bolton & Leigh Railway, which was a mere 7¾ miles long. The Company had received alternative routes and were unsure which to adopt. His reply was typically blunt: 'having the Sections of two before me the practicability of the one and the impracticability of the other is so obvious that it is unnecessary to make any comment on either.' He later went on to carry out a survey on the ground and sent in a detailed report in January 1827, in which he found numerous faults in the plans, particularly in the levels. Near the Leigh Canal, it was originally intended to bring the line to a point where it would make a junction with the proposed route for the Liverpool & Manchester Railway, but an alteration meant that the proposed line would be too low to make the smooth junction. The plans also called for two inclined planes, set close together so that the wagons could be easily moved from one to the other, but now they were to be a mile apart. As a result, 'an establishment of horses will oblige to be kept there, which will necessarily increase the rate of tonnage, as well as a loss of time'. In another place, a change in levels had been suggested to avoid the cost of building a bridge and creating a cutting, but as the slope would then be too steep for a horse to manage more than 8 tons, this was considered poor economics. He disapproved the line taken for the incline towards Bolton, and in particular the need to install a 50-horsepower engine. Stephenson pointed out that as the loaded wagons would be travelling in one direction, the incline could be largely self-acting, with the weight of the loaded trucks being used to help haul the empties. He felt a 10hp engine would be perfectly adequate. He criticised the construction of the wagons, which cost £24 each, yet were inferior to the ones being built for the Liverpool & Manchester at a cost of just £5.

With so much detailed criticism for what was, after all, a very short length of tramway, it must have been a most uncomfortable day out for the engineer, Mr Daglish who had drawn up the plans and accompanied Stephenson on his tour of inspection. The report was followed up by a letter with his own plans and costings that came out at £37,905 1s 6d, bizarrely the odd 1s 6d was tacked on to the cost of creating cuttings and embankments, which could only have been a fairly rough estimate at best. That same year he was consulted about a far more important route, a railway to link Birmingham and Manchester. The Birmingham promoters were clearly desperate to acquire Stephenson's services at any price, as he explained in a letter to Longridge, in which his pride in the reception he received is certainly not concealed.

I know you are scolding me for not writing according to promise but after telling you how I have been fagging almost night and day You will I am sure excuse me – I have now been through the whole of the Birmingham line except the Branches and the greatest part of it is marked out. It will be a very fine Line the Undertakers are in great spirits about it. On my arrival at Birmingham a meeting of the most wealthy of the subscribers took place who would not hear of any other executing their work but myself of course I gave way to their wishes as I had also received the news as mentioned in your letter for the extension of time for depositing the plans. They readily agreed to all my charges and I assure you it made me blush to ask it but the hardening lessons I had got from you made me stand to it and it was pleasant to find no one had the least objections – After all our business was settled the Company sat down to dinner you may imagine the style from what you saw at Sunderland – I think the greatest part of the Company had as much wine before dinner was over as would serve you and I to a great many – Foster is a warm hearted Gentleman he has accompanied me through the whole of their Line and I am sure he will not forget it as long as he lives – Some days fourteen hours without either bread or water rising at half past three and working till nine ten and sometimes twelve before we get to our quarters. Mr. Foster says he never slept so pleasantly in his life before closing his eyes when he laid down he opened them no more till he was called.

This was a gruelling schedule by any standards and gives a hint of the pressures Stephenson was under at this time in attempting to cope with all his different projects.

One of those projects was the Canterbury & Whitstable Railway and on his return to England, Robert took a special interest in this line. In March 1828 he wrote to a friend indicating that he was particularly glad to take charge of this project, because it was reasonably close to London: 'How strange! Nay,

The entrance to one of the tunnels on the approach to Liverpool.

say not strange, that all my arrangements instinctively regard Broad Street as the pole?' The attraction at Broad Street was Fanny (Frances) Sanderson, who he had obviously met before leaving for South America. She was apparently 'elegant' rather than beautiful and was also described as 'unusually clever'. His visits to the line under construction seem to have been rather more frequent than the job required, at the expense of the Forth Street Works. That problem was resolved when Robert and Fanny got married in June 1829 and came to live in Newcastle. He could now give all his attention to important works. His father certainly had need of him as his workload increased.

Once George was reinstated as chief engineer for the Liverpool & Manchester that took precedence over everything else. It was a line that presented far greater problems than any he had faced in all his previous engineering career. At the Liverpool end of the line there were to be three tunnels and a deep cutting at Olive Mount that had to be blasted and hacked out of sandstone. There was to be an immense viaduct over the Sankey Navigation and a smaller one over the Bridgewater Canal. The owners of these two waterways dreaded the arrival of the railway and had done all they could to prevent its being built, fearing for the loss of trade. They were right to be worried: although the Bridgewater still exists it carries no cargoes and the Sankey has long since been closed and has all but disappeared from the landscape. There were great embankments to be built, one of which over the valley of the Ditton Brook was more than a mile long and there was a 2-mile long cutting near Newton-le-Willows. There were sixty-three bridges across the line, one of which at Rainhill had to be built on the skew. It has been said that Stephenson puzzled over how to construct such a bridge, working out the problem by carving up a turnip. In fact, all he had to do was go across to the nearby Lancaster Canal to see how it had been done in the previous century. And there was the biggest problem of all still to be overcome: how to lay lines across Chat Moss.

Quite early on in the proceedings, errors were found in the calculations for the first of the tunnels at Edgehill and after the first shaft had been sunk and work begun on the pilot bore, it was found to be some 13ft off the correct line. Stephenson reported that this would have to be corrected otherwise it would threaten to undermine houses in Great George Street. The engineer in charge of that end of the line was Charles Vignoles and he was blamed for the mistake. It was the final straw in the relations between Vignoles and his chief engineer. In February 1827 he resigned. He gave his own version of his time on the railway in a letter to Edward Riddle immediately before his resignation.

The following outline of my connection with Mr. Stephenson must have the first place. After the royal assent had been given to the Railway Bill I was employed independently of anyone else to commence operations by marking out the line on the ground and preparing the drains on Chat Moss. In June, Mr. Rennie, who had been previously engineer to the company having absolutely refused either to consult with or participate in the slightest degree with Mr. Stephenson, vacated his appointment, in consequence of the directors making his co-operation a *sine qua non*. Mr. Stephenson was re-elected principal engineer in the early part of July 1826, and when he came to Liverpool he found me sole acting engineer.

Soon after this I delivered your letter, which from Mr S's subsequent expressions, I found gave him mortal offence, inasmuch as your friendly recommendations were construed by him as admitting me to be his *partner* instead of his *assistant*.

Mr. Josias Jessop, civil engineer (since dead) was soon called in as the consulting engineer, and he differed absolutely in many points with Mr. Stephenson. This was another cause of offence. I also acknowledge having on many occasions differed with him (and that in common with all the other engineers), because it appeared to me he did not look on the concern with a liberal and expanded view, but with a microscopic eye, magnifying details, and pursuing a petty system of parsimony, very proper in a private colliery, or in a small undertaking, but wholly inapplicable to this national work.

I also plead guilty to having neglected to court Mr. S's favour by crying down all other engineers, especially those in London, for though I highly respect his great natural talents, I could not shut my eyes to certain deficiencies.

All these circumstances gave rise to a feeling of ill-will on his part towards me, which he displayed on every occasion; particularly where I showed a want of practical knowledge of unimportant minutae, rendered familiar to him by experience.

I now proceed to answer his accusations. It is true that there was an error in the survey of the tunnel made by me, but it was one which might have been rectified without trouble or expense; and it was one which would not have originated if I had been here alone.

It is hard not to believe that Vignoles' complaints did not have a basis in reality and that Stephenson had allowed his prejudices to cloud his judgement of his assistant's abilities. However, Stephenson now had the team he wanted, with the works divided between three assistant engineers: Joseph Locke, John Dixon and William Allcard, with Daniel Gooch as chief clerk. They were employed and paid by the Company, and Locke, who had recently been working directly for Stephenson at the end of his apprenticeship at £100 per annum, now had a far more handsome salary of £400. These terms of employment were to cause difficulties in the near future.

The major undertaking inevitably called for a large workforce and Stephenson decided to employ men directly, rather than work through established contractors – the system he had used on the smaller colliery lines and the Stockton & Darlington. It appears to have been a somewhat shambolic system. In 1828, the Company asked Telford to prepare a report on progress and he sent an assistant, James Mills, to take a look at the workings. He was surprised, not to say horrified, by what he found. The workforce was organised under the three assistants:

Each has 200 day men employed and pays them every fortnight as *company* men for laying temporary roads, moving planks, making wheelbarrows, driving piles and, in short, doing *every thing* but putting the stuff into the carts and barrows which is done by a sort of men which is also under their direction and to whom they pay 3½d per yard to 5s as they think it deserves.

It was not a system Telford would ever have used himself, but it seemed to work in that progress was being made steadily in several parts of the work. There was one area, however, where things were definitely not proceeding very quickly, if at all: Chat Moss. According to local folklore, this 12 square miles area of peat bog was bottomless. That was obviously not true, but the workers found they had to go down 12ft before reaching solid ground. It was all too easy to walk into the morass, and local farmers used to tie planks to the feet of their cattle to prevent them from sinking. The idea was copied by the navvies and there was a dramatic demonstration of why this was such a good idea. Plank footpaths had been laid over the surface, but on one of his tours of inspection John Dixon lost his footing, fell into the bog and began disappearing into the ooze before the navvies were able to pull him clear. Running a railway over such a terrain looked at first sight to be a near impossibility.

The first step was to dig ditches to help drain the bog, but as fast as a ditch was dug the bog simply oozed back in again. Eventually the ditches were completed by constructing a simple drain by joining together a row of barrels, from which the bottoms and tops had been removed. The next step was to create a firm foundation for the rails. Soil was tipped into the bog and promptly sank from view. Stephenson then devised a new plan, probably inspired by the tough plants that spread over the surface, seemingly floating on the peat. He decided to make rafts of heather and brushwood and he reasoned if he piled enough earth on top, eventually a point of equilibrium would be reached. It was considered rather a bizarre notion to most spectators but it worked. At the Manchester end, conquering the bog proved more difficult. There was nothing for it but to go on pouring in more and more soil, which for week after week simply vanished beneath the surface. Recalling those days, some time later, Stephenson wrote: 'We went on filling in without the slightest apparent effect. Even my assistants began to feel uneasy and to doubt the success of the scheme. The directors, too, spoke of it as a hopeless task, and at length they became seriously alarmed.' There was no alternative other than to keep on tipping until the day eventually came when instead of disappearing a load remained above ground. Then it was just a case of building on this solid foundation until the bank stood a comfortable 5ft above the wasteland. On New Year's Day 1830, a single line track was laid over the Moss and Stephenson had the proud task of accompanying a party of previously sceptical directors over the 'impossible' terrain. Other engineering problems were large, but did not require unique solutions.

Deep cuttings and tunnels had been a commonplace on canals for many decades and the technology was well understood. The first essential for a tunnel was to lay out the line, and make a careful survey of the height of the ground all along the route. Once that had been done, shafts could be sunk to the appropriate depth at different points, and provided all the levels had been accurate, the bottoms of the shafts should all be at the same level and in line. The tunnellers could then work out from the bottoms of the shafts, using the bearings taken at the surface. Once the tunnel had been excavated to the appropriate size, it would be lined with brick unless it was passing through areas of very solid rock That was work that had been carried out on canal tunnels such as that under Standedge Fell for the Huddersfield Canal, that was an imposing 5,698 yards long. So, the technology was well understood, but that did not mean that the task was either easy or safe.

Among the many problems encountered along the way, the tunnels at the Liverpool end were to prove as troublesome as any. Construction of the main tunnel at Edgehill, once Vignoles had been sent on his way, was handed over to the care of young Joseph Locke. On 28 February 1827, he sent a report on his work in a letter to Robert Stephenson.

On the Tunnel we are going very well and I hope very correctly – at least I spare neither pains in watching every part of it. I assure you I have had a busy time of it since I came here – and that present prospect is even more busy … I have strove to assist and advance the interest of your father which in return has advanced mine and has ever placed that confidence in me of which I am proud … I know not how the manufacture goes on at Newcastle, I fear not so briskly as has done – I believe Mr. Longridge wishes to decline the Engine business until your return.

It was a heavy responsibility as the tunnel was built to an unprecedented scale. It was to be a mile and a quarter long, 16ft high and 22ft wide and had to be driven through a mixture of blue shale, rock clay, sandstone and earth. Fortunately, one of the main contractors for the work was William Mackenzie. He attacked the difficulties with great enthusiasm – enthusiasm that was not always shared by his assistant David Stevenson:

I have spent many a weary hour and I might say night, because Mackenzie would often after finishing his pipe and glass of brandy and water … go out

The viaduct carrying the Liverpool & Manchester Railway over the Sankey Navigation. As a result of the railway competition, the Navigation became derelict.

to one of the shafts which, as ill luck would have it, was close to his house and if, by further bad luck, he found a bucket going down, he would at once cry, 'Now then Stevenson, let us jump in and see what these fellows are about down below' and the whole night's expedition terminated in making our exit into daylight at 4 or 5 in the morning.

Around 300 men were involved in its construction. The work involved blasting: the most dangerous part of the operation. First a hole had to be drilled by hand into the solid rock. This was then packed with gunpowder, then rammed home with a metal rod at which point the men involved prayed there were no sparks flying that could set the whole thing off while they were still at work. The fuse was lit and the men scampered for safety. Once the explosion had brought down the rock and dirt, it all had to be cleared away and removed to the surface. The atmosphere in the tunnel was eerie; the candlelight reflecting from the water that constantly ran down the tunnel sides and collected in pools. The air was almost always filled with dust from the explosions and in this dim light the men stumbled to their tasks, their ears ringing from the detonations. Henry Booth, the company secretary, described the workings in his own history of the railway and reported that men sometimes had to be almost physically forced back into the workings when water levels threatened to flood them out or rumblings and cracklings in the roof threatened a collapse that would bury them alive. Somewhat surprisingly the Company agreed to visitors going into the tunnels to see the work for themselves. The more timorous walked a little way in from the entrance and rapidly scurried out again. Braver visitors could penetrate the depths, travelling just as the workmen did, being lowered down the shaft in a giant bucket. One who did, wrote that the scene that greeted him gave 'no contemptible idea of some infernal operation in the regions of Pluto'.

As work progressed on the construction front, there remained one unanswered question: what sort of railway would this be and how would goods and passengers be moved from one end to the other? The Act was vague and offered all kinds of unlikely users of the line: 'Chaises, Gigs, Coaches and Passengers and Cattle may pass on the Railroads'. The Company also envisaged carrying various commodities themselves, lumping together 'Persons, Cattle and Other Animals'. It was the first time that passengers and cattle had been linked together in this way, but the idea unfortunately appears to have re-emerged on the twenty-first-century railway system. The Company was undecided about what to do. Some had been to the colliery lines and been unimpressed by the slow, lumbering engines clanking their way down the tracks and proposed an alternative idea. They wanted to see a series of stationary engines, which would haul trucks and carriages between each other using cables. Stephenson was obviously going to be advocating locomotives, but as virtually the only supplier of these engines he could be accused of acting in his own interests. In any case, he was not advocating just using steam locomotives. There were inclines at the Liverpool end that would be worked by cable haulage. This seemed good ammunition for his opponents, who said, in effect – 'very well, if we are going to have to have cable haulage on one section, what is wrong with extending it to the whole line?' As no one could agree on which system to adopt, it was decided to call in outside experts to report on the virtues and shortcomings of the rival systems.

Early railways offered a wide range of options. The Monkland & Kirkintilloch Railway, opened in 1826, had followed the lead of the Stockton & Darlington in using both locomotives and horses. The S & DR had not proved to be quite the perfect testing ground that it might have been, as the mixed traffic caused havoc with schedules. Complex rules were drawn up regarding who had precedence, horse traffic or locomotives, freight or passengers. With single track working there had to be regulations covering how locomotives and coaches should react when they found themselves head to head on the same length of track. The rules seemed straightforward: the one that had passed the half-way point between passing loops had the right of way, and the other had to reverse to the loop they had already passed. But what about the horse-drawn coach: horses do not have a reverse gear. It was a less than perfect system. There was also the problem that had appeared with boiler explosions, suggesting to the locomotive's opponents that the machines were fundamentally unsafe. But at least the locomotive lobby could show there were signs that engine design could be improved.

Robert Wilson of Gateshead had produced a curious engine for the Stockton & Darlington, built with four wheels and four cylinders, each cylinder providing the drive to the wheel immediately below it. The engine was unsurprisingly not a success and it was sent to Timothy Hackworth at Shildon to see what he could make of it. He decided to simply strip the whole thing down and start again with a radically new design. He returned to a more conventional two-cylinder system, with a direct drive down to the rear wheels. These were then coupled to two other pairs of wheels, making this the first 0-6-0 engine. He also realised that he needed to provide more steam than the earlier engines had required and built it with a return flue boiler. Named the *Royal George* it was the most powerful engine working on the line. There was also another new design, this time from the Stephenson works. This was the first locomotive to be built with horizontal cylinders, but they were set on top of the boiler not below it, so drive had to be transmitted through a complex system of jointed connecting rods, earning it the nickname 'Old Elbows'.

As well as the railways that used locomotives there were others such as the Stratford & Moreton that had turned away from locomotives altogether and only used horses. One of the directors listed the arguments, some of which seemed valid: locomotives were expensive to buy and they needed heavier track on which to run because of their weight; they could be halted altogether in winter by snow on the line and, less convincingly – people were frightened of them. The enthusiasm that had greeted the opening of the Stockton & Darlington should have made it obvious that the latter was hardly valid, but there were railway opponents ready to argue the point. One of these was Thomas Greevey MP who wrote timorously: 'the quickest motion is to me *frightful*: it is really flying and it is impossible to divest yourself of the notion of instant death upon the least accident happening'. Then finally, the investigators would look at the various inclines in use to see how they performed.

The experts chosen for the report were James Walker and John Urpeth Rastrick. Both were experienced engineers and familiar with locomotives. They started their survey in January at the Middleton Colliery line and then proceeded through Durham and Northumberland. At the end they seem to have reached their decisions, such as they were, purely on economic grounds. They concluded that though it would cost more to erect stationary engines than it would to buy locomotives, the running costs of the former would be lower. They concluded that in the long term fixed engines would prove cheaper, apparently making no allowance for possible improvements in locomotive design. It was hardly a very convincing report and satisfied no one. Robert Stephenson wrote in some disgust to Timothy Hackworth:

> They have increased the performance of fixed engines beyond what practice will bear, and, I regret to say, that they have deprecated the locomotive engines below what experience has taught us. I will not say whether these results have arisen from prejudice, or want of information or practice in the subject.

Hackworth offered encouragement to George Stephenson:

> Do not discompose yourself my dear Sir; if you express your manly, firm, decided opinion, you have done your part as their adviser. And if it happens to be read some day in the newspapers – 'Whereas the Liverpool and Manchester Railway has been strangled by ropes', we shall not accuse you of guilt in being accessory either before or after the fact.

It was decided that there was an urgent need for a pamphlet setting out the locomotive case, and the task of writing was shared between Joseph Locke and Robert Stephenson, although it would be presented under George Stephenson's name. Their report *Observations on the Comparative Merits of*

Locomotives and Fixed Engines needed to address the question of relative economics that had been central to the argument in favour of fixed engines, which it did at some length, but it also made some cogent arguments against the latter system.

> Who can look upon 30 miles of Railway, divided into equal stages, with 40 trains of carriages, running at the rate of 12 miles an hour drawn by 20 different steam engines (a delay in any one of which would stop the whole), without feeling that the liability to derangement alone is sufficient to render the stoppages extremely uncertain? And in considering this long chain of connected power, with the continual crossings of the trains from one line to the other and subject to the government of no fewer than 150 men, whose individual attention is required to preserve the communication between two of the most important towns in the kingdom, We cannot but express our decided conviction that a system which necessarily involves by a single accident the stoppage of the whole, is totally unsuited to a Public Railway.

The committee now had to consider what course of action they should follow and the result of their deliberations will form the subject of the next chapter. Meanwhile a new problem arose. George Stephenson had, as usual, many different irons in the fire and one of his projects was a line between Manchester and Stockport. Being too busy to attend to it himself, he gave instructions to Joseph Locke to go and supervise the work. Not surprisingly the Liverpool Committee objected strongly, pointing out that Locke was employed by them not by George and as they were paying him a large salary to attend to their works they would not allow him to wander off to another line. This left Locke in an unenviable position. He had taken great pride in his work on the Liverpool & Manchester and was loath to walk away from such a great undertaking to go on to a far less significant project. On the other hand, George Stephenson had been his mentor and he owed him a great deal. He felt he had no option. He resigned and left for the Stockport line. He must have thought that this was to be his last connection with the Liverpool & Manchester, but he was to return later and face another personal dilemma. In the meantime, the battle between the fixed engine and the locomotive was to reach a decisive climax.

Chapter 9

RAINHILL

Rastrick and Walker had recognised that there was a problem with opting for the fixed engine option. If the committee opted for that plan they would have to build all the engines and engine houses to see if the system worked – and if it failed they had incurred a severe loss. On the other hand, they could issue a challenge to devise a locomotive to do the job, and if that failed then the loss would be nowhere so great. In fact, they had an even better idea. Why not hold a competition and invite engineers to submit engines at their own expense with the lure of a premium payment for the winner and the much more enticing prospect of many more orders to follow? There was an ideal length of track at Rainhill, which was on the level, along which locomotives could be tested. And if they wanted to make a comparison, there was an inclined section nearby where a fixed engine and cable haulage could be tested. There were a number of locomotive enthusiasts on the committee, notably the Treasurer Henry Booth. With his encouragement the committee passed a resolution on 20 April 1829 to authorise the trial at Rainhill with a prize of £500 to the winner – assuming any of the engines met the requirements they would lay down. If none of the engines did meet the standard then nothing was lost by the Company apart from some wasted time; only the disappointed engineers would suffer. The trial date was set for October that year. An advertisement appeared in the appropriate newspapers:

To Engineers and Iron Founders
The Directors of the Liverpool and Manchester Railway hereby offer a Premium of £500 (over and above the cost price) for a LOCOMOTIVE ENGINE, which shall be a decided improvement on any hitherto constructed, subject to certain stipulations and conditions, a copy of which may be had at the Railway Office, or will be forwarded, as it may be directed, on application for the same, if by letter, post paid.
HENRY BOOTH, Treasurer Railway Office, Liverpool, April 25, 1829

No doubt they expected a few cranks to apply and one or two respected engineers, but they were astonished by the number of letters they got from all kinds of people offering a wide variety of strange and wonderful suggestions, as Henry Booth recorded.

> From professors of philosophy down to the humblest mechanic all were zealous in their proffers of assistance. England, America and Continental Europe were alike tributary. Every element and almost every substance were brought into requisition and made subservient to the great work. The friction of the carriages was to be reduced so low that a silk thread would draw them, and the power to be applied has to be so vast as to render a cable asunder. Hydrogen gas and high-pressure steam – columns of water and columns of mercury – a hundred atmospheres and a perfect vacuum – machines working in a circle without fire or steam, generating power at one end of the process and giving it out at the other – wheels within wheels, to multiply speed without diminishing power – with every complication of balancing and counteravailing forces, to be the *ne plus ultra* of perpetual motion.

In the event, the majority of the entrants simply did not meet the criteria laid down by the Company, and would have been excluded in the unlikely event of their being built and able to work at all. The criteria were very precise. The first requirement was that the engine had to 'effectively consume its own smoke', a requirement of the Railway Act. In practice this meant using a smokeless fuel, coke. The engine could weigh up to 6 tons if carried on six wheels and up to 4½ tons on four wheels. The task set for the 6 ton engine was that it

> [M]ust be capable of drawing after it, day by day, on a well-constructed Railway, on a level plane, a Train of Carriages of the gross weight of Twenty Tons, including the Tender and Water Tank, at the rate of Ten Miles an Hour with a pressure of steam in the boiler not exceeding Fifty Pounds on the square inch.

For lighter engines, the load was reduced proportionally according to weight, so that a 5 ton engine would only need to pull 16⅔ tons and so forth. This may not sound unreasonable, but it was asking a lot of the engineers, given the current state of locomotive construction. George Stephenson had supplied William James with estimates of what could be expected of engines on the Liverpool & Manchester, and for a load of 20 tons, the average speed would have been little more than 4mph. Other conditions included the use of some

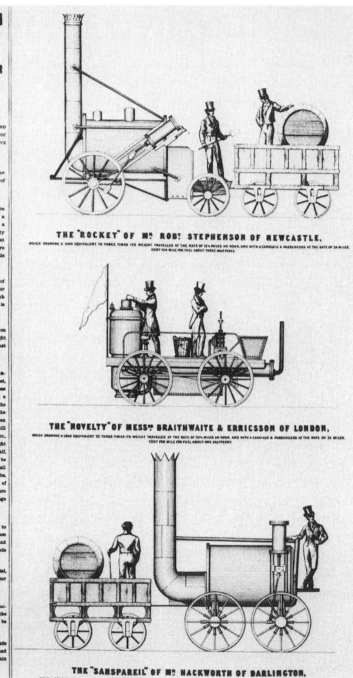

GRAND COMPETITION

LOCOMOTIVES

ON THE

LIVERPOOL & MANCHESTER RAILWAY.

STIPULATIONS & CONDITIONS

ON WHICH THE DIRECTORS OF THE LIVERPOOL AND MANCHESTER RAILWAY OFFER A PREMIUM OF £500 FOR THE MOST IMPROVED LOCOMOTIVE ENGINE.

I.

The said Engine must "effectually consume its own smoke," according to the provisions of the Railway Act, 7th Geo. IV.

II.

The Engine, if it weighs Six Tons, must be capable of drawing after it, day by day, on a well-constructed Railway, on a level plane, a Train of Carriages of the gross weight of Twenty Tons, including the Tender and Water Tank, at the rate of Ten Miles per Hour, with a pressure of steam in the boiler not exceeding Fifty Pounds on the square inch.

III.

There must be Two Safety Valves, one of which must be completely out of the reach or control of the Engine-man, and neither of which must be fastened down while the Engine is working.

IV.

The Engine and Boiler must be supported on Springs, and rest on Six Wheels; and the height from the ground to the top of the Chimney must not exceed Fifteen Feet.

V.

The weight of the Machine, WITH ITS COMPLEMENT OF WATER in the Boiler, must, at most, not exceed Six Tons, and a Machine of less weight will be preferred if it draw AFTER it a PROPORTIONATE weight; and if the weight of the Engine, &c. do not exceed FIVE TONS, then the gross weight to be drawn need not exceed Fifteen Tons; and in that proportion for Machines of still smaller weight – provided that the Engine, &c., shall still be on six wheels, unless the weight (as above) be reduced to Four Tons and a Half, or under, in which case the Boiler, &c., may be placed on four wheels. And the Company shall be at liberty to put the Boiler, Fire Tube, Cylinders, &c., to the test of a pressure of water not exceeding 150 Pounds per square inch, without being answerable for any damage the Machine may receive in consequence.

VI.

There must be a Mercurial Gauge affixed to the Machine, with Index Rod, showing the Steam Pressure above 45 Pounds per square inch; and constructed to blow out a Pressure of 60 Pounds per inch.

VII.

The Engine to be delivered complete for trial, at the Liverpool end of the Railway, not later than the 1st of October next.

VIII.

The price of the Engine which may be accepted, not to exceed £550, delivered on the Railway; and any Engine not approved to be taken back by the Owner.

N.B.—The Railway Company will provide the ENGINE TENDER with a supply of Water and Fuel, for the experiment. The distance within the Rails is four feet eight inches and a half.

THE "ROCKET" OF MR ROBT STEPHENSON OF NEWCASTLE.

WHICH DRAWING A LOAD EQUIVALENT TO THREE TIMES ITS WEIGHT TRAVELLED AT THE RATE OF 12½ MILES AN HOUR, AND WITH A CARRIAGE & PASSENGERS AT THE RATE OF 24 MILES. COST PER MILE FOR FUEL ABOUT THREE HALF PENCE.

THE "NOVELTY" OF MESSRS BRAITHWAITE & ERRICSSON OF LONDON,

WHICH DRAWING A LOAD EQUIVALENT TO THREE TIMES ITS WEIGHT TRAVELLED AT THE RATE OF 20½ MILES AN HOUR, AND WITH A CARRIAGE & PASSENGERS AT THE RATE OF 32 MILES. COST PER MILE FOR FUEL ABOUT ONE HALFPENNY.

THE "SANSPAREIL" OF MR HACKWORTH OF DARLINGTON.

The three locomotives that competed in the Rainhill Trials.

form of springing to support engine and boiler and the provision of two safety valves, one of which had to be out of reach of the driver. The latter requirement was aimed at eradicating the pernicious practice of tampering with the valve to increase pressure and performance – almost certainly the cause of explosions on the S & DR.

The Newcastle works began getting ready to design and build what was originally simply known as 'The Premium Engine'. Since Robert's return from South America, the organisation at the works had been brought back into good order and the young man was full of new ideas. He wrote to Michael Longridge in January 1828: 'I have been talking a great deal to my father about endeavouring to reduce the size and ugliness of our travelling engines, by applying the engine either on the side of the boiler or beneath it entirely'. He had the opportunity to put his ideas into practice when an order came from Liverpool for an engine to help with the construction process. After it was completed, the Company decided they didn't need it after all but agreed for it to go instead to the Bolton and Leigh Railway, where it was christened the *Lancashire Witch*. The most striking features were the cylinders, set at the side of the boiler and angled down at approximately 45°. This locomotive was the starting point for development of the engine for the Rainhill Trials. The decision was taken that they would go for a light, four-wheeled engine and it would incorporate similar angled cylinders driving the front wheels. That was just the first change that would distinguish the new engine from its predecessors.

It must have been obvious that the best way to increase the performance of the engine would be to improve on the method for raising steam. There were two elements that combined to create an efficient steam-raising unit. The first was suggested to Robert Stephenson by Henry Booth: the multi-tubular boiler. In this, the hot gases from the firebox, instead of passing down a single flue, whether doubled back or not, were passed through a number of small tubes, greatly increasing the area of hot metal in contact with the water. The same idea was arrived at simultaneously in France by Marc Seguin. The latter recognised that for this to be really efficient he needed to provide a strong blast of air to the firebox, which he achieved by means of a huge fan, geared to the locomotive. Robert Stephenson had a far more elegant solution. He went back to an idea first used by Trevithick: the blast pipe exhaust. The exhaust steam from the cylinders was allowed to escape from a narrow tube set into the bottom of the chimney, drawing air through the firebox. The elements were all in place in theory, but it was now down to Robert to produce working drawings and oversee the actual construction of a brand-new type of locomotive.

The new design was to have a separate water-jacketed firebox, and the 3ft 4in diameter boiler would have twenty-five 3in diameter copper tubes. They provided a total heating area of 138sq ft. This compares very favourably with the engine designed by Timothy Hackworth for the trial, which had a conventional return flue boiler with a heating area of 90sq ft but the boiler had to be much bigger to accommodate it at 4ft 2in diameter. In many ways the controls on the premium engine look familiar enough to anyone who has been used to the footplate of a steam locomotive, with one exception – there is no reversing lever. Modern valve gear had yet to be invented, so reversing was through slip eccentrics on the left side of the driving axle, worked through 'drivers' operated by a foot pedal.

The most pressing problem for Robert was how to install the tubes in the boiler. His first attempts involved putting screw threads on the end of the tubes and tightening them with nuts. These systems failed, so he then tried a new system of 'clunking' or riveting to fix the tubes. Things were going well at first, as he wrote to Henry Booth at the beginning of August.

> Since my arrival arrangements have been made which I expect will enable us to have the premium Eng. working in the factory say Thursday 3 weeks – This will give us time to make experiments or any alterations that may suggest themselves – The tubes are nearly all made, the whole number will be completed by tomorrow night they are an excellent job – the only point I consider at all doubtful is the clunking of the end of the tubes. The body of the boiler is finished and is a good piece of workmanship. The cylinders & other parts of the Engine are in a forward state. After weighing such parts as are in progress the following is an estimate of the weight … cwt 80 – 0. This weight I believe will cover every thing – The wheels I am arranging so as to throw two and a half tons upon the larger wheels in order to get friction on the rail. *Will there be any fatal objection raised to this?*

This was satisfactory up to a point, but it was found that when the pressure in the boiler was increased, the tube plates to which the tubes were fixed tended to bulge – 'the boiler end at 70lb per sq inch came out fully 3/16 of an inch' – distorting the tubes themselves. They had been made out of very thin metal to save weight – just ⅜in thick. So, he introduced stays between the plates to prevent them from moving and this solved the problem. He estimated that the system would withstand pressure of 150psi. This was well above the maximum pressure allowed for the actual trial, but he was aware that the judges would want to test the boiler at far above its working pressure, as an essential security precaution.

Robert was very aware that in a competition appearances matter and could influence judges, so he made every effort to make the engine appear as handsome as possible. 'The wheels of the Engine are painted in same manner as coach wheels and look extremely well. The same colour of painting I intend keeping up, throughout the engine it will look light which is one object we ought to aim at'. The colour he had chosen was a bright yellow, and the wheels themselves were made of wood with an iron, flanged tyre. Robert was able to write to Booth on 5 September that he had run the engine on the Killingworth line with very satisfactory results.

The fire burns admirably and abundance of steam is raised when the fire is carefully attended to. This is an essential point because a coke fire when let down is bad to get up again; this rather prevented our experiment being so successful as it would have been throughout. We also found that from the construction of the working gear the Engine did not work so well in one direction as in the other. This will be remedied…

We went three Miles on this Railway, the rate of ascents and descents my father knows – on a level part laid with Malleable Iron Rail, we attained a speed of 12 Miles per hour and without thinking that I deceived myself (I try to avoid this), I believe steam did not sink on this part. On the whole the Engine is capable of doing as much if not more than set forth in the stipulations. After a great deal of trouble and anxiety we have got the tubes perfectly tight. As requested by you in Mr. Locke's letter, I have not tried the boiler above 120 lb. The Mercurial Gauge and some other nick nacks are yet to be put on. On Friday next the Engine will leave by way of Carlisle and will arrive in L'pool on Wednesday week.

Around this time the *Premium Engine* was given a new, more enticing name – *Rocket*. In the event, there were to be few competitors, one of which proved to be of no consequence to the outcome. It was the work of Timothy Burstall, who had built a steam carriage in his home town of Edinburgh. Robert found him lurking around the works.

Mr. Burstall of Edinburgh is in Newcastle, I have little doubt for the purpose of getting information. I was extremely mystified to find that he walked into the manufactory this morning and examined the Engine with all the coolness imaginable before we discovered who he was. He had, however, scarcely time to take advantage of any hints he might catch during his transient visit.

Certainly, the locomotive he built for Rainhill, *Perseverance* had very little in common with *Rocket*. The design was closely based on his steam carriage of 1824, with a centrally placed vertical boiler. It was damaged on its way to the trials, when the cart carrying it overturned, and although it eventually arrived at the site, it took Burstall days to try and get it repaired. By the time he had done so, the trials were almost over, and although it was given a short run its performance was very poor. He was awarded a meagre consolation prize of just £25. There was also a strange contraption called the *Cyclopode*, entered by T.S. Brandreth powered by a horse walking inside a form of treadmill which did not even begin to qualify under the original terms of the competition. It was probably only allowed to appear at all because Brandreth was one of the Company's directors. That left just two more serious competitors.

As already mentioned, one competitor was Timothy Hackworth, who worked under difficult circumstances as he was still fully employed at Shildon. As a result, design work had largely to be carried out at night and he had to arrange for various parts of the locomotive to be produced in different locations. The main contractors were Longridge's Bedlington Ironworks who

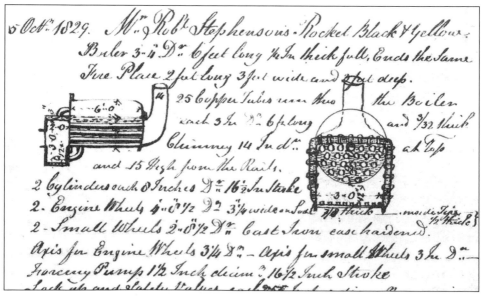

Part of John Rastrick's notebook, showing his sketches of the multi-tubular boiler on *Rocket*.

made the boiler and the cylinders were cast at the Stephenson factory in Newcastle. Various other, smaller components were provided by a number of companies. It was not the most satisfactory way of constructing a locomotive, and the work was only just finished in time for despatch to Rainhill, with no chance of running trials to test for flaws in the workmanship. It was a very conventional engine, largely based on the successful *Royal George* with the return-flue boiler, a pair of vertical cylinders providing drive to two pairs of coupled wheels. It was a large machine and it is surprising that it was not, like *Royal George* set on six wheels, which was quite allowable under the rules, and would have avoided later controversy. Like *Rocket*, the engine used exhaust blast, which was said to be so powerful that it frequently sent red hot particles of coke shooting out of the chimney. Hackworth optimistically named it *Sans Pareil* – 'without equal'.

The third entrants were faced with an even more hectic schedule than Hackworth. They were John Braithwaite and John Ericsson of London, and as far as the other competitors were concerned they were very much dark horses, but steeds with good pedigrees. Braithwaite's father, John Braithwaite senior was one of those rare creatures among inventors in that he actually made a lot of money out of his own inventions. He began with a small engineering business in St Albans and when that prospered moved to the capital. He designed a diving bell and used it himself on a salvage operation on the sunken East Indiaman, the *Earl of Abergavenny*, raising some £1,340,000-worth of goods from the wreck. When he died in 1818 the business passed to his two sons, John and Francis, and when the latter died John took full control.

The main business was manufacturing pumping engines and high-pressure steam engines. He did meet George Stephenson once in 1827 and at about the same time got to know a 24-year-old Swedish army officer, John Ericsson. Like his father, John Braithwaite recognised the importance of innovation and invention and in Ericsson he found the ideal companion. A number of useful devices came from the works, including the first steam-powered fire engine. It was used at blazes in the House of Commons and the Opera House, but the traditional firemen took exception to the rival and turned their hoses on the firebox. It was the end of the fire engine, but the ideas developed in making it were to find a new expression at Rainhill.

Ericsson had been highly successful in the army, proving to be a skilled and innovative surveyor, far more adept than any of his contemporaries, but his heart was never in it. His inventive mind was too constrained by military life and he managed to obtain extended leave, during which he was able to work with Braithwaite. He became so engrossed in this new career that he entirely forgot that his leave had actually come to an end and officially he was AWOL. Fortunately, his senior officers were lenient and instead of court martialling him, simply allowed him to resign.

Braithwaite and Ericsson heard about Rainhill more or less by accident, when they got news of it in a letter from a friend in Liverpool. With just seven weeks to the deadline, they decided to design and build a locomotive, which they very aptly named *Novelty*. It was indeed novel, owing nothing to any existing locomotive design. The earlier fire engine did not need to haul heavy loads, but it was essential that it got to the blaze as quickly as possible. The locomotive was designed to the same idea – speed was the essential. The first and most obvious difference was that the engine was very light, weighing less than 3 tons, and that included a water tank, slung beneath the frame – making it the very first tank engine. The vertical piston was connected to a bell crank and a horizontal connecting rod to a cranked axle – another first. Instead of a conventional firebox, there was a device rather more like a closed stove, from which the exhaust pipe snaked away, doubling back on itself, before bending vertically to form the chimney. The boiler itself was partly vertical surrounding the 'stove' and partly horizontal, wrapped round the convoluted exhaust pipe. Blast was provided by bellows, driven by the engine. This meant that the whole firebox was enclosed, and fuel had to be poured in from the top. One assumes the bellows were disconnected for this operation or the fireman could well have ended up minus his eyebrows. The boiler itself was sheathed in copper, which according to John Dixon gave it 'a very parlour-like appearance' like 'a new tea urn'. But to most who saw it, the engine looked decidedly sporty, with its sprung frame and light, spoked wheels. When it arrived at Rainhill, the gathering crowds made it the clear favourite. George Stephenson, however, summed it up very succinctly – 'nae guts'.

The trial officially began on 6 October 1829, but crowds gathered before that, many of them unsure exactly what was being tested. There were various descriptions in the press, and many referred to it as a race, and that seemed to be the general view among the spectators, which goes some way to explaining the general approval of *Novelty*.

The ground at Rainhill exhibited a very lively appearance; several thousand persons were collected from all parts of the country, amongst whom were several of the first Engineers of the country. A commodious tent has been erected for the accommodation of the ladies, which was graced by the beauty and fashion of the surrounding neighbourhood: the sides of the race-ground were lined with carriages of all descriptions – in short, the *tout ensemble* exhibited as much bustle and excitement as if the great St. Leger had been about to be contested.

But the event had nothing much in common with the St Leger – the prize would not go the swiftest but was to determine whether a steam locomotive could steam from Manchester to Liverpool and back again, at a reasonable speed, with a suitable load and without expending too much fuel. There was a very real possibility that none of the engines would succeed and the prize would go unclaimed. None of that mattered much to the vast crowd that gathered for the event, many of whom would never have seen a steam locomotive before. Some were excited at the idea of previously undreamed-of speeds, others apprehensive, worried by the stories that were circulating about the effects of these new-fangled machines – they would curdle the milk of cows, the sight of them would induce mass hysteria and 'experts' warned that they would most certainly explode. Anywhere that had rooms to rent out was packed by visitors and, as a local newspaper drily remarked: the landlady of the newly named Railroad Tavern would 'have substantial reasons for remembering the trial of Locomotive Carriages'.

The track was marked by white poles set a mile and a half apart with an extra eighth of a mile at each end for getting up to full speed at one end and slowing down at the other. The engines had to go up and down this track until they had covered a distance equivalent to that between the two termini, Liverpool and Manchester. They then, after a pause, would repeat the performance to simulate a return journey. The rules called for each train to pull a load equal to three times its weight, but there was a problem with *Novelty* as, unlike the others which had fuel and water in a separate tender, this one had everything on board. So, to be fair, the judges made allowances. This caused some snide remarks from one magazine about altering the rules at the last minute, but as the editor's adviser was Vignoles they could hardly be called unbiased. A far bigger problem literally arose with *Sans Pareil:* the locomotive was considerably overweight. Hackworth demanded that it was weighed again, and although the judges refused they allowed the engine to compete anyway. Heaven only knows what would have happened if it had won. There was, in any case, a certain amount of muttering about judicial bias. There were three judges, two of whom had practical experience with building locomotives themselves: John Urpeth Rastrick and Nicholas Wood. The argument was that they were both very familiar – and perhaps too familiar – with the Stephensons. But it is difficult to see how two experienced railway engineers could have been found anywhere who were not familiar with them. The criticism could not be levelled against the third judge, John Kennedy, whose only interest was in seeing an efficient railway established that would serve his very extensive cotton mill in Manchester.

The first day was merely an opportunity for the engines to have their initial test runs on the track. The first out was *Rocket* hauling a load of 12½ tons at an estimated speed of around 12mph, after which it ran light at about twice that speed. *Sans Pareil* was next to take to the track and the performance was judged to be not very different from *Rocket*'s. After that it was *Novelty* that gave the crowd the thrill of the day as it zipped along at high speed, on one run covering a mile in less than two minutes, a speed of over 30mph. The spectators loved it and the journalist extolled it.

> It seemed to fly, presenting one of the most sublime spectacles of mechanical ingenuity and human daring the world ever beheld. It actually made me giddy to look at it, and filled the breasts of thousands with lively fears for the safety of the individuals who were on it, and who seemed not to run along the earth, but to fly as it were on the wings of the wind.

If the prize could have been awarded there and then by popular acclaim there would only have been one winner. One might have expected George Stephenson to be concerned about this rival, but he would have been very well aware that travelling at high speed over a short distance when travelling light was no indication of how it would perform over a long distance with a heavy load.

The next day was to mark the start of the actual trial. The programme numbered the engines with *Novelty* at Number 1. Once again there was a flying start averaging 20mph on the first leg, but on the return the bellows broke and that was the end of that for a time. Hackworth was having problems with *Sans Pareil* and was not yet ready. The unhappy Burstall was still trying to put his machine together, but the crowd were treated to the unusual sight of the *Cyclopede* having a go. But the best it could do was reach a speed of 5mph for a short distance – it was hardly the railway future anyone was envisaging. Competition was called off for the day, but Stephenson took advantage of the occasion to make some fast runs just to prove he was a force to be reckoned with. Then the heavens opened, the rain came down and everyone scurried off home. It was only now that the judges finalised the rules. There should be ten double runs, there and back, then a pause for taking in more fuel and water, followed by another ten double runs. The amount of fuel used had to be measured, and to qualify there had to be an average of 10mph over the entire journey.

The following day, 8 October, was a triumph for the Stephenson camp. *Rocket* set off steadily but at a good speed, and all through the test the performance continued to improve, until on the very last lap George Stephenson opened up the regulator and *Rocket* lived up to its name, shooting along at over 30mph. It had pulled the stipulated load the full distance with no sign of a problem at an average speed of almost 14mph, well above the requirements of the competition. No one now could doubt that the steam locomotive was the answer to running a railway, not a series of cables hauling trucks and carriages along. The only question that now remained was – would anyone else match or even beat this performance? That should have been decided the following day, but no one was ready. Hackworth asked for more time and it was agreed that he should run on the Monday. Braithwaite and Ericsson had been busily making new joints for the pipe from the water feed pump to the boiler, but declared they would be ready to go the next day. The judges recommended that they wait until the Monday to join Hackworth, but they were adamant that all would be well and they wanted to go ahead. It turned out not to be a good idea. *Novelty* set out for its runs on the Saturday but after just one run it was clear that the joint had given way again, as water flew in all directions and the engine ground to a halt. Their day was finished. Their chances of winning anything were looking exceedingly slim.

There was now just one serious competitor left to challenge *Rocket* – Hackworth's *Sans Pareil*. There remained two problems with the engine: it was overweight by 7cwt and the rules had stipulated springing which was clearly totally absent. The judges very sensibly decided that the directors of the railway company would be interested in taking on the best engine and would not really want to be left with no choice and no means of comparison, so they allowed the engine to run. There was further delay and it was Tuesday before everything was ready and *Sans Pareil* set off again. At first, things seemed to be going well and the locomotive was averaging the same speed as *Rocket*. By the eighth run, however, it was clear that something was seriously wrong. Hackworth was struggling to keep the engine going and then, right in front of the grandstand, the engine came to a halt in a cloud of steam.

The water feed pump had failed with the inevitable result that not sufficient water had reached the boiler, which had overheated and the fusible plug did its job – it melted, allowing the steam to escape and thus avoiding an explosion. The engineer had begged the judges for one more try, but this time they were adamant. They had been measuring fuel consumption, and found that the Hackworth engine's was far too great – three times that of *Rocket*. Given that the engine was too heavy, unsprung and with horrendous fuel consumption they saw no point in him continuing.

The Wednesday was the last day of the trials, and *Novelty* was to make one final attempt to complete a set of runs. The engineers had been working hard to make repairs, and Timothy Hackworth had generously offered to help, whether from good will or from a sense that he would rather not see Stephenson win is uncertain. It was all to no avail, as the official report made clear.

> The engine returning westwards the second trip, the Joints of the Boiler gave way, as indeed they might naturally be expected to do from being so recently made. Which put an effective stop to the Experiment, so that the Engine and Train were obliged to run up by hand. Mr. Ericsson then declared to us that he would now withdraw his engine from all further competition so far as regarded the Premium.

It was all over and John Dixon wrote to tell his brother of the triumph.

> We have finished the grand experiment on the Engines and G.S. or R.S. has come off triumphant and of course will take hold of the £500 so liberally offered by the Company, none of the other being able to come near them. The Rocket is by far the best Engine I have ever seen for Blood and Bone united
>
> Timothy has been very sadly out of temper since he came for he has been growling on night and day and nothing our men did for him was right, we could not please him with the Tender or anything; he openly accused all G.S.'s people of conspiring to hinder him of which I do believe them innocent, however, he got many trials but never got half of his Seventy miles done without stopping. He burns nearly double the quantity of coke that the Rocket does and mumbles and roars and rolls about like an Empty Beer Butt on a rough Pavement and moreover weighed above 4½ tons consequently should have had six wheels and as for being on Springs I must confess I cannot find them out.

There was to be more grumbling by Hackworth after the event. In a letter he declared that there was nothing basically wrong with the design and construction, but he had been forced 'to put that confidence in others which I found with sorrow was but too implicitly placed'. He went on to say that the defects could all have been remedied had he had enough time. As we know, various components were made by different companies and Hackworth never stated which company was responsible for faulty workmanship. Later, however, a new version appeared – the failure was due to a cracked cylinder, provided by the Stephenson works. This was stated quite specifically by Robert Young in his 1923 biography of Hackworth.

Rocket **preserved** in the Science Museum, London. It had been modified in service, most obviously by lowering the angle of the steam cylinders.

Yet there was no mention of any such defect at the time, and certainly it is difficult to square that with Hackworth's own assertion that repairs could easily have been carried out at Rainhill. There is, however, more than ample evidence of other faults, notably with the boiler and the feed pump, neither of which was supplied by the Stephensons. None of which prevented the story growing that *Sans Pareil* had been nobbled by the Dastardly George and Evil Robert.

We cannot go back in time to test the reliability of the different engines that competed at Rainhill, but we can see the replicas that were built to celebrate the 150th anniversary. I had the good fortune of being asked to write and present the BBC TV programme, *The Rainhill Story* in which we followed the construction process of the replicas and I had a chance to see them perform on completion. *Rocket* was everything that one would expect it to be – a smoothly running, efficient machine, a truly impressive piece of machinery. It was built by Mike Satow's company Locomotion Enterprises, and they also undertook to build the replica *Novelty*. Here, history repeated itself and it scarcely managed to stagger out of the workshops. Unlike the original, it was destined never to steam at Rainhill at all, and when the celebratory cavalcade took place, the engine could only be seen, rather ignominiously, sitting on top of a flat-bed truck, unable to move under its own steam.

Sans Pareil had a very different fate in store. Very appropriately, the replica was constructed at Shildon, not at the old Hackworth workshops, but at what was then the British Rail depot. It was first steamed on a cold, damp November morning. It seemed to take an age for the pressure gauge to finally move and reach a modest 10psi, but as the pressure gently rose, there was a rather ominous bubbling and dripping from the feed pipe, a reminder of problems with the original. But all went well, though stoking looked very difficult, with an awkward narrow firebox by the chimney. But at last working pressure was achieved and the engine rolled out of the shed and moved off smoothly. The first impression was just how much bulkier it looked than *Rocket*, but that it also seemed an impressively powerful machine. The engineer's great-great-granddaughter Jane Hackworth Young was there for the occasion and was invited onto the footplate. At the end of the ride, she was clearly absolutely delighted by the performance and had no doubt that, if all had been fair and above board, the locomotive would have outperformed *Rocket*. Having seen both the replicas perform I felt disinclined to share her opinion – but was certainly not going to dampen her enthusiasm by saying so.

The Hackworth camp did get their reward in a way. When it came to the great cavalcade in 1979 at Rainhill, all the locomotives that were to take part on the opening Saturday, were gathered at nearby Bold Colliery. *Rocket* was to lead the parade, but just as the event was about to start, the engine was derailed and could not be got back onto the track – something was out of gauge. So, the only one of the contestants that appeared under steam that day was *Sans Pareil*. If there is an engineering heaven, Timothy Hackworth must have been looking down and laughing his head off.

It was as well that *Rocket* did win. *Sans Pareil* represented the end of a line of development that began with the first colliery engines, not the start of something new. However, Hackworth went on to have a successful career as an engine builder, including supplying the first engine to work a railway in Russia. *Novelty* had too many design flaws to be a model for anything. Ericsson, however, was destined to succeed in a very different area of development. He went to America, where he designed one of the very first screw propellers for a steam ship and *Monitor* the first ironclad battleship that saw service in the American Civil War. But it was *Rocket* that represented the railway future. There was to be controversy over who should take the credit for blast pipe exhaust, but it was only when it was combined with the multi-tubular boiler that it became a really valuable device. The movement of the cylinders from the vertical to an angle was a first step towards the eventual move to horizontal cylinders that would characterise later locomotives. There were contemporaries who criticised several features – including that it was too light, but it has to be remembered that the engine was not designed to work the line at this stage but to fit in with the specific requirements laid down for the competition. The engine would later be modified for use in service, as can be clearly seen in the preserved engine. The future of the steam locomotive was assured.

Chapter 10

THE GRAND OPENING

Whilst the question of whether or not locomotives were capable of running the railway was being decided, construction work was going ahead. One valuable member of the team was missing. Joseph Locke was away, working on the Manchester & Stockport line, though he was also to take a more responsible position on the Canterbury & Whitstable. Neither of these, however, compared in importance with the Liverpool & Manchester. He must have thought that his connection with the line was over, but he was to return in what turned out to be unfortunate circumstances at a later date.

The argument over Locke's employment was not the only disagreement between Stephenson and the company directors. In particular, James Cropper, who had been one of the leading enthusiasts for fixed engines, seems to have had a grudge against the engineer who had so decisively proved him wrong. He began arguing that, in spite of all evidence to the contrary, *Rocket* was not necessarily the right engine for the job. He suggested approaching Sir Goldsworthy Gurney who had built a steam carriage for use on the road, but that gentleman showed little interest in the idea. He then decided to champion Braithwaite and Ericsson, arguing that the only problem with their engine was not the design but the haste with which it was constructed. There were still those who were impressed by what they saw as the elegant, light, speedy engine and he persuaded his fellow directors to order two locomotives similar to *Novelty*. They were expensive, costing twice as much as the Stephenson engine, and proved to be as hopeless now as they had been at the Trial. *Novelty* itself was given a brief outing on the St Helens & Runcorn Gap Railway, and when that did not answer was reduced to the lowly role of a contractor's engine during the building of the viaduct over the Ribble for the North Union Railway. It was as well that the directors had also ordered four locomotives from Robert Stephenson at the conclusion of the Trial. They were named *Arrow, Comet, Dart* and *Meteor*.

Robert had made a number of changes, partly based on experiences at Rainhill and partly because he was no longer constrained by the limits set for the competition. He was able to increase the weight of the engine's 1½ tons, and the most obvious difference in the appearance was the reduction of the angle of the cylinders to near the horizontal. Internally, their diameter was increased from 8 to 10 inches, reflecting improved steam raising capacity. Inside the boiler, the tubes were reduced in size but increased in number to eighty-eight giving a greater heating surface. The new engines were both more powerful than *Rocket* but also thanks to the change in the cylinder positions ran more smoothly. The engines were a great success and in February, orders were put in for two more – *Phoenix* and *North Star*. Experience showed that further development was still possible, and cylinder sizes were increased once again by a further inch and the boiler slightly extended. The most significant change was at the chimney end, where for the first time there was a proper smokebox. A third engine, *Northumbrian*, brought even more changes. Steam raising was improved yet again, by introducing 132 tubes of 15/8in diameter, providing a heating area almost three times that of *Rocket*. The firebox was now an integral part of the boiler, a development that would be followed in all future steam locomotives. There was no doubt that as far as locomotives were concerned, the Company was being well served. One might have thought that Cropper having made something of a fool of himself by insisting on ordering the useless Braithwaite-Ericsson engines would retire from the fray, but he was not finished yet with tormenting the chief engineer.

Cropper and his supporters now arranged to employ William Chapman to inspect and report on the works. It was not unreasonable in some ways as Chapman was one of the locomotive pioneers, but he was also known to have annoyed Stephenson by denigrating the performance of *Lancashire Witch* to the directors of the Bolton & Leigh Railway. Most who knew of the antagonism now sat back and waited for the explosion. They did not have to wait long. Chapman took it upon himself to question one of the men about the locomotives, though as Stephenson wrote later: 'it is doubtful whether he understood the import of the questions, and it is still more doubtful if they were intelligible to any working mechanic'. Chapman, however, declared the answers unsatisfactory and immediately sacked the man. Now this was one of the trusted hands that Stephenson had brought with him from the north-east. It was all too much and Stephenson's blood was up. He let fly with a long, angry letter to the directors, which ended:

> This kind of interference with my duties as well as doubts and suspicions which had been expressed regarding the opinions I have from time to time given in different subjects connected with this work has occasioned me much uneasiness. I have been accused of jealousy and a want of candour in

A replica of *Planet* at the Museum of Science and Industry, Manchester: the locomotive represented the next stage of development after the success of *Rocket*.

the case of Mr. Brandreth's and Mr. Winan's waggons as well as in that of Mr. Ericsson's engine, and even of worse than this in the case of the Stationary v. Locomotive engines. In all these cases, instead of jealousy operating I confidently state that I have been only influenced by a disinterested zeal for the complete success of your work and by a laudable desire to support and establish my own credit.

May I now ask if I have supported your interests or not? Has Mr. Brandreth's carriage answered? Has Mr. Winan saved 9/10 of the friction? Was not Walker & Rastrick's report wrong? Has the *Novelty* engine answered your expectations? Have the *Lancashire Witch* and the *Rocket* not performed more than I stated? These facts make me bold, but they also stimulate me to still further improvements. But I cannot believe that you will permit me to be thwarted in my proceedings by individuals who neither understand the work nor feel the interest which attaches me to this railway. Allow me therefore to ask if you intend Mr. C to continue on the works?

The arguments were, as Stephenson well knew, unanswerable. The Company responded in the only way possible: Chapman left the workings. His opponents on the board had not quite finished with him yet. Stephenson had successfully tendered for a big winding engine for use on one of the inclines, but there was a penalty clause attached. If the engine was not delivered on site at the stated date and in good condition, there would be a £500 penalty. The engine was ready on time and was sent by ship to Liverpool. Unfortunately, the ship foundered and although the engine was recovered it could not be repaired in time to meet the due date. The clause had clearly been put in to ensure that the engineering firm responsible did a proper job, but it made no allowances for accidents in transit. The board refused to show leniency and demanded their pound of flesh. They had just awarded Stephenson his £500 premium – now they had got the money back again. The decision was legally correct but morally indefensible. All this bickering and constant criticism, together with money wasted on impractical machines, must have been intensely irritating to the engineer and could hardly have helped the smooth running of the operation. In the end, George Stephenson's reputation remained intact and his morale was to get a boost from an unexpected quarter.

Fanny Kemble was enjoying a huge success as an actor in London from her first appearance as Juliet in 1829 when she was just 20 years old. She was not only a beautiful girl, but was blessed with a lively intelligence and wit and had already written a play of her own that had been very well received. Like many in the fashionable world, she was interested in the new mechanical marvels on show in north-west England. She was fascinated by the locomotives and George Stephenson was, it seems, no less fascinated by her. He took the unusual step of inviting her to join him on the footplate of *Northumbrian*. Her account of the journey has been printed many times, but it is worth repeating for it captures in the way that no other does the sheer excitement of those days. Here she is going down the deep cutting at Olive Mount.

You can't imagine how strange it was to be journeying on thus, without any visible cause of progress other than the magical machine, with its flying white breath and rhythmical, unvarying pace, between these rocky walls which are already clothed with moss and ferns and grasses; and when I reflect that these great masses of stone had been cut asunder to allow our passage thus far below the surface of the earth, I felt as if no fairy tale was ever half so wonderful as what I saw. Bridges were thrown from side to side across the top of these cliffs, and the people looking down upon us from them seemed like pygmies standing in the sky.

Her obvious enthusiasm both for the novelty of the locomotive and the scale of the works must have been a tonic to George Stephenson, who continued with the journey to show off the other major features along the line, including the Sankey viaduct. When she had marvelled at the sights, he had one last treat in store for his charmingly beguiling guest as he opened up the regulator and the engine gathered speed.

> The engine having received its supply of water … was set off at its utmost speed, 35 miles an hour, swifter than a bird flies (for they tried the experiment with a snipe). You cannot conceive what a sensation of cutting the air was; the motion is as smooth as possible too. I could either have read or written; and as it was I stood up, and with my bonnet off 'drank the air before me'. The wind, which was strong, or perhaps the force of our own thrusting against it absolutely weighed my eyelids down. When I closed my eyes this sensation of flying was quite delightful, and strange beyond description; yet strange as it was I had a perfect sense of security, and not the slightest fear.

If Fanny was enthralled by the speed of her journey, she was equally delighted with her companion.

> Now for a word or two about the master of all these marvels, with whom I am most horribly in love. He is a man from fifty to fifty-five years of age; his face is fine, though careworn, and bears an expression of deep thoughtfulness, his mode of explaining his ideas is very peculiar and very original, striking, and forcible; and although his accent indicates strongly his north country birth, his language has not the slightest touch of vulgarity or coarseness. He has certainly turned my head.

Fanny Kemble's career as an actor was short lived. On tour in Boston, Massachusetts she met and married an American who took her home to a Southern plantation. The experience horrified her and she became a leading figure in the movement for the abolition of slavery.

The interlude with Fanny Kemble was a pleasant break in George's hectic life, for he was still juggling a variety of different projects, including the line he had inherited from James – the Canterbury & Whitstable. He was far too busy to take much of an interest in it himself, but both Robert Stephenson and Joseph Locke were to spend time in charge of operations. It was a somewhat absurd line, joining Whitstable Harbour to a village on the outskirts of Canterbury, just 6 miles away, but there was a rise of 200ft in between the two ends, which was managed by a mixture of inclined planes and the 828-yard-long Tyler's Hill tunnel. The engineers must have been gratified when the tunnel was completed to find that the bores, started from each end, met in the middle with almost perfect alignment. Their satisfaction, however, was short lived as just a month later part of the roof collapsed, injuring a workman. In spite of this setback, the line was opened in April 1830 and became the first railway in the world to offer a regular passenger service worked by steam locomotives – even if they only travelled part of the way behind a locomotive. The Liverpool & Manchester had been pipped to the post, but the opening of the modest line attracted little attention in the world at large, even if it was greeted by local enthusiasm. It was, in any case, a Stephenson engine that hauled that first train, the *Invicta*. She was based on the *Rocket*, but with significant variations. The cylinders were placed at the chimney end and the wheels were coupled in a 0-4-0 configuration.

Meanwhile work was progressing well on the major route. Chat Moss had been conquered, a single track had been laid and opened for traffic on New Year's Day, 1830. Things were, not, however, going so well with the tunnelling at the Liverpool end of the line. The main problem lay with the tunnel to what would eventually become the Lime Street station. Reports of surveying inaccuracies began to circulate. The Board decided to call back Joseph Locke to report, as he was familiar with that part of the line having been the resident engineer for some time. Locke had always had great confidence in George Stephenson, but now he found that there were indeed inaccuracies. According to Locke's biographer Joseph Devey, writing in 1869, 'several portions of the tunnel would never have formed a straight line, and in one instance, instead of meeting, would have given each other the go-by altogether'. Locke showed the report to the supervisor who had taken his place in the workings, who agreed it was a fair assessment and passed it on to the Board. Fortunately, there was time to correct the errors. The report resulted, however, in a souring of relationships between Locke and the Stephensons. George in particular regarded any criticism as a form of betrayal, and it would be some years before the old friendship between the two younger engineers would be resumed.

Robert Stephenson was still at work on devising improvements to his locomotives, and the result was *Planet* that was to prove to be the first of a large class of locomotives. This was an engine that looked very different from any of its predecessors. The engine had a separate frame that was set outside the wheels and built up of stout wooden beams, backed by iron plates. Stephenson had long had the ambition to make the engines look rather more elegant by tucking away some of the working parts. The outside frame allowed him to put the cylinders beneath the boiler, bolted to the firebox. According to W.O. Skeat in his book *George Stephenson: The Engineer and his Letters* the idea came from a conversation with Trevithick in South America, where the older engineer had discussed ways in which he had improved the performance of the Boulton and Watt engine. They were now used to drive a cranked axle. There was later controversy that suggested that he stole the latter idea from Hackworth, who had used a similar device on his engine, *Globe*. But the idea was not new: Robert could have seen it at work at Rainhill on *Novelty*. The new arrangement allowed for a larger grate on the firebox and he was able to slightly reduce cylinder diameter without any loss of power. The reversing mechanism was based on slip eccentrics as with the *Rocket* but their operation was quite different. Two long eccentric rods were passed between the cylinders to gabs, notches at the ends closest to the valves, which could then engage or disengage with a rocking shaft that controlled the actual valve movement. Once under way, the levers on the footplate continued to move backwards and forwards with the movement of the valve. As with earlier engines a replica was built and seeing it in action is quite a remarkable sight – one does not expect to see those sorts of moving metal parts on a footplate. The original was built to a 2-2-0 wheel arrangement with 5ft diameter drive wheels. The design was to prove highly successful, though the cranked axles proved difficult to forge and, in the early *Planets* were liable to break, though this was not the only problem with these early engines. George Stephenson alluded to this in a letter dated 11 October 1830 to Michael Longridge, who supplied many of the components for the engines.

Upon my arrival here I examined the broken wheels, and found that one of the hoops which has given way was scarcely at all welded. This says very ill for your Blacksmith's work and alarms me very much about the axletrees. For, should one of them break you are quite aware how serious an accident it would be. It is the cranked axletrees of the Engines to which I allude, The axletrees should all be numbered in your Works and the name of the Maker inserted in a book.

The opening of the Canterbury & Whitstable Railway, a line on which Robert Stephenson worked for a time as engineer.

It was not only in the field of mechanical engineering that new ideas were being tried out. The world's first passenger railway station was under construction at Liverpool Road, Manchester. Seen from the street it could easily be mistaken for a gentleman's residence, built in the late Georgian style. It looks reassuringly serene and perhaps calmed the nerves of passengers about to take their first trips on the mechanical marvels. The entrance for first-class passengers was through the front door of this station disguised as a mansion, while there was a second door to one side for less exalted passengers – the tradesman's entrance as Simon Jenkins has rather aptly described it. The booking office backed onto the embankment carrying the lines at first floor level. There were also private rooms set aside for the grandest passengers who preferred to travel in their own coaches, which were loaded onto special flat trucks. The preserved station and tracks are now home to the replica *Planet*. A goods warehouse was built opposite the single-sided station, with a capstan for winching trucks and wagons in and out.

Rolling stock also had to be built for the railway and the Company naturally turned to experienced coach builders for the more important vehicles. There were to be three classes of passenger coaches. The first class were four-wheeled vehicles that from the outside looked like three conventional stagecoaches stuck together. There was a seat outside for the guard, perched up at the top of the carriage. The second class were open-sided, though they had the advantage of a canopy to provide some protection from the weather. The third class were simply open trucks with benches. None of them would have been particularly comfortable, which perhaps explains why the wealthiest passengers preferred the comfort of their own, well-sprung coaches.

The date for the opening was set for Wednesday, 15 September 1830. It was recognised that, unlike the opening of the Stockton & Darlington, this would be an event of national importance. The principal guest was to be the Duke of Wellington. It was in some ways a slightly odd choice as he was known to have been less than enthusiastic about the idea of railways because, he said, 'They would encourage the lower orders to travel about'. The duke took a very dim view of the 'lower orders' in general and was an outspoken opponent of Parliamentary reform. This was not a view that would endear him to the people of north-west England. They still remembered what had happened in St Peter's Square Manchester in 1819. A meeting had been called to hear speakers argue for reform, and the event so alarmed the local magistrates that they called in the militia to disperse the crowd. They did so with incredible brutality slashing away with their swords, as the result of which fifteen people were killed and hundreds injured. To the people of Manchester, the Duke of Wellington was not the Hero of Waterloo but the Villain of Peterloo. Among those who had disagreed with the duke's reactionary views in Parliament was the local MP and railway enthusiast William Huskisson. The Company hoped that given the general enthusiasm for the new railway and the presence of so many other VIPs including Prince Esterhazy of Austria and the Russian Minister, Count Potacki, the crowds would forget party politics for the day.

There was certainly no lack of enthusiasm, and crowds poured into Liverpool, as the local paper reported. They came by road and by steamer, and the roads were packed with traffic. 'The horses on the road were worked to death: and so great was the scarcity of cattle, the Duke of Wellington could not, when his carriage reached Warrington, on Tuesday afternoon, procure more than two sorry jades to drag him to Childwell, the seat of the Marquis of Salisbury.' On the morning of the opening, as the crowds gathered, workmen were busy at work clearing away the last of the rubble from the entrance to the Edgehill tunnel and erecting railings along the top of the deep cutting at Olive Mount to prevent anyone tumbling over the edge. When the Duke of Wellington arrived, the band – somewhat inevitably – played 'See the Conquering Hero comes' and the Liverpool crowd cheered. He took his place in a specially prepared carriage.

The ducal carriage was a costly and splendid car. The floor was 32 feet long by 8 feet wide, supported upon eight wheels, which were partly concealed by a basement, ornamented with bold gold mouldings and laurel wreaths on a ground of crimson cloth. An ornamental gilt balustrade extended round each end of the carriage, and united with one of the pillars which supported the roof. Handsome scrolls filled up the next compartments, on each side of the doorway, which was in the centre of the carriage, protected with balustrading similar to that at each end. A lofty canopy of crimson cloth, 24 feet in length rested up eight carved and gilt pillars, the cornice enriched with gold ornaments and pendant tassels, the cloth fluted to two centres, surmounted with two ducal coronets. The canopy was, by the aid of a windlass in the basement, made to rise or fall, and so constructed that, when down, the coronets were concealed in the roof … the whole had a magnificent and imposing effect, in the Grecian style of architecture.

The Company had issued Orders of the Day. The eight available locomotives with their trains were lined up at Liverpool, with *Northumbrian* at the head and *Meteor* bringing up the rear. When all was ready a gun was to be fired and the first train set off, and then a second gun was fired signalling for the rest to follow. There was a planned stop at Parkhead to take on water, and at this point it was made clear 'the passengers are requested not to leave their carriages'. After that the procession was to move on to Manchester where there would be refreshments available before the passengers rejoined the trains for the return journey. It should all have gone smoothly, but the august passengers simply ignored the Company rules. At Parkside several got out and wandered around, apparently oblivious of the fact that the tracks were being used by fast-moving trains.

The Duke of Wellington's carriage had been shunted onto a different line, so that he could watch the arrival of the other locomotives. The duke decided that this was a good opportunity to make a friendly gesture towards his old adversary Huskisson and leaned out of his carriage offering to shake hands. Huskisson wandered across and stood on the track chatting. Suddenly there were shouts of 'Get in, get in'. *Rocket* was approaching at speed. Huskisson seemed bewildered, uncertain which way to go, wandered over the track and then tried to find a safe place by clinging to the door of the duke's carriage. There was no time for the driver to stop the engine, which caught the open door, threw Huskisson onto

The opening of the Liverpool & Manchester Railway: the start of the day in the Olive Mount cutting, Liverpool.

the tracks, where the train rolled over one of his legs, crushing the thigh. A Birmingham man Joseph Parkes lifted the stricken man from the rails.

'This is the death of me,' murmured Huskisson.
'I hope not, sir,' said Parkes.
'Yes, it is.'

Amid this confusion, George Stephenson began making preparations to get the victim to be taken to the nearest medical help. *Northumbrian* was uncoupled from its train and attached to a flat car that had originally carried a band of musicians. Huskisson was carefully laid on the car and then Stephenson personally took charge of the locomotive and sped off towards Eccles, reaching speeds of 36mph. It was a valiant effort but in vain. Nothing could save him and the man who had been such a stalwart supporter of the railway died on what should have been a day of triumph in which he had played a leading role.

The organisers were now faced with a dilemma. Given the tragedy at Parkside, should the rest of the day be cancelled or should they continue to Manchester? The duke, who unwittingly had been the cause of the accident, was reluctant to continue, but the officials were concerned that given the huge crowds that had gathered to see the procession, they had to carry on or face a possible riot. The duke reluctantly agreed, and *Planet* and *North Star* were coupled together and a long train formed behind them. The *Albion* newspaper reported the scene as the train approached Manchester. It was not exactly the reception they had hoped for:

> [T]he procession then dashed forward, passing countless thousands of people upon house tops, booths, high ground, bridges &c. and our readers must imagine, for we cannot describe, such a movement through an avenue of living beings, and extending six miles in length. Upon one bridge a tricoloured flag was displayed; upon another the motto of 'Vote by ballot' was seen; in a field near Eccles, a poor and wretchedly dressed man had his loom close to the road side, and was weaving with all his might; cries of 'No Corn Laws' were occasionally heard and for about two miles the cheering of the great body of the crowd were interspersed with a continued hissing and booing.

The reception at Manchester was, if anything, even worse, with repeated cries of 'Remember Peterloo'. There was a meal prepared but few had an appetite for celebration and the duke remained in his carriage, sitting in silence while the boos echoed round him. With all the changes that had been made, the plans were now in disarray, with locomotives and their coaches all needing to be marshalled into a fit order for the return. It was dusk before they got under way, and *Comet* was sent ahead of the main train, with the driver holding an improvised torch of tarred rope to light the way. It was a sad and gloomy procession that finally made it back to Liverpool at 11 o'clock that night.

The opening day may have been one of tragedy, but once the railway was opened for business it was obvious to everyone that this was the transport of the future, as the general public rushed to buy tickets in all the classes. What had begun just a few years before as a system to serve collieries with trains of creaking, slow moving trucks was about to develop into a nationwide system that would serve the whole community.

Chapter 11

THE SYSTEM EXPANDS

A number of new schemes were being put forward, in many of which George Stephenson himself had shares. In a letter to Nicholas Wood in November 1831 he listed his holdings as twenty-four in the Warrington & Newton, twenty-five in the Leicester & Swannington and twenty, held with Robert, in the Sheffield & Manchester. George had visited Leicester to discuss the line that would join the city to the Swannington coalfields in February 1829. It was only 16 miles long, but was considered important in reducing the price of coal to Leicester. George had carried out the preliminary survey, but it was Robert who was appointed chief engineer. This was a busy time for him as he was already involved in adding to the network, working on the Bolton & Leigh and the Warrington & Newton lines. He was also still in charge of the locomotive works, and there were grumblings in Newcastle that he was neglecting that side of the business. The only major engineering work on the Leicestershire line was the mile-long Glenfield tunnel, which turned out to be troublesome, as it had to be pushed through loose, sandy soil. There were two inclined planes, one at Bagworth, which was 946 yards long, but at a comparatively gentle slope of 1 in 29, which was self-acting as it sloped towards Leicester, the destination for the loaded coal trucks. The other at Swannington was a more demanding 1 in 17, up which the loaded trucks had to be hauled by a stationary engine. On 17 March 1832 the *Northampton Mercury* reported on progress in glowing terms:

Leicester and Swannington Rail-road – The driving and arching of the tunnel, on this new line of road, was completed on Saturday last, and the laying down of the railway will commence forthwith. The Leicester tunnel is a full mile in length, sixteen and a half feet high and twelve feet wide; and has been completed in the most scientific and satisfactory manner by the contractors, Messrs. Copeland and Harding, in the short period of eleven months. This, when we consider the seemingly hazardous nature of the operations, which were directed through an immense sand-hill, may be reckoned among the highest proofs of modern perseverance and skill.

Twelve miles of the Leicester and Swannington railway will open in May, and the whole line will be finished in September next.

Five locomotives were sent from the Robert Stephenson works, the first of which was *Comet* but someone had made a serious miscalculation: A locomotive with a 13ft high chimney was never going to go through the tunnel. The next engines, *Samson* and *Goliath* were initially 0-4-0s but they proved somewhat unstable and an extra pair of wheels were added to turn them into 0-4-2s. Robert Stephenson was so pleased with the result that he abandoned the 0-4-0 arrangement for later engines. However, they were somewhat underpowered, so he designed his first 0-6-0 locomotive, *Atlas*. The locomotive was also fitted with the newly invented steam brake. The idea was to be developed a lot further in 1833, when Robert Stephenson patented a new development, which was to have the usual flanges for carrying wheels but to leave the drive wheels without flanges. The engines came to be known as the *Patentees*, mostly with a 2-2-2 wheel arrangement, though other combinations for six wheelers were also made.

Samson's first run was plagued with problems. At one of the crossings, it hit a cart loaded with eggs and butter, which must have made an interesting mess on the tracks. Apparently, the carter had not heard the warning horn, so it was decided that something more effective was needed on the locomotive. George Stephenson designed and patented a steam whistle that proved highly successful, and was the basis for the whistles used on future locomotives. Although this was a modest line, it had resulted in two important changes in locomotive design. It was also to play an important role in the life of the Stephenson family.

Robert reported back to his father that in his opinion there were substantial reserves of coal in the area that had not yet been worked. George approached Joseph Sandars and Sir Joshua Walmsley to discuss the idea of developing the deep coal seams. They formed a partnership and bought land at Snibston and began sinking pits. Unfortunately, it was soon discovered that there was a 22ft deep stratum of hard rock to be worked through before the coal could be reached. The local men, inexperienced at this kind of work, were unable to cope, so a workforce was brought down from Killingworth. Three shafts were sunk, and once through the rock a thick seam of first class coal was reached. The mine was to prove highly profitable. George left his old home in Liverpool and moved down to be near the colliery, buying a handsome house, Alton Grange at

Ashby-de-la-Zouch. He was to remain there until 1838 when he moved to Tapton House, Chesterfield, a fine Georgian mansion set within extensive grounds. It was to be his home for the rest of his life.

It is rather surprising to find at this period of the early 1830s that a line was being promoted that was to be worked by horses. The citizens of Whitby were concerned that the port was in decline. It had a whaling fleet, some shipbuilding facilities and a substantial trade shipping out alum, but it was felt that there would be a great improvement in trade if they had better inland communications. In 1832, they approached George Stephenson and asked him to look into the matter and he reported back very favourably on the proposal for constructing a single track line from the port to Pickering. The line began near the harbour at Whitby and crossed the River Esk nine times before arriving at Grosmont via a short tunnel.

At Goathland there was a 1,500ft long rope-worked incline that connected the line to Beck Hole, where iron ore mines were developed. The remainder of the journey took the obvious line down the deep valley of Newtondale to Pickering. Passengers were carried at first in a coach not unlike that used on the Stockton & Darlington. Later the line was converted to steam operation and survives today as the North Yorkshire Moors Railway. The rope incline has gone, and the Grosmont tunnel has been by-passed but still remains in use for pedestrians. It is a superbly picturesque line, but was of minor importance in the greater scheme of things. It was in the Midlands and in the industrial North that the great changes were happening.

The obvious line of development was to unite the Liverpool & Manchester line with other main-line routes to link in with the most important towns and cities. A first stage would be to extend down to Birmingham and then to head further south to London. It was inevitable that the promoters would turn to the Stephensons for the first part of the plan. However, it was not quite as straightforward as they might have thought and expected. In 1824, an agreement had been reached to set up a company alongside the manufacturing company of Robert Stephenson to be called George Stephenson & Son. Michael Longridge was to take over the administration from a Newcastle office, and the company was to undertake every single aspect of railway construction, from preparing for the Parliamentary Bill to building the line and providing locomotives and rolling stock. There would be employees taking over all the necessary roles and the new company would also be responsible for contracting for work. It was using the George Stephenson brand name to attract customers, while the other partners would see to the

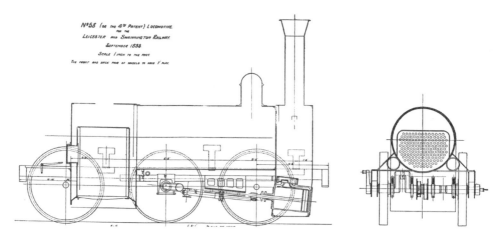

No.55 (or the 5th Patent) Locomotive
for the
Leicester and Swannington Railway.
September 1888
Scale 1 inch to the foot
The front and back pair of wheels to have 1 play.

An original drawing of the *Patent* locomotive for the Leicester & Swannington Railway: the end view shows the cranked axle.

financial affairs. A modern analogy would be the celebrity chef, who sets up a chain of restaurants and although his name might be over the door of each, he might never actually cook in any of them personally. The whole matter was further complicated by the fact that as well as this grand scheme, other less important developments were occupying the Stephensons at this time.

Many of the schemes going forward involved the new company, so that any necessary work was as likely to fall to Robert as it was to his father. One of Robert's first jobs was to survey and prepare estimates for a short branch line, the Kenyon & Leigh. It was only 2½ miles and one of the few obstacles in the way was the Leeds & Liverpool Canal that had to be bridged. Robert produced his estimates, which were rejected as being too expensive and he was told to come back with a cheaper version. He was not happy with the idea.

> This is one way of doing things, but proud as I am I must submit. I have tried in my cool solitary moments to look with patience on such proceedings, but, by heavens, it requires a great deal more than I have. I would patiently bear the alteration if they did it from principle: but knowing, and indeed hearing, them say from what the alternation does really spring, I cannot but consider it unworthy of Liverpool merchants.

In the event, Robert opted to use a cast-iron beam bridge for the canal crossing. This was a new technology and before construction began, extensive tests were carried on different castings. In this they were helped by William Fairbairn, who had already taken an interest in the use of iron and ran tests on different shapes for beams.

When the time came for serious consideration of a new main line to link the Liverpool & Manchester to Birmingham, the promoters automatically approached George Stephenson & Son to sound them out on taking over responsibility for planning and building their line. They were talking to a company whose principal was a very busy man. But this was a very important line and was given a suitably imposing name: the Grand Junction Railway. It was a confusing time, with the sudden enthusiasm for railway construction sometimes leading to conflicts of interest. The promoters of the Liverpool & Manchester had largely been Liverpool merchants, who certainly put their own interests first. So, when it came to talk of an extension towards Birmingham they began thinking of a line that would start on the south side of the Mersey. This left other interests to the north somewhat out in the cold, so they began looking for an alternative.

The first task was to conduct a survey of the route, which was to start at the Warrington & Newton line. That job was taken, not by George, but by Robert Stephenson. It was felt that George was too closely connected with the alternative route to become involved in this one. His proposed route passed through Sandbach, but it was opposed by the Marquess of Stafford, who also held the title 1st Duke of Sutherland, and was to become famous, or infamous, for instituting the Highland Clearances. In his early life he had been an active canal promoter, but he saw which way the wind was blowing and soon turned to the railways. It is not clear why he opposed the line, but he was such a powerful figure, who also had a 20 per cent interest in the Liverpool & Manchester, that his views could not be ignored. So, a second survey was carried out, this time by Joseph Locke. His route passed by Crewe, a name that was to become famous in railway history, but at the time was merely a grand house, Crewe Hall, and a hamlet.

There were some who disliked the new route and they decided to call in Charles Vignoles with the instructions to find a more direct line. He did as they asked, but it involved a massive and very expensive viaduct across the Mersey at Runcorn, with an alternative of an even more costly tunnel under the river. It was clear that this third proposal was never going to be adopted, so the Company returned to the route suggested by Locke, and began negotiations with the Warrington & Newton. This was a modest 4½-mile-long spur, which would require considerable improvements if it was to form part of a new main line, but the owners wanted far greater compensation than the Grand Junction was prepared to pay. Negotiations ground to a halt, and Locke was called back to see if there were any alternatives available. He concluded that even if it meant having to purchase all the £100 shares it was still the cheapest option. Eventually, agreement was reached and the Warrington & Newton shareholders had the satisfaction of walking away with a handsome £114 for each share.

The Company was highly satisfied with Locke's part in the planning and negotiations, but, of course, there was never any doubt in their minds that the contract would go to George Stephenson & Son. Locke would have hoped for a substantial role, preferably as resident engineer for the works, but Stephenson wanted to revert to his former practice, dividing the line into three sections, to be overlooked by assistants. Locke had already discovered the hazards of working in this way, having been forced to resign from the Liverpool & Manchester to keep his chief engineer happy, and he was also aware that he was no longer the favourite he had once been, following his report on the tunnel. He saw that taking on a role as a mere assistant was not a step forward in his career but a long pace in the opposite direction. He declined the offer.

Eventually, a somewhat dubious compromise was reached. George Stephenson was to be chief engineer, but Locke would be appointed as resident engineer for the whole of the northern half of the line, and in the event of George Stephenson being absent would take responsibility for the whole. According to Locke's biographer Devey, George merely remarked that he would never be absent and Locke would never have control of everything. It was typical that he would have seen anything else as unwarranted interference in his own grand plans. Now that the route had been agreed, the next task was to find contractors to undertake the construction.

Locke had been aware of the problems caused on the Liverpool & Manchester, and decided to organise his section of the line on a different basis. First of all he split the line into 10-mile sections, letting each one separately so that no contractor would be tempted to take on more than he could manage. He prepared detailed plans and specifications so that contractors would be very clear on exactly what they would be required to do. By the end of 1834, all the sections had been let on favourable terms. Stephenson, as usual, had preferred a far looser arrangement, but was still in disagreement with the various contractors by the time Locke's arrangements had been completed. The biggest difficulty appeared to be the huge difference between the prices

Drawn by G. Dodgson.   *Engraved by J. Stephenson.*

HAILING THE COACH, WHITBY AND PICKERING RAILWAY.

The Whitby and Pickering line was unusual for the time, in being single track originally and worked by horses.

Stephenson was offering and those considered reasonable by the contractors. When the Company investigated it became clear that the contractors had been given comparatively vague instructions and, being uncertain what was required, had upped their prices to make sure they did not lose out on the contracts. A very striking example was the estimate for a viaduct at Penkridge, for which the contractor was asking £26,000. Locke was asked to look into the matter, provided the contractor with detailed specifications as a result of which he dropped the price to £6,000. The directors were now faced with a dilemma. They had no wish to lose the services of the most famous engineer in the land, but on the other hand things had clearly gone badly awry. They came up with a proposal that was never likely to be accepted, that the two men should become joint chief engineers. The idea that George Stephenson might agree to share the position with his old apprentice was absurd and the inevitable result was that George, highly insulted, withdrew from the project altogether, leaving the works entirely in the hands of Joseph Locke. It was to be a start for the young engineer in what would become a highly successful career as engineer for many major projects both in Britain and in mainland Europe. In these works, he relied heavily on the contractor he had first met when planning the Grand Junction – William Brassey, who was himself to go on to become one of the most powerful railway contractors in the world.

Meanwhile, George Stephenson was considering railway schemes in many different parts of Britain. One important route under consideration was a line from Newcastle to Berwick. George Stephenson went to view the country and he soon came across a familiar problem: a great landowner who wanted to dictate where the line should go so that it had least effect on his property. In November 1838, he wrote from Berwick to his old friend Robert Brandling, describing his dealings with the local aristocracy.

> I called upon Lord Grey and was very kindly received by him. He appeared very desirous to have the Line carried west of his House and he pointed out a Line the levels of which I had taken and I found it to be quite out of the question to take the line in the direction he pointed out, as it would require a Tunnel upwards of a mile long or cuttings so deep that I could not recommend a Company to adopt. I made a full explanation of the nature of the ground to Lord Grey, he stated that he was very anxious that Lord Howick should be there, his Lordship was kind enough to ask me to drive with him, which I did. You may imagine the predicament I was in when all the Ladies seized me at dinner, I wanted your assistance very much to help me through as you have done on former occasions, I have every reason to believe that my explanations to him and his family were satisfactory. He has not yet consented but I believe he will not stand in the way of a great public good, and I trust when I see Lord Howick I shall be able to get matters put right

He went on to describe how the problem could be resolved.

> I find I can pass over one drive with an ornamental Arch without in any degree interfering with their comforts, and under the other drive in such a way as to hide the Railway from them and them from the Railway. My explanation to the family was satisfactory to some of them as to induce one of his sons to say at dinner that my Line was the best and think I was right.

In the same letter he described how his line would avoid giving offence to various other landowners, by ensuring the line never spoiled the view from their properties.

George Stephenson was the first person to be approached by many groups hoping to form a successful railway, among which was the proposed line from Manchester to Leeds. The idea for the line had been put forward as early as 1825, but it was only with the successful opening of the Liverpool & Manchester that anything positive was done. Once a decision to go ahead had been reached, the promoters decided, probably unwisely, to appoint Stephenson as joint chief engineer with James Walker, hoping that together they would be bound to combine their ideas to sort out the best possible route. In the event what they got were two entirely different proposals. Walker took a direct line, 37 miles long that ploughed through the hilly terrain with extensive engineering works. Stephenson preferred a more meandering route, following the Calder valley, which was 52 miles long but required far less engineering and had the added advantage that it could also serve such important manufacturing centres as Rochdale, Oldham and Halifax. The Company wisely decided on the latter, but Parliament was still not convinced that a railway that appeared to fulfil the same function as the existing transport system of the Rochdale Canal and Calder and Hebble Navigation was necessary. An Act was finally obtained in 1836 for a route from Manchester that would join the North Midland Railway south of Leeds. It was destined to become part of the ever-expanding empire of the man who would come to be known as the Railway King, George Hudson. Hudson and Robert Stephenson had actually met at Whitby in 1834, and had got on well, in spite of, or possibly because of, their very different personalities. They shared a boundless enthusiasm for developing the railway system, and each in his own way. Hudson's great achievement was the pulling together of smaller lines to create the Midland Railway. Robert's great achievements still lay in the future. The great difference between the two was that Hudson was to end his career in disgrace, while Robert was to live his entire life with his honour unquestioned.

The main engineering feature was the summit tunnel at Littleborough, just over a mile and a half long. There were the usual skirmishes with opponents, representing the various affected waterways, and also trouble from a few chancers who saw the arrival of a railway as a way of making extra cash. A quarry owner, Samuel Turner, demanded compensation for the line's effect on his stone quarry. The Company offered him £500. He turned that down and demanded £1,500. When the Company refused, he took them to court, a decision he soon regretted: the court awarded him £475 and told him to pay the expenses.

Two transport routes across the Pennines: the railway between Leeds and Manchester pierced the hill through this tunnel at Littleborough, while the Rochdale Canal climbed across via locks.

The principal difficulty was the summit tunnel which, at 2,885 yards long, was then one of the longest railway tunnels yet attempted. Stephenson took Thomas Gooch away from his post on the Liverpool & Manchester and put him in charge of operations. The young man who had started his working life as an apprentice at the Newcastle works now had the responsible post of resident engineer on a major line. Construction on the line began in August 1837. The work was not easy and in the early years it advanced so slowly that the Company became exasperated and dismissed the contractors, finishing the job with directly employed labour. In all, fourteen shafts were sunk and a vast amount of rock was extracted, some of which was later to be used in constructing the promenade at Blackpool, which was rather appropriate since this was the resort favoured by so many of the mill workers along the route of the line.

It was hoped to have the entire line opened by the end of 1840, but in December of that year, news reached Manchester that there had been a collapse in the tunnel, and rumours spread of carnage among the workforce. Fortunately, although there was a collapse, it was less serious than reported and no one was killed. George Stephenson went to the site with Gooch to inspect the damage. They discovered a band of blue shale below the invert, the curved lower section of the tunnel lining. As a result, the weight of the arch had forced the invert up for a length of 80 yards. It was a setback but it was reckoned that six weeks' work would be needed, but in the meantime a service could be run at either side of the tunnel.

Often George Stephenson was called in at an early stage as a consultant, though later he was to leave the actual construction to others. One particularly troublesome route was the proposed line from Newcastle to Carlisle, in which two factions argued for years: should it run north of the Tyne to Newcastle or south to Gateshead? Stephenson had preferred the former, but eventually the line was to run south under the direction of Francis Giles. He had learned his profession as a pupil of John Rennie, assisting him on a number of canal schemes. He first came to the public's attention when he ridiculed the notion of ever building a railway across Chat Moss. Given Stephenson's dislike of anything or anyone connected with the Rennie family and his general dislike of opposition, Giles was not likely to be looked on with a favourable eye. He made his opinion clear in a letter to Nicholas Wood in November 1831.

> I think Mr. Giles must be afraid of not holing right when he speaks of driving an expensive drift, for there is no occasion for it whatever, in fact it is safer and far less expensive without it. If Giles were in as bitter repute in the North than he is here he would not long remain on the N'Castle & Carlisle Railway.

The forecast proved all too accurate – Giles soon went. He was to have one more important line under his control – the London & Southampton Railway – and his stay there was also to be brief. His job of chief engineer was soon taken by that other Stephenson protégé, Joseph Locke.

As the network spread in an often haphazard fashion, the moment arrived when Robert Stephenson was to step onto centre stage in the role of chief engineer for one of the country's most important routes.

Chapter 12

LONDON AND BIRMINGHAM

The idea of constructing a line to link the capital to the important industrial centre of Birmingham was not new. The first proposal had been made by William James in 1820, which was to run from London through Oxford to join up with his Moreton-in-Marsh tramway. Nothing came of that, but four years later the Birmingham and London Railroad Company employed John Rennie (senior) to survey a route, which began at the docks by the Thames, avoided built-up areas of the capital and proceeded through Banbury and Bicester. That idea was never followed up. Next on the scene was that much-maligned engineer Francis Giles, and his route was different again, passing further to the east. The Stephensons may have had a very poor opinion of this gentleman, but the line chosen by Robert Stephenson when he was appointed chief engineer took a very similar route.

In fact, all these railway engineers had been preceded by the canal engineer William Jessop when laying out the Grand Junction Canal, now part of the Grand Union. The eventual railway would closely follow this earlier transport system for much of its length. When Robert Stephenson came to make his own survey, he would certainly have been aware of what the canal builders had done and the difficulties they had faced. Jessop had created a deep cutting through the Chiltern Hills at Tring, and further north had been forced to construct two long tunnels. Life for the railway builder would not prove any easier.

The Bill for the London & Birmingham faced the usual barrage of opposition from the canal companies and stagecoach proprietors, but by now such arguments were looking somewhat careworn. The success of the Liverpool & Manchester was there for all to see, and the various disasters that had been predicted had not appeared. That, however, did not prevent the House of Lords rejecting the Bill on its first appearance. It was only a temporary setback – the Bill passed the House of Commons with a large majority in 1833 and Robert was able to get to work. He set up an office in London, at first in Duke Street, then in Great George Street, and he and his wife moved to the capital. Initially they bought a house in St John's Wood but soon moved to Haverstock Hill, which would be their home for the rest of their married lives.

The London & Birmingham Railway closely followed the line of the Grand Junction – now Grand Union – Canal for much of the way.

The essential surveying work had laid down the line to be followed, which now had to be staked out and levels taken. It was essential to produce estimated costs and these depended to a very large extent on the amount of earthworks that would be required. Robert set about this task thoroughly, starting by taking levels at every chain: the surveyors' chain was 22 yards long. This gave an accurate profile of the whole route and it made it clear just where major earthworks would be needed. Trial borings were made in areas that required either deep cuttings or tunnels to determine the different make up of the land, which varied enormously from the dense London clays to the chalk of the Chilterns and the sandy soil further north. Different terrains demanded different approaches. The slope of cuttings varied from 2:1 in the London area to 1:1 in the chalk at Tring. All the embankments were to have 2:1 slopes, and the tunnels would have a two-brick thick lining. With all this information, Stephenson was able to work out just how much earth would have to be removed and how much piled up for embankments, and so produce what should be accurate estimates. Drawings had to be prepared for the whole route for the contractors, an immense task. There were 105 drawings for the first contract, which then required to have three more copies made. Altogether, producing the working drawings took the equivalent of 832 man-days. But all this was theoretical and based on the assumption that the work would run smoothly and there would be no unpleasant surprises along the way. In the event, neither of these criteria was met and, as with so many building projects before and since, costs escalated.

Once contracts were let out, work could begin. Choosing contractors was always a tricky business. The lowest contracts might well be suspect, so contractors were required to provide sureties of 10 per cent of the contract price. Work was to be paid monthly for 80 per cent of the work done, until the surety figure was reached. Theoretically that should have ensured that each contractor had enough capital to carry out everything that had been agreed. In practice, eight of the thirty contactors failed to finish the job. Eventually the Company was forced to take on some of the contracts themselves.

Work began at the London end, where the terminus was to be at Euston, not far from the spot where three decades earlier Richard Trevithick had tried to interest backers in his steam locomotive. The first stage at that end of the line involved making a cutting through the London clay right in the heart of Camden Town. The chaotic scene was described by Charles Dickens in his novel *Dombey and Son*.

Houses were knocked down; streets broken through and stopped; deep pits and trenches dug in the ground; enormous heaps of earth and clay thrown up; buildings that were undermined and shaking, propped by great beams of wood. Here, a chaos of carts, overthrown and jumbled together, lay topsy-turvy at the bottom of a steep, unnatural hill; there confused treasures of iron soaked and rusted in something that had accidentally become a pond. Everywhere there were bridges that led nowhere; thoroughfares that were wholly impassable; babel towers of chimneys, wanting half their height; temporary wooden houses and enclosures, in the most unlikely situations; carcases of ragged tenements, and fragments of unfinished walls and arches, and piles of scaffolding, and wildernesses of bricks, and giant forms of cranes, and tripods straddling

Barrow runs in the deep cutting at Tring.

above nothing. There were a hundred thousand shapes and substances of incompleteness, wildly mingled out of their places, upside down, burrowing into the earth, aspiring in the air, mouldering in the water, and unintelligible as any dream. Hot springs and fiery eruptions, the usual attendants upon earthquakes, lent their contributions of confusion to the scene.

Dickens was writing to entertain his readers, rather than give a strictly accurate account of the workings, but it probably gives a fair indication of how it seemed to the ordinary citizen. However, the illustration by J. C. Bourne in Chapter Twelve shows that the reality was not too different from the novelist's description, with a great gash through the heart of the built-up area. And the work was not without its frustrations. On one occasion when a cutting was virtually complete and work was beginning on the retaining walls, a heavy rain storm loosened the clay and sent it sliding back down to where it had started weeks before. Even so, Stephenson still remarked that he would rather work in the London clay than with some of the other types of material met in different parts of the workings.

As the workings spread north, there were new challenges to be met. A mile-long tunnel was needed at Watford. The system of construction was well established. Because levels had been accurately assessed, a series of shafts could be dug to just the right depth along the line of the tunnel. Material could be lowered down and spoil brought up by means of a horse gin at the top of the shaft. This was a simple device by means of which a horse trudging round a circular track, turned the drum, wound with cable that stretched down the shaft. It was at one of these shafts that catastrophe struck in 1835. According to the official report on the accident, the contractor went down the night before to inspect the works, and decided that the wooden supports could be removed to allow the bricklayers in to start on the lining. As the night shift was at work, the tunnel suddenly began to collapse at the foot of the shaft, and then the shaft itself began to cave in.

> The man who attended the Gin heard a cry of 'ware' that the ground fell at the same instant and so suddenly that his Dog was buried in the abyss, the gin and Gear carried down & that he only escaped by being tangled in part of the machinery above ground. That the candles of the men at work on the length tunnel in the next adjoining shaft on the north were blown out by the rush of air through the heading or driftway when the ground fell.

Ten men were named as being among the fatalities in the accident and an eleventh who was also killed was never identified.

The next major obstacle to be overcome was the chalk ridge at Tring. This was an immense undertaking that required nearly one and a half million cubic yards of spoil to be removed to create the 2½ miles long cutting. By the middle of 1837 there were thirty-one gangs at work, usually eight men to a gang. A series of barrow runs was established to bring up the spoil. Planks mounted on trestles stretched to the rim of the cutting. A rope was attached to the barrow, which then ran up over a pulley to a horse, which walked away from the rim to draw up the laden barrow, steered by a worker. Coming down with the empty barrow was not that much easier, the man galloping down the planks covered with greasy clay, the empty barrow trundling behind him. The problems posed were described by the engineer, Robert Rawlinson and although he did not work on the London & Birmingham, the system would have been just the same.

> The practice of running, though common, is dangerous, for the man rather hangs to than supports the barrow, which is at once rendered unmanageable by any irregularity in the motion of the horse. If he finds himself unable to control it he endeavours by a sudden jerk, to raise himself erect; then throwing the barrow over one side of the board, or 'run' he swings himself round and runs back to the bottom. Should both fall on the same side, there is great risk of the barrow with its contents falling on him before he can escape.

Working the barrow runs was hard and dangerous and only the strongest stuck to it. Rawlinson reported that it was not unknown for beginners to get half way up and freeze, and that would be the end for them as far as that type of work was concerned. The actual cutting work itself often involved blasting with gunpowder – at the Blisworth cutting further north it was estimated that around 100,000lbs of powder were used. The actual material to be shifted was mixed with clay and marl resting on a bed of limestone.

The spoil from the cuttings was not wasted if there was an embankment to be built nearby. Most of the banks were constructed by end tipping. Material was laid down until it had reached the required height, then trucks were run along the partially finished bank, and so the whole was gradually extended. Like the barrow runs, the work was not without its dangers. A horse would be harnessed to a truck full of spoil and would set off towards the end of the embankment. It would gradually go from a walk to a trot. Then, at the last minute, the horse was unhitched, pulled to one side, and the truck sped on to crash against a barrier. The truck was designed so that when it was brought to that abrupt halt, it tipped up, shooting out the spoil down the slope to where the navvies were waiting down below. It was a matter of nice judgement on the part of the spreaders at the foot of the slope to be near enough to the load to get to work quickly – but not so near that they were buried beneath it. Moving train-loads of spoil also seems to have created problems, and several accidents were reported, largely it seems because men used to illegally hitch a ride. Occasionally trucks got out of control, and it was not unknown for as many as twenty trucks to be smashed in a major pile-up.

It was not just the men who had troubles with working on embankments: they were often a nightmare for the engineers as well. The 40ft high embankment at Brent on the outskirts of London and the bank near Watford

The approach cutting to the Watford tunnel.

gave particular trouble as Robert described in a report on their condition in February on the line up to Tring.

> The permanent road is in tolerably good order, except on the Brent embankment, near London, and on the Colne embankment near Watford. Both these works have continued to subside, with scarcely any intermission, more or less rapidly since their formation, the former from the slippery

nature of the material which composes it, the latter from the unsoundness of its sub-stratum in the valley of the Colne. The gradual subsidence of embankments left no other remedy than maintaining the level of the railway by the constant supply of new sound material adopted for ballasting.

It was by no means the only embankment that was to cause trouble, and the troubles did not end when the line opened. The Blisworth bank slipped just two years after completion, sinking by an alarming 8ft, and an army of men had to be deployed at once to build it back up again.

The greatest challenge facing railway engineers were the tunnels. It was not simply a case of making a large hole through a hill and then ordering up bricks for the lining. Kilsby tunnel in Northamptonshire was to provide Stephenson with a major headache. In his initial borings he had originally aimed for a shorter route further to the east, but he had hit quicksand. The test shafts sunk along the line of the Kilsby tunnel showed a mixture of boulder clay, lias clay and gravel with some limestone. It seemed a much better option. This was engineering on a massive scale: the tunnel was to be 2,398 yards long, with a maximum depth below the surface of 132ft. The opening was to be 27ft 4in high and 14ft wide, with a 27in brick lining. This would require a lot of bricks. Local brickworks were simply not big enough to supply that quantity, so the Company had to make their own. Robert Stephenson's report of April 1836 gave raw statistics for the requirements for Kilsby tunnel, which are worth quoting because they give a good idea of the industrial scale of the operation.

> To erect a steam clay mill with kilns etc sufficient to supply 30,000 bricks per diem: say total quantity of bricks required 20,000,000 then 10,000,000 to be made the first season, and supposing 6,000,000 may be obtained from the open cuttings at the two ends of the tunnel and the neighbouring brickworks, 4,000,000 will be required from tunnel clay, then average number of working days in the season say 15 x 30,000 = 4,500,000.

Work began with sinking shafts, four in the middle and northern part of the tunnel and all went well. It was just what Robert had expected, as he explained when he gave his evidence to Parliament before the passing of the Act, when asked if there would be problems at Kilsby; 'Very easy indeed; in all clays it is very easy to tunnel, unless there be a great deal mixed with sand'. Unfortunately, that was exactly what they did find when they sank shafts near the southern end – not just plain sand but the one thing they had hoped to avoid – quicksand.

It was a major problem: as fast as the tunnel was excavated, the water and sand flowed back in again. Tests were made to see if a change in alignment would help, but the results showed there was no alternative route that would avoid the quicksand. Somehow it would have to be drained away. The standard approach would have been to cut a new channel along which the sand and water could be pumped out. This proved ineffective, so Stephenson decided that the only option was to sink pumping shafts and install two powerful steam engines. Up to this time he had been working in collaboration with the contractor Joseph Nowell, but when he died quite suddenly his sons declined to take over the work. So it was left to Robert to employ direct labour and supervise the work himself. The first stage was to sink a 12ft diameter shaft for two pumps, worked by a 10hp engine, later followed by a second shaft. More shafts were sunk and a railway built above the tunnel to facilitate the work. It was a frustrating time – and the site became known as 'Quicksand Hill'. But the sand was slowly conquered. Water was being pumped out at the rate of 1,800 gallons a minute, reducing the quicksand down to the level of the tunnel floor. By January 1838 Robert was able to announce 'The drainage of the quicksand is now completed'. The first 585 yards of tunnelling had taken eighteen months to complete: the remainder, over a mile long, a mere six, largely uneventful, months. During that time 1,300 men had been employed – and the Northamptonshire Infirmary reported that it had treated 124 navvies for injuries.

All the tunnels on the lines presented problems of one sort or another. The 1100-yard long Primrose Hill tunnel in London was different from the others. The first 21 yards at either end were made by creating a deep cutting and then covering it over. The remainder was more conventional, but hit big problems. Work was carried out from four shafts, with timbering to support the sides and roof as the bricklayers followed on immediately behind the excavation. But it was soon apparent that the London clay was swelling out. The timbering proved inadequate and the clay forced mortar out between the bricks and crumbled the edges. It was necessary to bring in much stouter timbers to keep the clay at bay.

Another problem facing Stephenson was the necessity to build bridges over both the Regent's and Grand Junction Canals. It would have been difficult, if not impossible, to use masonry as the necessary timber centring would have effectively closed off the busy canals. The answer had to be iron bridges. Suspension bridges had been very successfully used for road traffic, but had proved disastrous when first tried on the railways. Captain Sam Brown, one of the pioneers of suspension bridge construction, had built one for the extension of the Stockton & Darlington Railway, but the effect of a train running over it was alarming, as Robert described it: 'I have heard it stated that when the engine and train went over the first time, there was a wave before the engine of something like 2ft, just like a carpet.' The experiment was not repeated, so bridges based on cast-iron beams were used instead.

The surveying and construction of the London & Birmingham was an immense undertaking. It might have been thought that this would have been quite enough to occupy Robert, but he was consulted on another major project in the south of England – the proposed line from London to Brighton and the South Coast. There were two groups, both hoping to build the line. One of them engaged Charles Vignoles, the other Charles Cundy, who had

The foot of one of the great ventilation shafts in Kilsby tunnel.

surveyed a proposed ship canal from London to Portsmouth, a scheme that never materialised. With the possibility of two rival Bills reaching Parliament, Robert was asked to give an opinion. He was given leave of absence from his work on the London & Birmingham, mainly to visit the Newcastle works, but he was able to look over the rival plans. The Vignoles' route was direct, involving heavy earthworks to cross the North and South Downs. Cundy avoided the problem by heading further west and then turning south through Dorking. Robert's report favoured the Dorking route, but was highly critical of Cundy's survey, which was full of major errors. This really did little to decide the matter, but in 1835 a third group approached Stephenson and asked him to survey the best route on their behalf. There was a problem as he was contracted to work full time on the London & Birmingham, but they were generous and realistic: this was a big opportunity for Robert, and as they did not wish to lose his services they increased his salary and gave him leave to act as consultant engineer.

Robert Stephenson now needed an engineer to act on his behalf and he appointed George Bidder, already at work as an assistant on the London & Birmingham. Unsurprisingly, already having come down in favour of the Dorking route, he proposed something similar, leaving the London & Southampton Railway near Wimbledon, and dividing at the southern end between Brighton and Hove. The supporters of the more direct route had not, however, abandoned the fight, and eventually brought in Stephenson's old adversary Sir John Rennie to prepare a new plan. In the end it was the direct line that won out and would become the London, Brighton & South Coast Railway. This must have been a big disappointment for Robert. It would have been very convenient to have had a line near his home in London, and would have given him more time with his wife. As it was, he seldom managed to spend more than a Sunday with her. On the other hand, the London & Birmingham had shown how much they valued his services: his new salary of £2,000 a year was immense for the time. Not that everything always went quite as well with his employers.

On the whole Stephenson's plans were accepted by the Company, but there was one area of disagreement: the nature of the permanent way itself. Robert had recommended the use of fish-bellied rails, set on the Stephenson patent chairs and mounted on stone blocks – the system adopted for the Liverpool & Manchester. The Company, however, were not keen on paying the royalty on the patent and decided to mount a competition to find the best system, with a hundred guinea prize for

The Cutting at Camden Town

the winner. In the event the prize was not awarded. However, an expert, Peter Barlow of the Royal Military Academy, was called in to give an opinion, as he was a recognised authority on the subject of iron rails. He recommended parallel rails instead of fish-bellied. The Company also looked at what Joseph Locke was doing on the Grand Junction, where he was using heavier rails at 62lbs/yard that could be set further apart than the lighter rails, so reducing the number of stone sleeper blocks needed. In the event, this was the system adopted, which was not exactly a good result for Stephenson, nor in the event did it turn out to be a wholly satisfactory solution. It proved difficult to keep the rails aligned. Transverse wooden sleepers were used on embankments.

Another area of contention was the siting of the London terminus. The original Stephenson proposal was for a station near the Regent's Canal, and when that was rejected one at Marble Arch was proposed, which was also turned down and the third suggestion for ending at Maiden Lane was no more successful. Eventually the present site was approved. This was a prestige project so an architect was called in. Philip Hardwick's previous work included the substantial buildings round St Katharine's Dock and a new hall for the Goldsmiths Company. His Euston buildings bear no resemblance to what one can see at the present station. The main train shed was comparatively plain, with pitched, glazed roofs carried on iron pillars. There were two separate platforms for arrivals and departures. Anything that the actual station may have lacked in grandeur was more than made up for by the immense entrance in the Doric style, usually known as the Euston Arch. The train shed had been developed many times after the opening, but through it all the Arch remained until, in July 1961, the Transport Minister Ernest Marples signed the order for its demolition. There were protests from many architects, and notably from Sir John Betjeman; but to no avail. The other notable feature of the London terminus was the approach from Camden Town. The 1 in 68 gradient was considered too much for the locomotives of the day, so the final section between the two depended on cable haulage. Hardwick also designed the Birmingham terminus at what was to become Curzon Street Station. This has suffered the opposite fate from that of Euston: the classical arch has survived in lonely isolation as the station has gone.

One other element required to run the railway was, of course, the locomotives and rolling stock. The Company decided that while Robert Stephenson was employed by them as their chief engineer it would be inappropriate to allow him to supply the locomotives. They went instead to Edward Bury of Liverpool, and although they found Robert's dual role unacceptable, they had no problem in also appointing Bury as the man in charge of their mechanical engineering department, able to order his own engines. Bury was a passionate advocate of four-wheeled locomotives, where Stephenson had already moved in to six-wheelers. Bury's argument was that these engines were cheaper, which was true, and lighter, which was also true. He then proceeded to a rather more dubious argument that the lighter engines would not require as much power to move themselves, somewhat overlooking the fact that they were also required to haul trains as well. Apart from being light, they also suffered from a badly designed firebox that made raising steam difficult. So it was that, in the early years, every passenger train had at least two locomotives and sometimes three, with four for freight – while on one memorable day a train of forty-five goods wagons required an astonishing seven locomotives. It was not clear that the Company had got themselves a good bargain.

The original, rather modest station at Euston.

By 1845, the inadequacy of the Bury locomotives had become all too apparent. The Company Secretary R. Creed wrote to Robert Stephenson & Co that October:

> I am desired to say that our Company are prepared to deal with you for a supply of Engines to an extent that would probably make it worth your while to devote your establishment to the execution of our orders exclusively.

The order was to be for all classes of locomotive, and although the Stephenson Company declined to work exclusively for the London & Birmingham, they did begin a regular supply of six-wheeled engines. They were to continue to supply locomotives when the following year, the London & Birmingham was amalgamated with the Liverpool & Manchester and Grand Junction to form the London & North Western Railway.

The whole line was finally completed on 21 June 1838 when the final brick was laid on the top of one of the vast ventilation shafts at Kilsby with a silver trowel and was officially opened on 17 September. In many ways it was a triumph, a 111-mile route that had involved immense engineering works on a scale that had never before been attempted, and in the face of so many unforeseen difficulties. The Company, however, were not exactly overjoyed at the cost. The original estimate had been for £2,400,456 but the final sum was £5,500,000. The cost per mile had ended up twice that of the other major route under construction at the time, the Grand Junction under Joseph Locke. But it would be grossly unfair to try and make a direct comparison, given the far more difficult circumstances faced by Stephenson – Locke had no Kilsby to contend with for a start. Robert Stephenson freely admitted that he had totally failed to meet the original estimates, but pointed out that all too often contractors had failed and he had been forced to employ direct labour, while at the same time being urged to move forward to completion as rapidly as possible. By any standards it was a great achievement, overcoming immense obstacles. To have had Stephenson locomotives hauling trains over the Stephenson tracks from the start would have made the triumph complete. There was, however, the consolation that if the London & Birmingham did not want their locomotives at first, there were plenty of other customers, no longer just in Britain but overseas as well. There would be no shortage of work for Robert in the foreseeable future.

Robert Stephenson never shied away from work, but he did appreciate the little time he had with his wife and small group of intimate friends. In particular George Bidder and his family. Like most of his friends, Bidder was also a work colleague, having a post with Robert in Great George Street office. The closeness of the family connection was emphasised by letters he wrote to 10-year-old Bertha Bidder, one of which shows how sympathetic he was to children's feelings.

> I have received with much pleasure the beautiful little short purse you have been so very kind as to knit for me. It is exactly the kind of purse I wanted, for several young ladies have made me a similar present, but they are generally so long and covered with such heavy metallic ornaments that I found it very inconvenient to wear them. The consequence is that they were laid aside and I have now got nearly a drawer full of them. Yours, however, is so neat, elegant, & compact that you may rest assured it will not share the same fate, but be worn in remembrance of your romping with me.

It seems a shame that Robert had never had a child of his own to romp with and to encourage so charmingly. But then given his increasingly hectic life, there would have been precious little time for romping anyway.

Chapter 13

THE NEWCASTLE WORKS

By the end of the 1830s the Stephenson works were without doubt the leading manufacturers of steam locomotives in Britain – which, in practice, meant that they were also world leaders. Yet the actual machinery available was surprisingly limited, as Sir George Bruce explained in an address to the Institute of Civil Engineers in an address of 1887. He was looking back at his own time as an apprentice at Forth Street.

> In 1837 there were no small planing or shaping machines – there was only one slotting machine the use of which was very restricted. Wheels were driven onto their axles by sledge hammers, wielded by strong arms alone. Steam hammers were, of course, unknown, and only hand labour was available for the ordinary work of the smith's shop and boiler yard, with the exception of the punching and shearing machinery. Riveting by machinery, and especially by hydraulic machinery which has wrought such changes, and without which some work done now would hardly have been practicable at all, was unknown. It is scarcely credible, but it is a fact that there was not a single crane in Robert Stephenson's shop in 1837. There were shear-legs in the yard, by which a boiler could be lifted onto a truck, and there were portable shear-legs in the shop, by the skilful manipulation of which, at no little risk of life and limb, wonders were done in the way of transmitting heavy loads from one part of the shop to another. And the only steam-engine in what was the most important locomotive shop in the world of that day, was a vibrating pillar engine, with a single 16-inch cylinder and 3 feet-stroke. The heaviest planing machine in Robert Stephenson's works in 1837 weighed probably not more than 3 tons.

Having had the privilege of seeing the manufacture of the replica *Rocket* at various stages it makes it even more remarkable that the original was constructed with such comparatively primitive equipment and machinery. It is a tribute to both the organisation and the skill of its workforce. But, as Robert Stephenson pointed out, they were unlikely to retain their virtual monopoly for very long and other engineers had the advantage of building

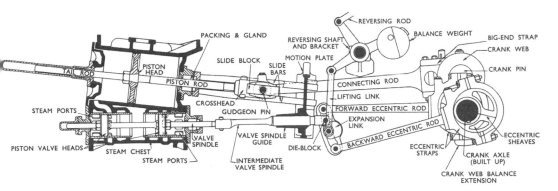

The Stephenson valve gear: the illustration comes from a twentieth- century manual for engine drivers, so shows some differences from the original mechanism, notably the use of piston rather than slide valves.

on the foundations laid down in Newcastle: 'Rivals however are now coming into the field who have not to begin by expensive experiments. There is no groping in the dark, or at least there ought not to be.' To maintain their leading position, Stephenson had to constantly be looking for new advances in locomotive technology.

Reference has already been made to the developments made in improving the original *Planet* class of engines, but it is worth looking at them in a little more detail. A problem that had appeared on the Liverpool & Manchester was the breaking of the crank axles, which Robert believed was caused in many cases by the unequal pressure on the flanged driving wheels when going round curves, hence his introduction of the flangeless drive wheels on that axle. The development of the six-wheeled engine also enabled him to use a bigger boiler. This had a further advantage: the greater heating surface meant that the fire in the firebox need not be so intense to produce the same steam pressure as before. This meant that the effect of the exhaust steam blast could be reduced, which in turn allowed for an easier release of steam from the cylinders, resulting in freer running. The other main improvement was the steam brake, the action of which was described applied to his new six-wheelers.

[It] consists in applying the force of small extra steam-pistons fitted into suitable cylinders, which by turning a cock can be supplied when required with steam from the boiler in order to act upon a double brake, or pair of clogs, which are applied to the circumference of the tires of the said main-wheels without flanges and of the two additional small wheels.

The first of the new engines was built for the Liverpool & Manchester and was later called the *Patentee*. In spite of Robert Stephenson's claim that the new boiler would have a larger heating area than the *Planets'* it was actually slightly less, as the heating tubes were now more widely spaced, which was shown to be more effective. The new arrangement also meant that the size of the firebox could be increased, so that taken altogether steaming was certainly more efficient in the new engine.

One area which saw steady development through the first years was the valve gear. In all the early engines this was operated via eccentrics. The first versions used two fixed eccentrics but in 1834, Hawthorn introduced an engine with four eccentrics. Stephenson saw the advantage of the system, adopted it and improved upon it. The first engine from the Newcastle works to use the new system was No. 136 of 1836. There was later a whiff of controversy when the Stephenson works supplied an engine to the Baltimore & Susquehanna Railroad in 1850, reporting that a Colonel Stephen H. Long was threatening to sue, as he had taken out a patent in America for a four-eccentric gear. Nothing seems to have come of this. In any case, there was to be a major development that changed valve gear for ever. In all the early versions, there had been a fixed cut off point for steam entering the cylinder: it was rather as if a modern motor car had only two gears, one forward and one reverse. The new system would allow the cut-off point to be varied.

The first successful version was developed by John Grey who patented what became known as the 'horse leg' gear in 1838 and it made its first appearance a year later on a Liverpool & Manchester locomotive, *Cyclops*. He then took up a post as locomotive superintendent on the Hull & Selby Railway, where he used the device on several engines. Quite why the device never achieved general acceptance is something of a mystery. In his patent he made it quite clear that he saw the advantages of having variable cut-off, but either other engineers failed to notice the patent or the line was too far away from the main developments. It was never widely adopted. The breakthrough that did revolutionise locomotive design took place at Forth Street – and no engineer was going to ignore anything that came from the famous works at Newcastle.

It began when the works was looking for ways to improve the existing gear, which involved an X-shaped gab gear for the four eccentrics. It was difficult to work in practice, and it was William Williams who first drew up a design for a different type of gear. He was a 'gentleman apprentice', in other words a young man whose parents had paid for him to be taught engineering. He devised a slotted link, with the forward gear eccentric coupled to the top and the reverse gear to the bottom of the link. The links were raised and lowered via the reversing rod, operated from the footplate. This enabled the change to be made smoothly. With reversing lever in the full forward position, the piston moves the full length of the cylinder before the steam is cut off; but if the lever is then moved back towards the reverse position, steam is exhausted earlier and the remainder of the piston travel is aided by the expansion of the steam before it reaches the exhaust port. So, much as a car is started in first gear and then the gears are moved up as it gathers speed, so on the locomotive, the gear is set in full forward to provide maximum effort for starting or for steep climbs, then eased back once everything is well under way. It made for economical and smoother running. A model was sent from the works to Robert Stephenson, who wrote back in August 1842: 'On the first blush it is very satisfactory and I sincerely hope will prove really so … If it answers it will be worth a Jew's eye and the contriver of it should be rewarded.'

At this point a controversy arose. William Howe, a pattern maker at the works, now claimed that it was his design not Williams'. However, when in 1870 it was proposed to hold a testimonial for Howe, acknowledging his invention of the link, there were objections from engineers who had been contemporaries of the two men. It is difficult now to disentangle the truth of the matter, but one thing seems clear. The original idea, the basis for the whole thing, was entirely down to Williams, though Howe may have played a role in modifying it to create its eventual form. But, whoever was responsible, neither of them ever had their name attached to the invention: it was universally known as the Stephenson linkage, and remained in use for decades to come.

Robert Stephenson was well aware that the growing popularity of railways in Britain would lead to many new manufacturers emerging, but there was also a growing interest abroad and it was only natural that the engineers from other countries would come to see what was happening in Britain. In France, the first railway was a modest mineral line at St Étienne, but in 1826 the Seguin brothers advanced a much more ambitious scheme to link St Étienne to Lyons and Marc Seguin visited England in December 1827, returning home in February the following year. He had extended meetings with George Stephenson, who was rewarded for the consultation with a fee of 12,500 francs. The meeting also resulted in the order of two locomotives from the Newcastle works: one of which was sent to M. Hallette, described by Marc Seguin as a 'distinguished machine constructor at Arras', while the second was used by Seguin himself as a model for further engines. Both engines were the two-cylinder variety then in use on the Stockton & Darlington.

Other engineers in those early years came from even further afield. Horatio Allen was resident engineer for the Delaware & Hudson Canal Company. This was an unusual enterprise in that there was a formidable obstacle right across the route of the canal – the Allegheny Mountains. To overcome this difficulty, two inclines were built. The packet boats on the canal were designed so that they could be divided in two and then hauled up

The locomotive *John Bull* built for the Camden & Amboy Railroad seen at the Columbia Exposition of 1893. Originally built as a 0-4-0 it was later modified and a cowcatcher added turning it into a 2+2-2-2.

and down the inclines on wheeled carriages. The central summit section between the two was a railroad and Allen's visit to Britain in 1827 was to assess whether or not it was possible to work this line with locomotives. As a result, he came in his own words 'to a decided conviction as to the future of the locomotive as the tractive motor power on railroads for general freight and passenger transportation'. He reported back to the Company and was sent back to England with instructions to visit the Stockton & Darlington, Killingworth and Hetton Railways and to purchase four suitable locomotives. He was given detailed instructions on the size and weight of locomotive required for the 4ft 3in gauge railway. It was clear that the Company expected all the orders to go to Robert Stephenson & Co. but in the event he ordered one from them and the other three from Foster and Rastrick of Stourbridge. The Stephenson engine was the first to arrive, reaching New York in January 1829, but it was not immediately put to use.

The engine that was tried was the *Stourbridge Lion*. As no one had driven a locomotive in America before, Allen took it upon himself to take the footplate for the first trial run, which included crossing a trestle bridge over the creek. Allen declared himself well pleased – and probably greatly relieved to have survived the experience. The spectators were less impressed. The bridge had creaked and groaned, and on inspection it was discovered that many of the rails had cracked and broken under the weight of the locomotive. That was the end for the time being of the use of steam engines on the line – it is doubtful if the Stephenson engine even got steamed at all. However, other railroads showed an interest in Stephenson locomotives. The president of the grandly named Camden & Amboy Rail Road & Transportation Co. had already visited the Newcastle works and put in an order for a *Planet* type of locomotive, which was when delivered was identical to other *Planets* with the exception of the use of a newly developed round firebox. Later it was given a more American appearance by the addition of a cow catcher at the front. Initially known simply as Number 1, it was later named *John Bull* and did excellent service. The original has been preserved and a working replica built.

Not everyone interested in railway construction took the trouble to make the trip to England. Leopold I of Belgium invited George and Robert to visit his country to give advice on developments. They arrived in May 1835 and had lengthy discussions about how a State Railway system could be developed, linking Brussels to the other main cities. The idea for developing the system had already been put in hand by the Belgian engineer, Albert Simons, who in 1834 had ordered three six-wheeled engines from the

Stephenson works. However, the king clearly felt that the English engineers' experience was invaluable and George was made a Knight of the Order of Leopold. The Stephensons returned to Belgium for the opening of the line from Brussels to Mechlin on 6 May 1835, with all three Stephenson engines taking part. The account of the day was reprinted in England.

> At a quarter past twelve o'clock the King being at the station, near the Boulevards to witness the ceremony, the departure of the steam-carriage train was announced by a salute of artillery. Immediately three files of ten carriages, each carrying nearly a thousand persons, began to move, drawn by the *Flèche*, the *Stephenson* and the *Éléphant*. The passage from Brussels to Mechlin occupied fifty three minutes. On their return the *Éléphant* took in tow all the thirty carriages that had been drawn, by the three locomotives, and would probably have reached Brussels in half an hour, had it not been obliged to stop at Vilvorde for a fresh supply of water. In the evening the Minister of the Interior gave a public dinner to 200 of the principal persons, natives and foreigners, who were present at the ceremony.

If they did manage to squash 100 passengers into each carriage it must have been a very uncomfortable ride. Back in London, George called on the Belgian ambassador simply to ask him how he should address the king as he wanted to thank him for his hospitality and the honour he had received. He was obviously very impressed by his treatment when he arrived and sent up his card.

> This done we were order'd up immediately, where he and several Belgians were at breakfast and he received me in as kind a manner as King Leopold did, and stated that he was very glad indeed to have the *honor* of my acquaintance. He seemed quite delighted with what had taken place in Belgium about the Railway.

The Stephensons were back in Belgium for the opening of the line from Brussels to Ghent and once again they were treated with immense respect, and dined with the king. On a later visit Robert received a knighthood to match his father's.

Not all dealings with European promoters went as smoothly. The promoters of the *Bayerische Ludwigbahn* from Nuremburg to Fürth contacted the Company to ask them to supply locomotives. The line, though grandly named after King

Ludwig of Bavaria, was actually a very modest mineral line. When they got the costs from Newcastle, they declared that due to the exchange rate between Britain and Germany the price was too high. They turned instead to a German manufacturer to make their locomotives, but the enterprise failed. They had no option and were forced to use Stephenson locomotives after all. A replica of the first locomotive *Adler* is now in the museum at Nuremberg and is regularly steamed. Most of the locomotives supplied to European railways were of the *Patentee* type with 2-2-2 wheel arrangements, but there was one notable exception. In 1837, the Company built *La Victorieuse* for the Versailles Railway, with a 0-4-2 arrangement. This was one of the largest engines built so far, with large cylinders – 15in diameter and 18in stroke, with a bigger than usual grate and boiler. The engine weighed in at 13 tons, compared with *Adler*, which was a modest 8 tons.

One of the most interesting examples of a Stephenson locomotive supplied to a European railway is *L'Aigle* built in 1846 for the Avignon & Marseilles Railway, which is now preserved in the Cité du Train at Mulhouse. This is an example of a new design developed by Robert Stephenson, the long-boiler locomotive. The *Patentees* had been a success, but the increased size of the firebox had not been accompanied by an increased heating area in the boiler. The result was that fireboxes were likely to overheat. He was reluctant to increase the diameter of the boiler, as it would have put too much strain on the leading wheels, so the only answer was to increase the length of the boiler. He was also reluctant, however, to increase the wheelbase, so he put all three sets of wheels under the boiler, leaving an overhanging firebox. Soon other modifications were made. The single plate frame was placed inside the wheels. In 1843, he made yet another change, this time setting the cylinders outside the frame. The new long boiler engines were a huge success in France, and the works were kept busy supplying them for the Marseilles & Avignon and the Paris-Orleans railways. The design was to form the basis for most French locomotives for decades to come.

In spite of the international success of Robert Stephenson & Co., relations between Robert himself and the Quaker partners who had initially financed the Company, Michael Longridge and Edward Pease, were not always comfortable. Robert received complaints that he was not paying sufficient attention to the works, to which he rather angrily pointed out that it was the work he was doing outside Newcastle that was bringing in the orders. In spite of his time-consuming civil engineering projects, Robert always took a keen interest in the mechanical engineering side. But there were times when he found the activities of the partners exasperating. He had his own particular contact at the works, the Chief Clerk, Edward Cooke, who was also his wife's uncle. When news came through that Longridge was considering leaving the partnership and setting up on his own to manufacture locomotives, it was to Cooke that he revealed his annoyance.

> 'I shall read Longridge and Pease a lesson by post in a day or two; they shall either rescind the £200 resolution or else I shall go out of the thing altogether. Indeed there is scarcely one thing that they have done that I will not undo – the resolutions are conceived and phrased in a style which I will not put up with from those who have done nothing for the concern for many years past and only began to show an interest in our proceedings after I had succeeded by my own resources and those of my father in establishing a character for the firm. The impudence of a Quaker is beyond estimate by Heavens!'

The exact cause of this outburst is unknown but the general sense of dissatisfaction and anger is plain enough. Fortunately, the Stephensons could rely on a good team to manage the mechanical side of construction. Those who worked at Forth Street certainly earned their pay. The regulations for the drawing office of 1846, show a working day that started at seven in the morning and ended at six at night, except on Saturdays when they went home at four, but the rules also stated that they might be required to work even longer hours 'whenever business requires it'. They did, however, have half an hour for breakfast and an hour for dinner. And, as the rail system expanded, business must often have demanded those extra hours. In 1846, the Company had orders for an astonishing 224 engines.

Among the overseas orders that came in during the early years of railway development was one from Russia, where the Stephenson works provided two locomotives to work the line that was to be built linking the Imperial Summer Palace at Tsarokoe Selo to St Petersburg. The choice of route reflected the fact that it was Czar Nicholas I who was the driving force behind construction. As Duke Nicholas he had visited England and had been to see the Middleton Colliery Railway and he had been decidedly impressed by this new form of transport. At first the idea was that the engineer M. E. Cherepanov would visit England, study engines at work and come home and build ones to copy the best that Britain had to offer. He chose a Stephenson engine as his model, but perhaps he had not paid enough attention to detail, for his engine was a failure. The Russians would have to buy British after all. There was one minor problem facing the engine builders back in Britain: the Russian gauge was originally based on local units: 2 *arshim* 5 *vershak*. Fortunately, the Russians recognised that this might bewilder the British, so they opted for the nearest value in feet – so the line was to be 6ft gauge. Building a locomotive for these dimensions was a new experience for Forth Street, but it was experience that was to prove useful when a new gauge was mooted for a British main line.

When George Stephenson built his first locomotives they were designed for the Killingworth track at 4ft 8in. It worked well enough, and he saw no reason to change it, though an extra half inch crept in along the way. He did

L'Aigle **a** long boiler locomotive built for the Marseilles-Avignon line in 1842, on display at the Cité du Train in France.

not, it seems, ever ask himself the question: what would be the best gauge for a modern rail system that would eventually cover the whole country? But a young engineer called Isambard Kingdom Brunel did. He had no previous experience of railways, but he had been appointed to build a suspension bridge over the Avon gorge at Clifton, and the Bristol merchants were impressed by his efforts. So when it was decided to promote a line to link their city to London, it was Brunel they appointed. He opted for a wholly new system. Instead of the conventional transverse sleepers, he opted for longitudinal sleepers running the whole length of the track, with metal ties – and the rails, which were also built to a new design, were to be 7ft apart. This, the engineer claimed, would make for smoother, faster running and would, as an added advantage, make fitting the working parts to the engine much easier given the extra space between the wheels. At first, it was suggested that the new line should join the London & Birmingham at Euston, but that idea was rejected. As a result, Brunel had no need to worry about fitting in with an existing system: what was now known as the Great Western Railway (GWR) could be treated in isolation. Nevertheless, the directors were understandably cautious and sought expert opinion. One of them, John Hawkshaw, wrote to Robert Stephenson who replied on 1 October 1838.

> The extent of inconvenience we experience in the construction of locomotive engines of moderate power (say 14 inch cylinders) for a gauge of 4 foot 8½ inches, is very small indeed. In our early engines an additional width of 3 or 4 inches would have facilitated the arrangement of the working gear and eccentrics: but this has since been simplified, and our latest arrangement of these parts leaves scarcely this small increase of width to be wished for. The construction of engines for Russia for a six foot gauge, leads us to believe that that a considerable increase of expense is attendant upon increased width: more especially if the power of the engine is considered to bear any relation to the width of the gauge. If the power or dimensions of the engine be kept the same, the additional expense consequent upon increase of gauge will not be very considerable.

Brunel had no manufacturing facility at first, so orders were placed with Tayleur & Co of the Vulcan Foundry and Robert Stephenson for locomotives. Brunel was very clear on what he wanted. His first requirement was speeds of 35-40mph, and he was convinced that this would require locomotives with large driving wheels. Tayleur certainly met that requirement constructing

8ft diameter driving wheels, with the axle boxes for these wheels above the frame. As a result, the top of those wheels were almost level with the top of the boiler. Stephenson had already the experience of building wide locomotives for Russia, and the Company had recently constructed a pair of locomotives for the 5ft 6in New Orleans Railway. Unfortunately, America was going through a financial crisis and the Company was unable to pay, so Forth Street had two engines on their hands. They were both of the *Patentee* type and it was comparatively straightforward to extend the axles to meet the Brunel gauge. One was named *Morning Star* and retained the 6ft 6in diameter driving wheels that had been designed for America, but on the second engine, *North Star* they were increased to 7ft.

North Star was a powerful engine, and in general was a scaled-up version of the earlier *Patentees* – with an 8ft 6in long boiler with 167 tubes, 16in diameter cylinders and a wide, deep firebox. The performance was exemplary. On a trial run before the line was open, the engine hauled a train of ten carriages with around 200 passengers over 22 miles at an average speed of 28mph. On a later trial with a 45 ton load, the speed reached 38½mph – just what Brunel had hoped for. In 1837, Daniel Gooch was appointed locomotive superintendent to the GWR. He had worked for a time the previous year in the Forth Street drawing office during the period when the Russian engines were being built – and he had original drawings in his possession, which is interesting as one of the rules stated that no drawings should be removed from the office.

Robert Stephenson and Brunel were never close friends. Their temperaments were so very different that it was never going to be likely, but they had great respect for each other and at critical times in their careers would look to each other for support. They certainly differed strongly on the best way to build a railway, but when the directors of the GWR asked Robert to give his views on the broad gauge, he refused. He explained why in a letter to Brunel in August 1838 that says a great deal about the relationship.

I find it quite out of my power to form a report on your permanent way – I have written to Sandars declining to do so. I have carefully considered what I saw with you the other day at Maidenhead and I am compelled to say that my former views as to the increased width of the Rails as well as the plan of laying them remains unchanged, you will I am sure readily see how unpleasant my position would be, if I expressed myself in an unequivocal manner in my report: and to do otherwise would be making

North Star: the Newcastle works provided the locomotive for the Brunel broad gauge line between Bristol and London.

myself ridiculous since my opinions are pretty generally known – To report my opinions fully therefore would do harm instead of good to the cause in which you are interested and this I am sincerely desirous of avoiding.

It was a letter that could only have pleased Brunel. The two engineers were quite content to disagree with each other about the track, but would not do anything that would harm the other's career. But the argument about the Stephenson and the Brunel gauge would not go away, though it would be many years before it was finally resolved.

Another area of controversy arose later between Brunel and the two Stephensons: the atmospheric railway. This was an idea that had been around since the beginning of the nineteenth century, when George Medhurst first suggested sending letters down a tube using air pressure. Then he developed it further by suggesting a means of communication by sending a piston down a tube. From that it was a small step to suggest that if there was a way of attaching vehicles to the piston it could be the basis for a means of transport. The first experiment was made by H. Pinkins, who devised a system with a piston in a pipe, with a slot in the top. A flange on the piston protruded through the slot and it could be attached to the vehicle. The whole system would be kept airtight by a heavy leather flap. The idea was not taken up until 1840, when Clegg and Simonds patented a system that was essentially the same as the Pinkins' version and this time the idea was taken seriously. Two railways using the idea were built: an extension of the Dublin & Kingstown and the London & Croydon. Parliament set up an enquiry to look at the merits of the system. Those in favour included Charles Vignoles, William Cubitt and Brunel. Among the most prominent opponents were George Stephenson and Joseph Locke. The latter had already made out the case for using locomotives instead of cable haulage for the Liverpool & Manchester, and one of the most powerful arguments against this new idea was exactly the same. The system was worked by having a series of engines that would pump air out from in front of the piston, allowing air pressure on the opposite side to push it forward. But should there be a fault in just one of them, then the whole system was inoperable. No decision was reached, and Brunel famously went on to build his atmospheric railway to extend his Great Western Railway from Exeter to Plymouth. He had even, rather cheekily, tried to bring the system to the heart of Stephenson territory, proposing to use it for a line from Newcastle to Berwick. That idea was rapidly rejected, which was just as well as the Atmospheric Railway proved to be a disastrous failure. The future of the locomotive looked safe for many years to come.

Chapter 14

THE REALM OF THE RAILWAY KING

George Hudson was born in 1800 near York, the son of a farmer. He went on to become a successful businessman: a partner in a firm of drapers. His situation changed dramatically in 1827 when he received a legacy of £30,000, equivalent to roughly £3 million today. He saw that the developing railway system offered a potential for investment and profit. When a line was proposed to link York to another intended route from Leeds to Selby, he purchased 500 shares, giving him a controlling interest. But his ambitions went far beyond that modest line: he wanted to make York a major rail centre, with connections north to Scotland and south to London. In 1834, he met George Stephenson in Whitby to discuss his plans.

The meeting proved a success and the two men got on well together. This is perhaps surprising, given that Hudson was a bombastic man and, it later transpired, fraudulent, while Stephenson was honest and downright. But, of course, it would be some years before Hudson's criminal activities came to light. And one can see why Stephenson found him agreeable. As we have seen, George had a deep distrust of many men from the south of England, and London in particular, and here was a Yorkshireman who, like the engineer, had never lost his strong local accent. Above all they not only shared a passion for railways, but also a vision of how a vast inter-connected network could be established. Hudson had the money and the political influence: Stephenson had the practical experience – it seemed the obvious partnership.

Plans went ahead for three lines that would connect with the existing system: the Birmingham & Derby Junction Railway, the North Midland from Derby to Leeds and the York & North Midland to complete the route. All these lines would be surveyed by George Stephenson. There was one other new line being promoted in the region, which was not part of the Hudson scheme – the Midland Counties, which was to link Birmingham to other important centres, such as Leicester and Nottingham. This was to cause a clash of interests when it came to presenting Bills to Parliament.

There were two areas of contention. The Stephenson Birmingham & Derby Junction line had included a branch to join the London & Birmingham at

Hampton in Arden, and the Midland Counties, whose engineer was that old adversary Charles Vignoles, had a line along the Erewash valley. To avoid the duplication in routes, the Birmingham & Derby Junction offered to drop the Hampton route if the Midland Counties abandoned the Erewash. But when the latter's Bill came before Parliament the Erewash route was still there. At this point the Hampton branch was promptly reinstated, and the Birmingham & Derby received its Act of Parliament in 1835. The actual work of construction was overseen by Robert Stephenson.

The North Midland had an easier passage through Parliament, but offered greater engineering challenges. The most obvious direct route from Derby to Leeds passes through Chesterfield and Sheffield. The great advantage of this line was that Sheffield was a major manufacturing centre, which would provide a considerable amount of business for the railway. But this consideration was less important to George Stephenson than the fact that the region was hilly and difficult, and there was a much more attractive route to

When the line of the North Midland Railway met the Cromford Canal, the railway company had to build an aqueduct to carry the waterway across the line.

be had by passing further east and Sheffield itself would have to be served by a branch line, the Sheffield & Rotherham Railway. Not surprisingly, the citizens of Sheffield were not overjoyed with the notion of being stuck out at the end of a branch line, and money was raised to pay Joseph Locke to carry out a second survey to incorporate a direct route. He produced a plan that necessarily involved heavy earthworks, cuttings, embankments and numerous bridges. An aqueduct also had to be constructed to carry the Cromford Canal across the line. The North Midland opted for the Stephenson route. That too was to have its fair share of problems, in spite of being laid out in good part along the Derwent valley.

Although Stephenson had avoided Sheffield, the line still required 7 tunnels and 200 bridges, with deep cuttings and embankments. George was involved in so many schemes and Robert had his hands full with other projects, so the actual construction had to be left in the control of Frederick Swanwick. He had actually begun studying Classics at the age of 17 at Edinburgh University, but was soon wooed to the world of civil engineering and was apprenticed to George Stephenson at 19, working on the Liverpool & Manchester, and driving *Arrow* at the opening. He did a good job. A feature of the line was the elegance of the stations, designed by Francis Thompson. Not everyone was impressed. Francis Whishaw in his book *the Railways of Great Britain and Ireland* (1840) wrote scathingly:

> We cannot but deplore the growing evil of expending large sums of money on railway appendages. Instead of cottage buildings, which, for the traffic of most of the intermediate stopping pace on this line, would have been amply sufficient, we find the railway literally ornamented with so many beautiful villas, any one of which would grace the sloping lawn of some domain by nature highly favoured.

One important function of stations was to allow passengers a chance to literally relieve themselves in the days when trains had no toilet facilities. At Wingfield, the toilets were placed under the water column that supplied the locomotives, and which now served the extra purpose of flushing the lavatories.

Although George Stephenson was not involved directly in the construction of the line, it was while work was being done on the tunnel at Clay Cross that he saw the potential for developing the mineral resources of the area. It was his interest in this prospect that was largely responsible for the move to Chesterfield. A company was set up with Hudson, his old partner Joseph Sandars and William Claxton to develop coal mines at Clay Cross and the limestone quarries at Crich. Developing the latter required the construction of an immense bank of limekilns at Ambergate beside the Cromford Canal and a transport system to link quarry and kilns. It was a happy marriage of interests: the poorer quality coal from the mines could be used in the limekilns.

In October 1840, Stephenson's solicitor wrote to the owners of Crich offering to rent the site and to pay the owners a penny farthing for stone and 2*d* for lime 'and any damage done to the surface, to be settled by competent judges'. Stephenson also undertook 'to make and maintain a Railway from Crich Cliff to the Cromford Canal and my Limekilns near Amber Gate and to commence the formation of the Railways soon as the consents of the Landowners are obtained'. The railway was narrow gauge and, rather surprisingly set at one metre, rather than in feet and inches. It was partly operated by rope haulage on the steep inclines and by locomotives on the level sections. It was very successful, and was worked right up to 1957, during which time about 6 million tons of stone were carried. The quarry site is today home to the National Tramway Museum – but these are electric trams, not the trams of mineral railway days.

Hudson and Stephenson had a common interest in developing railways in the north-east: the former wanted to turn York into a major rail centre, the latter dreamed of a through route to the Scottish border, passing through Newcastle. There was no reason why the two ambitions could not be united. The result was first to extend southwards from York to link in with the York & North Midland. This was a comparatively straightforward route, with no heavy gradients, long sweeping curves and no great earthworks. The Act was passed in 1836 and the line was opened throughout in 1840. This was a major development: passengers now had a through route all the way from York to London, with a journey time of approximately 14 hours. It seems a long time by today's standards, but appeared almost miraculous when compared with the four days taken by the coaches on the Great North Road.

When first opened, trains stopped at a temporary wooden station just outside the city walls at York. Later the walls were pierced and a more substantial station built. It is doubtful if today anyone would be allowed simply to smash a hole in such ancient works, but such was Hudson's influence in local politics that no one could oppose him. But it proved inconvenient when routes were extended northwards, as trains had to reverse out, rather than simply continue straight out and on their way. It was to be several years before a better solution was found and the present magnificent station was opened in 1877.

Developments further north were influenced by a line that should in theory have had no bearing on the matter: the Stanhope & Tyne Railway. If one looked at a map of the region, you would dismiss the idea as wildly impractical and probably not worth the effort. The aim was to link extensive limekilns at Stanhope to South Shields, with a branch to the coal mines at Medomsley. The start of the line was to be 800ft above sea level in the heart of the Durham moors, climb to a summit at Whiteleahead at 1,140ft and then drop down virtually to sea level at the mouth of the Tyne. As if that was not enough of a problem to contend with, the route would have to cross the ravine of Hownes Gill, 800ft wide and 169ft deep. It was promoted by a group of industrialists and mine owners, led by the brothers William and John Harrison. At this point a certain amount of nepotism seems to have crept in as the man appointed to the post of chief engineer was a 24-year-old relative, another William Harrison. He was Robert Stephenson's assistant on the London & Birmingham. Although his relatives may have had complete confidence in him, the young engineer was rather less sure about tackling such a daunting task, and Robert was called in as consulting engineer.

Robert was still busily engaged in work on the Liverpool & Birmingham, but he accepted the assignment in September 1832. Even he was not too sure about how all the problems would be solved. He wrote to his father the same month: 'There are several stationary Engines to be erected and there is one I want to have your opinion upon as an application of an Engine in the manner I propose is entirely new and I want you to see the situation.' Most of the engines Robert referred to were working in the usual way, using cable haulage to move trucks up and down inclines. One of these at Wetherhill worked a long incline. Built in 1833 by Hawks and Co., it had a single vertical cylinder, connected to an overhead flywheel and worked the winding drum. It is a rare survivor of this type of engine and is now in the National Railway Museum in York. But Robert's 'new' engine was designed to work to overcome the chasm of Howes Gill.

The young engineers were daunted by the notion of bridging the gill, so Robert's idea was to have two railed inclines, one from each rim to the bottom of the gill. The mineral trucks would arrive at the top, be turned on a turntable through 90 degrees and loaded onto platform wagons running on the railed track. The winding engine was situated at the bottom of the gill

The original York station: the railway arrived through an archway cut right through the ancient city walls.

and worked both inclines simultaneously, the weight of the descending trucks partially helping raise the ones ascending on the opposite side. Trucks were changed from one incline to the other at the foot of the two slopes via another turntable. It was claimed that there could be a truck movement every five minutes. All in all, this whole railway was a curious affair, partly worked by locomotives, partly by horses and partly by a number of stationary engines. Given Robert Stephenson's strongly stated opinion on the latter when arguing for locomotives on the Liverpool & Manchester, it is a little surprising to find him accepting just such a situation here, but given the nature of the terrain there was little choice. Over the years, problems with the stationary engines were to plague the line, just as he had prophesised.

Robert had agreed to take his fee of £1,000 in shares, without considering the implications: because the Company was unincorporated, as a shareholder he would be held personally responsible for any serious debts they might incur. In fact, the Company was to prove hopelessly irresponsible. They borrowed funds, and used their existing capital to invest in another railway, the Durham Junction Railway, linking the Hartlepool Railway to the Tyne via the Stanhope & Tyne. The Company continued to operate until 1840, but the revenue never matched their expectations: the demand for the limestone was not as high as hoped, and the transport costs on this odd, hybrid line were high. They might have staggered on, but one of the directors was also director of another company, and when that went bankrupt, the creditors gathered, demanding immediate cash payments. The money was not there and the shareholders were required by law to make good the deficit. To his horror, Robert Stephenson received a demand for his share of the joint responsibility; funds to repay a staggering total debt of £1.4 million had to be found by the shareholders. The situation was dire and Robert's solicitor advised him to take the initiative and call an extraordinary general meeting of the shareholders.

The result of the meeting was a decision to dissolve the old company and form a new incorporated company. The existing shareholders would still be liable for the old debts. Robert was faced with the fact that he already owed his father money and that he would need to find £20,000 for his share of the company debt. His only solution was to sell off his share in Robert Stephenson & Co. He bore the loss bravely, as he spelled out in a letter to Edward Cook.

Your view as to my wishes respecting one half of my interest in the factory is exactly what I wish. The transaction is not intended to be otherwise than bona fide between my father and myself. The fact is, I owe him nearly £4,000, and I have not the means of paying him as I expected I should have a month or two ago. All my available means must now be applied to the Stanhope and Tyne. On the 15th of this month I have £5,000 to pay into their coffers. The swamping of all my labours for years past does not now press heavily on my mind, It did so for a few days, but I feel now master of myself; and though I may become poor in purse, I shall still have a treasure of satisfaction amongst friends who have been friends in my prosperity.

The shareholders raised £350,000 to pay off the debts and a new company was formed, the Pontop & South Shields Railway. The top half of the old Stanhope & Tyne was sold off and the remainder was run by the new company, of which Robert Stephenson was appointed chairman in 1843. It was now an important link in the developing north-eastern network, and was to play a role in the developing story of the push to the north and create a dilemma for Stephenson.

As the Stanhope & Tyne collapsed in financial chaos, Robert was approached by Joseph Pease, a member of the family that had played a leading role in promoting the Stockton & Darlington and later in funding the Newcastle works. It would be fair to say that they had played a crucial part in the careers of the Stephensons. Now he approached Robert, asking him to take over work on the Great North of England Railway, which was to link the Stockton & Darlington Railway at Darlington with Newcastle. Work had begun on the section linking York to Darlington, but it had proved unsatisfactory and the original engineer, Thomas Storey, had resigned. Robert recommended that all the efforts should be concentrated on the southern end of the line, and that nothing should be done at the time to develop the route northwards to the Tyne. This made a great deal of sense, since once that section was opened, which should happen quite quickly, the Company would start to enjoy the revenue. There was also a possibility that developments to the north could be arranged to the benefit of Robert's new company. At this stage things became more complex.

George Hudson had his own plans for extending his rail empire north to Newcastle and on to Scotland as well. There was already a rival in the field: over to the west Joseph Locke was busily constructing a route of his own that would head up from Carlisle to Glasgow and then across to Edinburgh. Hudson was determined that York should be the heart of any route from London to Scotland. He proposed a quite different route north of Darlington, which would incorporate the struggling new line – and Robert Stephenson helped with the survey. There was a clear clash of interests here, but the Hudson line would bring much needed funds to hard-pressed shareholders of the failed Stanhope & Tyne. To Pease and the Quaker community of Durham, it was a betrayal. For Stephenson it had been a dilemma: it was not merely the immediate financial gains, but he had been an integral part of Hudson's grand schemes and it was a connection he was loath to lose. In the event, it was the Hudson line that won the battle.

Hudson's ambitions were immense. He bought out the shares in the Great North of England and now was able to control the whole route and plan the next extension north to Berwick. It is hardly surprising that Robert Stephenson wanted to share in the enterprise. He worked on the survey of the northern route up to Newcastle, where the next major challenge had to be faced: the crossing of the Tyne. But that still lay in the future, as did Hudson's catastrophic fall, once his fraudulent handling of shares was disclosed.

These were difficult times for Robert in many ways, but his problems with railway construction were overshadowed by a personal tragedy. According to H. M. Walmsley, 'Mr Robert Stephenson has said that he never had but two loves in his life, his wife and his father'. But by 1840, Fanny was clearly in poor health. In a letter to Edward Cook, he wrote in good humour about Fanny and a relative having bought plaids 'and in a season or two they expect to be designated scotch lassies'. But it ends: 'Fanny I think is going on well although she is still grazing on macaroni and occasionally a little marine flesh, vulgarly called fish'. She was obviously not in good health and that year she was diagnosed with cancer. They had never been able to have children, and Fanny apparently knew how much Robert hoped to pass on his knowledge and expertise to a son, just as his father had done for him. When Fanny knew there was no cure, she pressed Robert to marry again in the hope of getting an heir, but he never did. On 4 October 1842 his diary entry read: 'My dear Fanny died this morning at four o'clock. God grant that I may close my life as she has done, in the true faith, and in charity with all men. Her last moments were perfect calmness'.

Robert's only concern now was work. He sold the house in which he had been happy and moved closer to his office in Westminster. But misfortune dogged his steps. He had just moved in when there was a fire and many of his possessions were lost in the blaze. One of the great loves of his life was gone, and the other, his father, was coming to the end of his career.

Chapter 15

GEORGE STEPHENSON'S LAST YEARS

As early as 1837, George Stephenson was thinking of easing off his hectic working life. On 13 August he wrote to Michael Longridge:

> I intend giving up business in the course of two or three years when I shall be able to devote more time to my Friends. I have had a most delightful trip amongst the Cumberland Lakes, I should have liked to have remained a month to fish. I intend going again next year if I have time & have a large party with me – I hope you will accompany me.
>
> I want to take in 30 or 40,000 acres of land in the West of England of England I think it will be a good scheme.

This is one of the very few letters in which he even mentions anything approaching taking time off for such a simple pleasure as fishing in magnificent scenery. His plans for the West Country never materialised, but by the following year he had moved to Tapton House, which was to provide him with a great many happy days as work became less pressing. It was not in the best of condition, but it enjoyed a magnificent situation on a hilltop site and although the grounds were as neglected as the house they offered real opportunities for improvement – a task which was to give the new owner much pleasure in years to come. But when he first moved in, business remained his main occupation. There were the immediate tasks of establishing the new Clay Cross Company on a sound footing and the ever-pressing need to give his attention to new routes. We have seen in the previous chapter how he had become heavily involved with the Hudson schemes in the north-east, but that was by no means his only involvement with railways. One of the lines on which he was consulted was the Preston & Wyre Joint Railway: a company formed both to build the line and construct docks at the mouth of the Wyre at Fleetwood. Stephenson in his report gave as much attention to the harbour side of the business as he did to the railway itself, Fleetwood had, in fact, only been developed in the nineteenth century – and there had even been talk of naming the town New Liverpool.

Although Stephenson was overoptimistic in his assessment of its potential to overtake the port in the Mersey, Fleetwood did develop as a major fishing port. At the same time he was looking at ways of improving the connections, with a coastal route to Liverpool. This, for Stephenson, was the ideal terrain for railway building: flat and trouble free. He began with eulogising the proposed new harbour, before making his suggestions for the new line.

With respect to the Harbour of Wyre, I need say but little as it must be obvious to everyone that the fact of its possessing a safe entrance at all times of tide combined with its extremely favourable situation with reference to the Ports of Belfast, Drogheda, the Isle of Man, and other adjacent places must render it a desirable station for the steam vessels which now start from Liverpool and I do not doubt that on the completion of the Railway the owners of these vessels will find it in their interest to use it.

In the next place, a Railway being in a rapid progress from Glasgow to Ayr which will have the effect of materially shortening the sea voyage from Glasgow to Lancashire, your harbour will evidently offer much superior advantages to steam vessels from Ayr than the Port of Liverpool.

The subject to which I would, however, more particularly direct your attention is the great benefit which your line will derive from the formation of a Coast Line from Liverpool to Preston, a distance of about thirty miles, and which line would be extremely inexpensive in its construction. It needs little more than a reference to a map of that part of the country to convince you how materially this line will assist the Preston and Wyre Railway and I cannot urge upon you too strongly the propriety of taking measures to get the line forwarded.

All that I shall want from your Company will be to procure the consent, the owners of the land between Liverpool and Preston, as I feel confident that I shall be able to raise money required to make the line. As many of the Landowners as possible should be induced to take a sufficient number of shares to qualify them for seats in the Direction.

Supposing this line to be made from Liverpool to join your line near Preston, it will then be necessary for you to endeavour to get the Cumberland people to form a Harbour on the north side of the Duddon Sands, from which place to Whitehaven the line will be almost a dead level, and from Whitehaven to Maryport is also nearly a dead level. The country from Maryport to Carlisle is also extremely favourable and an Act has been obtained for the line, part of which is in course of execution.

The route which I have now described appears to be the only practicable line from Liverpool to Carlisle, as the enormous sum required for making a Railway across Morecambe Bay is too great and the scheme too hazardous to be attempted unless it should be taken up by Government, and the making of a Railway across Shap Fell is out of the question. It is therefore clear that the line I have described is the practicable line for a Railway Communication with the West of Scotland.

The letter is interesting for several reasons. Firstly, it shows how George Stephenson, even when he was asked to report on a minor line was always looking at the wider picture, seeing it not in isolation but as part of an ever-expanding network. This was one of his great strengths. On the other hand, his preference for selecting routes that created the least problems for engineers often led him to promote unnecessarily devious lines. He was quite right to say that crossing Morecambe Bay would never be practicable, but when it came to the route north to Carlisle he overestimated the difficulties. The latter was to provide the main line up the west coast to Scotland, and was to be built under the direction of his former apprentice, Joseph Locke. Crossing Shap remained a challenge throughout the age of steam, but it was a challenge that was met on a daily basis, admittedly often with considerable difficulty. Banking engines were always available to aid the ascent. His thoughts on persuading landowners not only to sell their land but to take shares in the Company chimed with his philosophy that railways were best run by directors who had a direct interest in their success, not just as shareholders but as citizens who were feeling the benefit of this new form of transport. One can see the logic in this attitude, but as local lines were joined up making an ever more complex web, the disadvantages of having to deal with a proliferation of small private companies became evident. The coastal line would eventually be built, and the Preston & Wyre Railway would suddenly find itself almost overwhelmed by passenger trains on certain days of the year, following the construction of a branch to Blackpool. Wakes Weeks, when the Lancashire mills closed their doors for the holiday saw tens of thousands heading for the popular resort. That was one trend George Stephenson had not foreseen.

In the early years at Tapton House, he was still heavily involved in consultations on railway projects, developing his mining interests in the Chesterfield area and acquiring land. But as the pressures of work eased he was able to spend more time developing the grounds around his house.

He became an enthusiastic gardener, but never quite lost his interest in innovation. One of the tasks he set himself was growing straight cucumbers, not perhaps comparable with developing a nationwide transport system, but a problem that interested him. He solved it by the simple expedient of putting the growing cucumbers in glass tubes. In developing his interest in horticulture, he became friends with the head gardener on the neighbouring estates of the Duke of Devonshire at Chatsworth, Joseph Paxton. The latter had designed a number of huge glasshouses to grow 'exotics', imported plants. George Stephenson also decided to follow his example and had a number of greenhouses built on his property. He did not, however, attempt anything on the scale of Paxton's Great Conservatory, a glasshouse that was 272ft long, 123ft wide and 67ft high. The largest glass building of the time it cost a massive sum of £33,000 to build. George Stephenson may have been wealthy, but not on the scale of the Duke of Devonshire. Paxton was later to have dealings with Robert on an even grander glasshouse.

As a young man George had loved wildlife and especially birds. Now that he had an estate of his own, he could enjoy such pleasures again, as Smiles wrote in his biography:

> He had favourite dogs, and cows, and horses, and again he began to keep rabbits and to pride himself on the beauty of his breed. There was not a bird's nest upon the grounds that he did not know of, and from day to day he went round watching the progress which the birds made with their building, carefully guarding them from injury. No one was more closely acquainted with the habits of British birds, the result of a long, loving, and close observation of nature.

Close observation paid off when it came to another of his ventures: beekeeping. He had hives near his house at the top of the hill, but was not getting as much honey as he expected. He then noticed that the bees were mostly collecting their nectar in the valley, and were struggling to fly back up again. This was a problem with a simple solution: take the hives to the meadows. His estates, which he was constantly expanding, kept him busy. His coal and limestone interests were thriving and they too took up a great deal of his time. But there were still railway matters to be attended to.

In 1844, he was approached to give an opinion on a proposed line from Birmingham to Shrewsbury via Wolverhampton. He gave a very carefully considered opinion, pointing out that the line between Wolverhampton and

Tapton House, Chesterfield: George Stephenson's home during his later years.

Birmingham would be extremely expensive, due to the likely very high costs of land purchase – a view he had already expressed earlier. In his opinion it would be far better to try and make a connection with the Grand Junction. He offered to go over the land again if it was thought necessary, but felt that on the whole there would be no great changes in his opinions on the matter. This was just one of a whole number of proposals going forward in the 1840s, many of which floundered because of the bewildering number of existing companies that had to be consulted, but this one was particularly interesting. Shrewsbury was also a destination for the rapidly expanding Great Western broad gauge empire. Whilst the two systems were quite separate, no one seemed to think it unreasonable to have two major rail networks with incompatible systems in one comparatively small country. Whilst they were still quite separate, no specific problems arose, but it was inevitable that both systems were not only trying to expand, but were competing for routes. One such battle occurred over who should build the route linking Oxford to Wolverhampton, a contest won by the Great Western. But then in 1845, the two systems met head to head at Gloucester. Travellers from the south arrived by broad gauge; those from the north by Stephenson gauge. As a result, passengers planning a through journey had to change trains – as did goods and livestock. It was a recipe for confusion. One can imagine the scene when all the passengers from one train headed for the other, meeting an equally large crowd trying to go in the reverse direction. At this stage, Parliament decided that the issue needed to be settled and appointed a Gauge Commission to look at the question and make recommendations.

The commissioners were a slightly unlikely mixture. The first on the list was clearly qualified to speak on railway matters: Lieutenant Colonel J. M. F. Smith, former Inspector General of Railways. The others were presumably selected for their sound common sense and, having no previous connections with railway companies, lack of bias. They were the Astronomer Royal, George Biddell Airey and Peter Barlow, Professor of Mathematics at the Royal Military Academy. They were to call a vast number of witnesses: managers, engineers and secretaries of all the major railway companies; locomotive builders, military engineers and important representatives of rail users. By the time the enquiry was over, 48 witnesses had been heard and 6,500 questions had been asked and answered. The engineers who were called represented a roll call of most of the great names in the industry, but everyone was aware that the most important witnesses would be those representing the Brunel and Stephenson camps: Daniel Gooch and Robert Stephenson.

George and Robert prepared their case with care and one of the witnesses, a naval officer Captain Laws, paid them a great compliment: 'Mr Robert Stephenson will tell you that there is no difficulty in making an engine as powerful on 4ft 8½in gauge as can be used with safety upon any other gauge. Now his opinion and that of Mr George Stephenson I would rather take than any other man's.'

The commissioners had been listening to evidence for three months when Brunel came forward with a suggestion that it would be valuable to test the performances of locomotives on the two systems, a test which he was certain would demonstrate the superiority of broad gauge and settle the whole question in his favour. He was aware that the majority of witnesses heard so far had favoured the other side and he saw this as an opportunity to turn the arguments in his favour. His original suggestion was that the two systems should be tested over a distance equivalent to the whole of the line from London to Exeter, but as it would have been impossible to find a strictly comparable line, the idea was rejected. Instead, the trial was to be held on two stretches of level track of equal length: between London and Didcot for the broad gauge and between York and Darlington for the 'narrow' gauge. The Brunel colours were carried by a *Fire Fly* Class locomotive, *Ixion* while the Stephensons were represented by a long boiler 4-2-0. *Ixion* had a best run that reached a commendable speed of 60mph hour while the rival only managed 53mph. Brunel was keen to point out that the trials showed the superiority of his engines in many ways, not just in the matter of speed but also in economy and smoothness of running. But the arguments were in vain. The commissioners had said they would note the results and take them into account, but they never said or implied that they would be the decisive factor. When it came down to practicalities, there was one inescapable fact: 1,900 miles of 'narrow' gauge already laid, far greater than the Great Western system. Looking at a possible future unification of the whole system, there was no contest. To convert the Stephenson gauge to broad gauge would be ruinously expensive. One has only to think of the cost involved in enlarging every tunnel and viaduct on the system, not to mention pushing station platforms further apart. On the other hand, converting the broad gauge would be comparatively simple. It was decreed that no more broad gauge should be laid. Later a temporary unification was obtained by adding a third rail to the broad gauge system to allow it to be used by all locomotives. By 1892, the last broad gauge track had gone.

George Stephenson was delighted by the result but it had not really proved anything. The locomotives were not strictly comparable. For example, *the Fire Fly* class had 7ft diameter drive wheels against the 5ft 6in of the long boiler. So, was the difference in performance due to the width of the track or other factors? We shall never know. Gooch never developed his locomotives to any great extent following the Commission's findings, while on what was now the standard gauge, speeds that would top the 100mph mark would be achieved by the beginning of the twentieth century. Similarly, we shall never know if a broad gauge would have proved a more efficient and comfortable system in the long run.

The 1840s were years full of railway schemes, many of which seemed to need the imprimatur of George Stephenson. A typical letter of February 1845 mentioned that he had been sent plans for the proposed railway from Middlesbrough to Redcar, and he intended to look over the route, but hoped to be able to catch the last train back home from Darlington. He ended the letter: 'what a Railway World this is! When is the bustle to be over?' But the bustle was not limited to Britain and he was still much in demand in Europe, where he was regarded, in effect, as the ultimate authority on all matters to do with railways.

Shortly after his Redcar excursion he was back in Belgium again this time to examine the 105km route between the River Sambre near Charleroi and Vieaux on the Meuse. Originally William Cubitt had been appointed as consultant engineer, but for some reason was no longer in charge. As a result of the survey, a Belgian engineer De Grandvoir was appointed as resident engineer, with Robert Stephenson as consultant engineer. This proved a very useful trip for George, as the proposed line served the very productive Belgian coalfield, where many new ideas had been tested. His companion for the journey was an old friend Thomas Sopwith, an expert on geology and especially coalfields. Stephenson found many interesting features, including new drainage methods and improved winding gear: ideas which he intended to use in his own mines when he got back home.

George Stephenson's standing was as high as ever in Belgium, and the chief director of the National Railways gave a banquet in his honour. It was all immensely flattering: a bust of the engineer was on display, crowned with laurels and a model of *Rocket* was later brought in and set under a triumphal arch. After this grand affair, Sopwith and Stephenson were invited to a private meeting with King Leopold where they discussed different aspects of the coalfields. Stephenson gave an explanation of coal strata using his hat as a model. Afterwards, he commented 'By the way, Sopwith. I was afraid the King would see the inside of my hat. It's a shocking bad one'. He was to make another trip to Belgium, this time to advise on the West Flanders Railway. This was not a single line but a complex network, which linked a number of different centres.

Amongst all this activity his wife Elizabeth died: George's memorial plaque and hers can be seen in Holy Trinity Church in Chesterfield. She was 68 years old. They had been married for twenty-five years, and both the Stephensons mourned for her: she was not only a much-loved wife, but she had always had a wonderful relationship with Robert, not something that can always be guaranteed between stepmother and stepson. But her death did nothing to ease the relentless pressure on George's time. By the end of the year he was off to Europe again, this time to Spain to survey a possible route that would link Bilbao to Madrid and then on to the coast on the Bay of Biscay. This was a formidable undertaking. The countryside between Bilbao and the capital was hilly, but that between Madrid and the Bay of Biscay was worse, as the Sierra de Guaderrama lay directly across the most direct route. This was a scheme being promoted by an Anglo-Spanish Company, but negotiations with the Spanish authorities had been protracted and unsatisfactory. For work to begin, the Company would have had to make a considerable deposit, known as 'caution money', but they needed assurances that their conditions would also be met and that appropriate funding would be available.

A leading promoter was Sir Joshua Walmsley of Liverpool who was both a friend and admirer of George Stephenson. In the biography by his son Hugh Mullineux Walmsley, published in 1879, there is an account of how the two men first met in the 1820s, and Sir Joshua's personal view of the engineer.

> Curiosity induced me to make Mr. Stephenson's acquaintance. At that time I shared the fear of those who regarded the railway scheme as Utopia, but I soon learned to have utter faith in Stephenson's genius, and better still, I learnt to love the man, to revere his truthfulness and honesty, and value his brave, tender heart. A close friendship ensued, we spent much of our time together, and I never met a more consistent man, or a more agreeable companion.

When Stephenson heard of his friend's difficulties with the Spanish authorities, he offered to go with him to Spain to cover the proposed route and give his professional opinion on its viability. He made no charge, although it would prove an arduous trip of two months. For the first part of the journey they were accompanied by the contractor, William Mackenzie, who was then working on the Orleans to Tours Railway, and had the opportunity to view the works. For the Spanish section they travelled in an open barouche. Walmsley's account of that journey is worth quoting in some detail, as it gives a rare personal insight into George Stephenson's personality in the words of a man who knew him well. As they travelled the engineer's 'keen eye was ever on the alert'.

> Though abounding with difficulties Stephenson asserted that they could be overcome, while at the same time he fully justified my refusal to deposit the caution money. On reaching Madrid, Stephenson dictated one of those lucid reports he excelled in, setting forth the obstacles and consequent heavy cost, at the same time showing the importance of the line, and making stipulations in favour of the Anglo-Spanish Company.

There then followed a series of meetings with the Spanish government's representative, General Nervaer, but they all ended in 'great shows of patience, great speeches, and nothing else'. The general offered to stage a bullfight in their honour, not an event that was likely to appeal to the animal-loving Stephenson. Eventually their patience ran out, and they gave official notice that unless they got some satisfactory progress within the next couple of weeks they would head for home. Nothing happened, so they were back in the open barouche drawn by a team of mules, heading for the high Pyrenees. It was a journey that was wearisome but not without its incidents and even humour.

> 'The old man', says Sir Joshua, 'usually sat with a map spread across his knees, and a pencil in his hand with which he marked down very accurately, the villages as we passed … One day, after a weary ascent of several hours, he looked up and said "Walmsley we'll reach the summit in ten minutes." "Nay, we've passed it already, we're going down," I answered. This reply was almost too much for the old man's equanimity, always easily ruffled at contradiction. "You know nothing about it, it will take us ten minutes to reach the summit, I tell you," he said testily. After a short silence he threw down the map. "This map is all wrong," he growled. "Nay, it was I who was wrong," he added, correcting himself a minute after. "How did you know we were going down that time?" "While you were buried in your map I caught sight of a stream, and we were going down with it," I answered, laughing. The old man joined in the laugh. "Better look at nature than all the maps; you've beaten the old man for once."'

As they went on their way over perilous roads with precipitous drops, Stephenson became concerned that the muleteers were driving far too quickly and risked wrecking the carriage. He attempted to get them to slow, but the men just thought it was a joke that they had made their English passengers afraid. They simply speeded up. Stephenson recognised the game they were playing, so he stood up in the carriage urging them to go much faster, shouting and clapping his hands, which had the desired effect. They slowed down. Their next adventure came when they reached France and had to cross a chain bridge across the Dordogne. Once across, Stephenson asked Walmsley to go back across with him. He 'walked very slowly with his head down' and at the end he announced that in his opinion the structure was unsafe and that at some time in the future it would give way. He felt it essential to pass on this information, but the local mayor listened politely then waved them goodbye. A few months later the engineer's prophecy tragically came true. A regiment of soldiers was marching over the bridge when it collapsed and many were killed.

Walmsley repeatedly referred to the engineer as an 'old man', suggesting that he was somewhat frail, but when they reached a railway construction site, Stephenson seemed to rediscover all his old vigour and energy. He watched the local navvies at work, excavating and filling barrows with spoil, in what seemed a not very efficient manner.

'Their posture is all wrong', he said, jumping out of the carriage with the natural instinct that impelled him to be always giving or receiving instruction, he took up a spade, excavated the soil and filled a wheelbarrow in half the time it took any of the men to do it.

A cartoonist's view of the chaos caused by the break of gauge at Gloucester station.

He then grabbed a heavy mallet and threw it as far as he could and indicated that the French navvies should try and match him. None of them could, but a large crowd gathered round him. The interpreter explained to them that this was 'Stev-i-son' at which they all burst out in loud cheers.

By the time they reached Paris, Stephenson was plainly far from well. It had been an exhausting journey and the accommodation had not always been good. However, he insisted on staying long enough to fulfil several engagements. However, when they got to Le Havre for the boat home, Walmsley rushed him straight in to see the ship's surgeon, who diagnosed pleurisy and bled him 'copiously', which Walmsley felt saved his life. It is not a course of treatment that would be recommended today. Pleurisy can be caused either by a virus or a bacterium – or in a few cases can be a result of pneumonia. The bacterial form is now treated with antibiotics – the viral form usually clears up in time without specific treatment. Stephenson's treatment would only have weakened him. When they reached England, Walmsley took him to the Adelphi Hotel in London, where he remained for six weeks recuperating. During that time his friend acted as his nurse, carer and amanuensis. Convalescence did not, however, stop him working and he was soon dictating papers on railway topics and discussing the topics and people of the day. One interesting point that emerged was his view on George Hudson. His initial friendship seems to have disappeared and although Hudson was still the Railway King, Stephenson was increasingly aware that he was not the honest man he had once appeared to be, saying:

> No one approved more than he did the pluck, the strong will, and business capacity of Mr Hudson, qualities that had lifted him from his small draper's shop in York to the arbiter of the fortunes of millions in England: but that no eminence could be held by unprincipled means.

Stephenson was also still thinking about how the railway system should develop over the country as a whole. One idea that he dictated was the construction of a line from the Derbyshire coalfield to London that would be used exclusively for freight. He had come to the conclusion that the country needed to have two rail networks not one: a dedicated freight line and the other to be used only for passenger trains. This would he felt be far safer than the present system. When he had fully recovered he returned to Chesterfield, where he resumed his enthusiasm for gardening. According to Walmsley he was particularly proud of his vines, melons and pineapples – and would only admit one rival as being worthy of consideration – Joseph Paxton.

Back in Tapton House he wrote to Michael Longridge on 22 November 1845 and gave a few more details of his Spanish expedition.

> I have had a most extraordinary journey in Spain. I crossed the Pyrenees 5 times, and rode on horse back 50 miles around the mountains seeking out the lowest pass – we had our carriage drawn up by bullocks to the mountain passes where a carriage had never been before – we passed just under the snow range.

He estimated that they had travelled 3,000 miles in thirty-three days. It is hardly surprising that he felt exhausted by the end.

Although 1846 was inevitably a far less eventful year for George Stephenson, it did result in a patent being granted jointly between himself and William Howe for a three-cylinder locomotive. Given the controversy over who had ultimate responsibility for the Stephenson linkage, it is interesting to find Howe having equal billing on the patent. The idea was mainly to counteract the swaying motion produced by two-cylinder engines, where the cranks were set at right angles, so that the thrust of the connecting rods alternated, first on one side, then on the other. In the new engine, the two outside cylinders were set on the same dead centre so that everything moved up and down in unison on either side. The locomotive showed its paces with a special train on 7th May 1847 when it ran between Wolverton and Birmingham, covering the 41 miles in 42 minutes, with a maximum speed of 64mph. In spite of this success, only two of these engines were built at Newcastle.

A long-standing problem among British engineers was the lack of technical education and one effect of the lack of an advanced technological institution was that there was nowhere where practical engineers could meet to discuss ideas. The first attempt to remedy this was the formation of the Society of Civil Engineers in 1771, later renamed the Smeatonian Society after the great engineer's death. Among its members was John Rennie, but it was considered rather elitist. A new generation of younger engineers set up their own organisation, the Institution of Civil Engineers, in 1820. In its early years it was dominated by the London-based engineers, the majority of whom had spent most of their working lives in the construction or roads and canals. The first president was Thomas Telford who was, at best, unenthusiastic about railways, if not downright antagonistic. A story was told by Smiles that Stephenson had applied for membership but was turned down. It seems to have little foundation in fact. This was a group led by just those London engineers with whom he had argued and battled for years. It is hard to imagine him wishing to join them. He himself firmly stated in a letter to J. T. W. Bell of 27 February 1847:

> I have had the honour of Knighthood of my own country made to me several times, but would not have it. I have been invited to become a fellow of the Royal Society and also of the Civil Engineers Society, but I objected to these empty additions to my name.

There was more than a touch of arrogance about this: to become a Fellow of the Royal Society would be for most a cherished honour, but it probably reflects his deep-rooted objection to all London institutions. He was, however, an enthusiast for the general idea of technical education.

As early as 1834 he presided over a public meeting in Newcastle called to discuss setting up a Mechanics' Institute. It was not particularly well attended, but it did result in an Institute being formed, which eventually became well known and influential. He regularly talked at this and other Institutes, including Leeds during the period he lived in the north, and when he moved to Tapton House he was a regular speaker at Belper and Chesterfield. He was an enthusiastic supporter of the British Association for the Advancement of Science, and addressed the Mechanical section on numerous occasions. At the root of his ideas on education was his awareness of how he had suffered in his early life from the lack of it. At the same time, he was equally aware of the value of the work he himself had done in bringing forward his own apprentices and assistants. The idea that science and technology could be combined to their mutual advantage was still comparatively new. While some universities, especially those in Scotland, were doing valuable scientific work, the older English universities lagged far behind. George Stephenson was not particularly interested in theory, but he did believe in the correct teaching of sound mechanical principles. It was inevitable that when the idea of setting up an Institution of Mechanical Engineers, along the lines of the Civils was mooted, he would be a keen supporter.

The prime mover for the establishment of a Mechanical Engineering Institute was J. E. McConnell, who by 1846 had become the chief mechanical engineer at the locomotive and carriage works at Wolverton on the London & Birmingham. The first meeting was held at the Queen's Hotel in Birmingham on 7 October 1846 and a committee was appointed to agree on a set of rules. The next meeting was held on 27 January the following year, with McConnell in the chair. The rules were formally approved and Stephenson was formally elected president. His first address was a very personal one, describing his early years at Killingworth. He was a great supporter, not only giving talks but also making a donation of £100 to help fund the various activities of the new Institution. Among the issues he addressed, many were concerned with safety. He wrote about a proposed system for a new type of continuous brake that could be operated from the footplate and would automatically apply brakes to all the carriages in the train. In the same paper he looked at ways of improving communications between the driver at the front and the guard in the rear of the train. As well as promoting his own ideas, he also enthused over a new type of pressure gauge invented by Sydney Smith of Nottingham. He continued making contributions for the rest of his life, his final paper being a comprehensive demolition job on a proposed new form of rotary engine.

The formation of the Institution was not the only major event in his life at this time. Ellen Gregory, the daughter of a farmer from Bakewell had been Stephenson's housekeeper for some time. But the relationship had obviously developed in new directions. While he was in London in 1847, he wrote to her on hearing that she had been ill. This was not a letter to be dictated to a secretary: it was one he would write himself. In it he addressed her as 'My dear Glen' and after enquiring after her and explaining his movements, he ended the letter: 'I shall be home to be with you at the end of the week'. He signed it 'I am dear Glen your loving friend'. This was not the letter of an employer to a housekeeper and in February 1848 they were married.

The wedding was a very quiet affair, so quiet that even Robert was not told about it until after the event. He was hurt by this and Joshua Walmsley took it upon himself to effect a reconciliation between father and son. Not being invited was perhaps only part of the problem. Robert had been very close to Elizabeth, George's second wife, and might well have thought it very strange that his father should now remarry. He had never considered remarrying himself, even though he had still been quite a young man when his wife Fanny died. The marriage was, however, destined to be short lived. At the end of July 1848, George became seriously ill and once again he was plagued by pleurisy. This time there was to be no recovery. He died on the 12 August. He was interred in the graveyard at Holy Trinity Church, Chesterfield under a plain slab with just his initials. Even in death he preferred simplicity to obsequious honours. Among those who came to pay their respects was his old friend, Edward Pease, who was then 81 years old, and still a devout Quaker. He sat through the funeral service, of which he clearly disapproved, with his hat firmly set on his head. At Tapton House he met Robert and they had a long chat in which he tried to comfort the son by telling him that it was probably 'a kindness that his father was taken' as 'his habits were approaching to inebriety'. There were many tributes paid, though many seemed to share with Edward Pease an acceptance that the man was not without his faults. But they also made it clear that these were of no account when set against his achievements. The local paper the *Derby and Chesterfield Reporter* expressed it as well as any: 'He seemed the impersonation of the moving, active spirit of the age'.

Chapter 16

LINES TO HOLYHEAD

In 1838, the Chester and Crewe Company asked George Stephenson to look at the possibility of extending their line to serve the mail service to Ireland, either by following the existing route taken by the road coaches to Holyhead or by developing a new port at what was then a tiny fishing village near the tip of the Llŷnly Peninsula now called Porthdinllaen. He recommended the Holyhead route but it was not until the following year that the Company decided to go ahead with the scheme, and asked Robert Stephenson to carry out a detailed survey and supply suitable plans they could then present to Parliament. The route he proposed was 84½ miles long, and the first part from Chester presented a number of challenges, but none that were exceptional for the time. The first difficulties appeared at the start of the line, where it left the city via a 405 yard tunnel to be blasted through the red sandstone and that was followed by a forty-five-arch viaduct, culminating in a bridge across the River Dee. The latter must have seemed of minor importance compared with what lay ahead, but it turned out that there was a major problem, which would only appear later. The line hugged the coast up to the point where the land rose up to Great Orme Head and it turned inland towards Conway, now Conwy. Here the wide mouth of the river needed to be crossed, before heading off towards Anglesey and the next, even greater challenge, the crossing of the Menai Straits.

It was obvious to Robert Stephenson that it was solving the problem of these two latter crossings that was key to the whole enterprise, and a large number of possible solutions were considered and rejected. Thomas Telford had solved the problem when constructing the Holyhead Road by building two imposing suspension bridges. As mentioned earlier, the previous attempt to build a suspension bridge for use by rail traffic had been a failure, and the history of the Telford bridge at Menai only reinforced the idea that it might not be usable by locomotives. During the construction process, it had been seen to distort in the wind and had to be strengthened. An alarming account appeared after the opening, when coach passengers reported their vehicle swaying badly during a crossing, but investigation showed that this was

The collapsed bridge over the Dee near Chester.

not due to movement of the bridge but the alcoholic content of the driver. That was a false alarm, but Robert Stephenson rejected the idea of building a second bridge of similar design. But if a suspension bridge would not take a locomotive, perhaps the Telford bridge could be put to use in a different way. The idea was that one of the two roadways would be laid with tracks. Trains arriving from Chester would uncouple wagons and carriages, which would then be pulled in small groups across the bridge by horses, then they would be reunited with another locomotive on Anglesey. There was, however, a problem. The approach from the Chester side was by a road that was too steep to be worked by locomotives, so an embankment would have to be built up to reach the level of the bridge deck. The bridge authorities agreed to the idea, offering to rent out the space for an annual payment of £200, but they stipulated that the approach embankment had to be temporary. This clearly made the whole scheme unworkable, so Stephenson was faced with the necessity of building a bridge of some sort. He faced precisely the same problem that had confronted Telford: the insistence that the bridge should be a minimum of 105ft above the high spring tide level to allow shipping to use the Straits and that there should be no piers that would interfere with navigation. There was one natural feature that would help with the latter condition. Right in the middle of the Straits was an outcrop known as the Britannia Rock. That at least could be used to hold one supporting structure, but the problem of what form the bridge should take was still to be solved.

Edwin Clark, the resident engineer in the project, wrote a very full account *The Britannia and Conway Tubular Bridges*, published in 1850. Much of it is taken up with technical reports, but it also contains an invaluable account of those years by Robert Stephenson himself, in which he described the several ideas that were considered and rejected. The first was for two cast-iron arches, each with a 350ft span, but the difficulty was how to erect them, even assuming spans of such a width could be supplied. There was no possibility of using the conventional method of building them up on centring – the wooden frame on which the arch would be built – as that would interfere with navigation. Stephenson discussed it with Isambard Brunel. The latter had devised an ingenious system for constructing an arch. The voussoirs were to be built out from a central pier and tied back to it by iron bolts. As the arch developed at an equal rate on either side of the pier, the two sides would be in balance. After the arch was complete, the bolts could be removed. This might have worked at Menai but not at Conway, as there would be no central pier. So that idea was rejected.

The next idea Stephenson considered was to construct the entire arch on floating pontoons, so that when completed it could be jacked up into position. This time it was the Admiralty who flatly refused to allow anything of the sort to happen, as it would necessarily interfere with the shipping lanes. At this stage the idea of a suspension bridge was brought forward again. In this version, the platform would be made rigid by the use of trusses. This had been tried successfully when a suspension canal aqueduct had been constructed at Fort Collins in Colorado. Stephenson at once saw that there was a problem. In the canal aqueduct the load 'is constant and equally distributed, and all the strains consequently fixed both in both amount and direction. In a large railway bridge it is evident, so far from these conditions pertaining under any circumstance, they are ever varying to a very large extent'. Once again, Brunel suggested a solution. Instead of chains, he proposed using hollow, curved tubes to hold the deck. But Stephenson decided that given the nature of the sites, they would be too difficult to construct.

At this stage, Stephenson went back to an idea of his own that he had first used in the construction on the Hertford & Ware branch of the Northern & Eastern Railway. He had to construct a bridge over the river at Ware to carry road traffic. He had used ordinary wrought-iron boiler plates held together by angle irons to create cells that joined together to form a very rigid structure. This he felt was a much better way of achieving a rigid deck for a suspension bridge than the trussed form and he began to work on a new version in which the trains instead of travelling on top of this tubular structure could actually travel inside it. He still envisaged it being supported by suspension chains, but he was sufficiently confident of this new version to put it forward as a practical proposal. There was some criticism of the design, and several engineers suggested that rather than the rectangular tube of the original version, one with an elliptical cross section would have greater strength. Stephenson was unconvinced and when he looked at his own ideas he realised that in effect, the thick plates at top and bottom of the tube were acting just like the top and bottom of an I-shaped girder. If that was the case, then there was probably no need for suspension chains at all.

At this stage a Commission was appointed to investigate whether the Holyhead route was feasible – in effect was the tubular bridge a practical solution to the problem of the two crossings? If they decided against, then the Company would almost certainly have been forced to give up the route and go for the other option and head for Porthdinllaen. One of the leaders in the investigation was Sir John Rennie who, in the past, had scarcely been seen as a supporter of the Stephenson family. But on this occasion the go-ahead was given for the Holyhead route. This did not mean that work could begin straight away on construction. The tubular bridge was still an idea on paper, and even Stephenson had no proof that it would work, but he was now convinced of the basic idea: 'I began to regard the tube as a beam' – and it was on that basis that he submitted his plans to the Chester & Holyhead Railway Co. The idea was now considered by General Charles Pasley, Inspector General of Railways, who advised him to retain the suspension chains, simply to be prudent.

Stephenson now sought advice from the sector where working with wrought iron on large projects had now became a standard practice –

shipbuilding. John Laird reassured him that the strength of wrought iron had been thoroughly tested. He then heard of an accident that had occurred at the Blackwall shipyard. An iron ship, the *Prince of Wales* was being prepared for launching when a cleat in the bows gave way and it plunged forward: the bows hit the bottom of the river and the stern was left stuck on the quay. It was, in fact, acting as a long iron beam only supported at either end. There was minor damage but the integrity of the hull remained unimpaired. It was a convincing demonstration, so Robert Stephenson now felt able to move forward, but still needed a partner in the enterprise who was familiar with this form of metal construction. He turned to the established shipwright William Fairbairn, with the idea of setting up a series of experiments to find the best possible design. At Fairbairn's suggestion another expert was added to the team, Eaton Hodgkinson FRS, professor of mechanical engineering at University College, London, who had done a great deal of experimental work on the strength of iron structures. Unfortunately, relations between him and Fairbairn deteriorated rapidly, and they ended up scarcely able to consult over anything, which did little to further the experiments.

Rather surprisingly, it seems that Clark was unaware that while cast iron was known to be weak in tension but strong in compression, wrought iron had precisely the opposite characteristics. With this in mind, the eventual form of the tube that emerged was rectangular as Stephenson had originally planned: an oval shape was stronger, but the difference was too small to justify the extra complications and cost of construction. The top and bottom were designed as cellular structures and were thicker than the sides. But this design was only achieved after a great deal of effort, involving experiments and calculations by all concerned. The dimensions that were decided on for Menai were tubes that were 450ft long, 30ft high and 18ft wide with a total weight of 600 tons each. The results were now made public. Edwin Clark described the reaction.

> Everyone had some doubts and fears to be overcome as soon as these details became known: direst warnings came in on all hands, suggesting every imaginable apprehension, and Mr. Stephenson appeared at times disheartened when he withdrew, as was his daily custom, to give instructions on the subject, and to deliberate on the weighty difficulties. Very few are aware of the powerful anxiety that falls to the lot of the engineer in circumstances of such deep responsibility; he can be satisfied with no uncertainty or doubt – and what other foundations were possible?

FLOATING THE
HOLYHEAD AND CHESTER RAILWAY TUBULAR BRIDGE,
AT CONWAY.
6th March 1848.

Manoeuvring one of the tubular bridge sections into place at Conway.

The experiments over, there still remained doubts. It was by no means certain that what worked in laboratory conditions would behave as well when scaled up to full size. It was decided to have one final test. A one-sixth scale model would have to be built, and work began on that in December 1845. It was only when tests on that proved satisfactory that the actual work of constructing the bridges at Conway and Menai could begin. These preliminaries have been described in some detail, simply because it is all too easy to think that Stephenson simply looked at the problem of bridging the two waterways, came up with a solution and that was it. As is now obvious, many alternatives were first looked at and even when the general idea of tubular bridges was accepted, there was still an immense amount of experimental work to be done, in which Stephenson, Fairbairn and Hodgkinson all played their part, even when two of the group were at loggerheads. The relationship between Fairbairn and Hodgkinson had steadily deteriorated: Fairbairn, the practical engineer was all for pushing ahead and getting on with the job in hand; while the academic Hodgkinson kept fussing over tiny details. Clark attempted mediation, with little success: 'They continue to hate each other enthusiastically'. Hodgkinson seemed to want experiments to go on and on, but Stephenson eventually had to call a halt. In March 1847, he wrote to Clark asking him to inform Hodgkinson of his decision:

> If I had my own way he should go on experimenting until the last day but I am driven by many considerations to put an end to them now but I will go into the consideration of any suggestions he may have regarding two or three additional experiments when I come down.

In its final form, the tube was to have a single cellular structure at both top and bottom, though at one time a double layer had been proposed for the top. The day had finally arrived to authorise the start of construction. Fairbairn suggested building the tubes on floating barges, an idea that had already been rejected. Instead, the tubes were to be fabricated on site and when completed loaded onto pontoons so that they could be raised into place. The Conway was to be the first to be tried, being the simpler of the two. It was to be built right next to the Telford suspension bridge, and the approach from the north was to use part of the embankment built for the Holyhead Road. However, because of the slope of the beach on the castle side, the abutments at that end had to be set further back. Ports were left at the top of the stonework for suspension chains that it soon turned out would never be needed. There were two tubes, one for each set of tracks.

The once peaceful spot by the river became a cacophony of hammering. Once iron plates were delivered from Liverpool they had to be riveted together by hand. There was, however, one surprisingly modern feature: the machine that drilled the holes for the rivets was controlled by punched cards. On 6 March 1847, the first tube was ready to be installed. Robert Stephenson was understandably anxious: he had always been concerned that many things could go wrong with the system of floating out the great iron tubes. On the day he was on hand to watch over everything and Brunel came along to give moral support. Clark had to watch from a distance, sitting in a carriage, as he had just suffered a most unfortunate accident at the works, which resulted in his having one toe amputated. Stephenson's worries proved all too well founded, when one of the pontoons broke free from its moorings and ended up stuck against a rock. As a result, the tube was no longer correctly aligned, and nothing could be done until the next high tide when the pontoon could be freed and repositioned. That proved to be a difficult operation and it was only on 11 March that the tube was finally in position. On 8 April, the hydraulic jacks were in place, and the actual lift went smoothly and quickly. On 18 April, Robert took his place on the footplate of a locomotive and steamed through the tube. By 1 May, the line was open for single line traffic.

Although one tube was now in place, Robert was still looking for help and reassurance. On 6 August he wrote again to Brunel, asking him to join him on site to 'give me the aid of your thoughts about these tubes both as to the riveting and hoisting'. The second tube was floated into place on 12 October and everything seemed to be going smoothly, until a crack appeared in one of the crossheads on a lifting jack. Packing was quickly added to ensure there was no damage to the tube, and the lift proceeded carefully and without further incident. With Conway now more or less completed, the pontoons and tackle were towed round the coast to Menai and the greater challenge of the Britannia Bridge.

This was a more formidable task than Conway, not simply because of the greater size, but also because of the dangerous currents and high tides in the Menai Straits. By now Fairbairn and Hodgkinson had left the team, but a friend of Brunel's, Captain Christopher Clayton, joined them, providing valuable expertise, not just in ship management but also in salvage operations. Stephenson remained anxious and became quite ill, and was ordered by his doctor to leave his office and set off to Windermere for a rest. He did not stay away for long. The site at the Straits was a great bustle of activity as the tubes were assembled on a wooden platform that stretched for over half a mile from the wharf. It was a scene that mixed technology with brute force: many of the plates that arrived by ship needed to be straightened, which required nothing more complex than battering with 40lb sledge hammers. The procedure was the same as at Conway but as with the first tube, there were problems that for a time looked as if they could only lead to disaster.

The initial attempt to launch the first tube had to be called off thanks to an accident with one of the capstans. The following day, the workers had to grapple with a strong wind and high, fast-running tide, and it was late in the evening before everything was again under control. The first objective was to get one end of the massive tube up against the Anglesey pier where it could be secured. The foreman in charge called Rolfe was supervising the operation, but it seemed that the tube was swinging too far and would miss the pier and they tried to correct it using the capstan that carried the cable to the tube. Then coils jammed, and the force of the moving tube out on the water dragged the capstan from the ground. Rolfe acted quickly, grabbed the free end of the cable and shouted for help. Crowds of spectators joined him, grabbing the line in a desperate attempt to bring the tube to shore. It was a battle, but it was a battle that was won. With one end now secured, the capstan at the opposite end was set to work and with no further alarms, the whole tube was secured in position and ready for lifting. Stephenson turned to Brunel who was once again there to support his friend, and simply announced that he was going to bed. He certainly needed the rest, for as he said the next day, worry about the project had kept him awake at night for three weeks, and aged him ten years.

Once a start had been made, the work proceeded comparatively smoothly, though once again there was a problem with one of the hydraulic jacks. Fortunately, Stephenson had noted how close disaster had been during the Conway lift and had extra safety measures in place. On 5 March the last rivet was driven into place and Robert Stephenson boarded the first train to cross the Menai Straits. By the end of the month, the line was open to a regular service. It was a triumph; but there was a sour note. A story began to circulate that credit for the work did not really belong to Stephenson at all, but that the honour should really go to Fairbairn, a view that was repeated by several leading figures, and if not actually propagated by him, never denied by Fairbairn himself. In some ways it was a repeat of a familiar story: Stephensons against London experts. There seems very little if any doubt that the whole idea of a tubular bridge came from Robert, and that although he relied heavily on his two collaborators for their expertise, he remained the chief engineer in charge of the whole project.

Stephenson had always been concerned and worried about these two crossings: in the first place, whether they could be made at all, then, once he had come up with the idea of the tubular bridge, whether such a novel idea would actually work. Once the first Conway tube was up and in use, he must have felt a great relief to know that the design was indeed practical. He still had the Britannia Bridge to worry about, but he must have felt that there was nothing else on the line that would cause any serious problem. There was another major river crossing on the line, across the River Dee. Designing and building that must have seemed far less of a problem, using established methods. Yet it was this bridge that threatened to end his entire career.

Robert's original idea had been to cross the river by a conventional five-arched viaduct in brick, and a start had even been made. Then it was discovered that there were difficulties with setting the piers, and opted instead for a three-arched version, with stone piers joined by iron spans. There was a problem with long cast-iron spans, not simply with their ability to take heavy loads but with actually acquiring them. There was a limit to the size of beam that the foundries could produce and even if they could be produced there were difficulties transporting them. Various solutions were suggested, including the use of iron beams of different lengths, clamped together, suggested by Peter Barlow, elder brother of the better known railway engineer, William Barlow. The method preferred by Robert Stephenson was the trussed iron bridge. Cast-iron beams of different lengths were bolted together and, in theory, suitably reinforced by wrought-iron ties. For the ties to be effective, the anchoring point had to be high enough above the deck, so that the ties met the deck at a steep angle. In that case, they would act rather like the chains of a suspension bridge. If, however, the angle was shallow, their effectiveness was limited or even non-existent. Robert had earlier worked with George Bidder to build this sort of compound girder bridge over the River Lea. There seemed to be no problems, and this was the method chosen for the Dee crossing. The iron ties were never securely anchored, but the bridge passed inspection and was opened to traffic at the end of October 1846. It was intended to use it for construction trains while work continued on the rest of the Chester & Holyhead route, but the Shrewsbury & Chester Railway had running rights and they began working the line with passenger trains.

At first everything seemed to be going well, but disaster struck on 24 May 1847. The driver of the train reported hearing a cracking noise, and convinced there was a real danger opened the regulator wide to try and get his train clear of the bridge. The locomotive made it safely, but the coupling broke and the tender on which the unfortunate fireman was busily breaking up coal plunged into the river. He died along with a guard and two coachmen travelling in the first van. Miraculously only two passengers died, though sixteen were injured. With a disaster on this scale, an inquest and technical enquiry were necessarily set up. There was, however, from the start a conflict of interests. For the Chester & Holyhead Company, the ideal outcome would be if it was found that the locomotive had derailed, causing the damage to the bridge. For the Shrewsbury & Chester, the accident was

The Britannia Bridge across the Menai Straits in its original appearance: part was recently destroyed by a fire.

entirely due to a failure of the bridge itself. Experts would be called, but the final verdict would lie with the inquest jury.

At the inquest, Robert Stephenson appeared as the only representative of the engineering staff who had designed and constructed the bridge, assuming full responsibility for it. Several senior engineers spoke on his behalf, including his friend Brunel. He must have been concerned when he heard Joseph Locke was to give his views. Relations between the two Stephensons and Locke had been strained following the latter's critical – but entirely fair – report on the Liverpool & Manchester tunnel. Not only that, Locke was known to disapprove of the use of cast iron in railway bridge construction. In the event, he spoke up on Stephenson's behalf and the two men, if they never returned to the easy friendship of their early years, were reconciled. The other individual whose reputation was on the line was the inspector who had passed the bridge as safe, General Pasley. In evidence he admitted that he had approved it more or less on the grounds that other bridges of a similar type had been completed and used without mishap. However, he also hit on the great flaw in the construction: 'I consider that the tension bars are of very little use; indeed the tension bars are connected with the girder alone, forming part of it and have no independent support.' The only voice raised in opposition to the theory that the accident was caused by a derailment came from the engineer from the Chester & Shrewsbury, Henry Robertson. His views stood little chance of being heard, when set against those of some of the most famous engineers in the land. At one time it was thought that there might be a manslaughter charge, but at the end of the inquest the jury brought in a verdict of accidental death without apportioning any blame. It is now all too clear that the compound girder design was fundamentally unsound and that, as General Pasley had suggested, the tie bars did nothing to counteract the downward forces on the beam. In other words, Robert Stephenson had made a terrible error of judgement.

It was without doubt the darkest episode in Robert Stephenson's career and had things worked out differently could have been a catastrophe for him. One has only to think what happened after the terrifying Tay Bridge collapse in 1879 which left its engineer Thomas Bough a ruined man: he died the following year. Robert Stephenson was to go on to other great works, but the strains of the accident and the construction of the tubular bridges left their mark. He had never had the robust physique of his father and the stresses of those years had seen a general deterioration in his health.

Chapter 17

HOME AND AWAY

The city centre of Newcastle sits high above the banks of the Tyne and before the railway arrived, the main river crossing was by a low level bridge, now demolished and replaced by the present swing bridge. The idea of a high level bridge had first been proposed by Thomas Telford in 1825, but nothing came of it. The Newcastle architect and civil engineer Benjamin Green was next on the scene. He had designed the handsome headquarters for the city's Literary and Philosophical Society and was an experienced bridge builder, having designed suspension bridges over the Tyne at Scotswood and the Tees at Whorlton. His high level bridge was intended only for road traffic, but once approval had been given for the Newcastle & Berwick Railway to construct a bridge at that site, the situation had changed. A separate High Level Bridge Company was formed and Robert Stephenson was invited to present his design. He proposed a dual purpose bridge for both road and rail traffic.

This was to be a massive structure, with a total length of 1,370ft and standing 146ft above the river. The bridge consisted of five stone piers linked by bow string iron decks, the lower carrying road traffic, the upper the railway. These consisted of cast-iron arches, the bows, in which the thrust of the arch on the piers was balanced by wrought-iron ties, the strings. The piers themselves were not solid throughout. Most of the lower pier consisted of a pair of pillars, each 7ft by 4ft 8in in cross section, united at the top by an arch immediately below the road deck. The foundations for the piers consisted of timber piles encased in concrete. The driving of the piles marked a significant advance in technology. James Nasmyth had recently invented a steam hammer, originally designed to forge a crank shaft for Brunel's ship the *Great Britain* when the engineer was still thinking in terms of a paddle steamer. The principle was simple: steam power was used to lift the hammer head, set in a vertical frame, and then when the pressure was released it fell under gravity. This was now adapted for pile driving.

It is interesting to note that given the acrimony that surrounded the question of who should be given the honour of being named as originator of the tubular bridges, the argument over who should claim the glory this time

The High Level Bridge across the Tyne at Newcastle, photographed a century ago, with a steam train visible on the upper level.

was of a very different nature. One of Stephenson's former assistant engineers, Thomas Harrison, was the principal engineer and Stephenson the engineer in chief. Harrison declared firmly that 'The plans for the High Level bridge have been applied under my direction: the designs are not mine, but my friend Mr Robert Stephenson's' while Stephenson stated equally firmly that he had no right to claim any credit – 'upon Mr Harrison the whole responsibility for the erection lies' and that he himself had done nothing 'beyond drawing the outline'. Whoever was ultimately responsible, and it would seem fair to let them share the credit, it was and is a magnificent structure and still dominates the river.

The line northwards from Newcastle to Berwick had been a source of conflict for some time, largely caused by the objections being raised by Lord Howick, who wanted the line moved. Michael Longridge was keen for it to keep to the original route so that it could serve his ironworks at Bedlington. He wrote to George Stephenson to get his views and received a very forthright reply in a letter of November 1843.

I am rather astonished at Lord Howick's observations about the line passing Howick. It does not go through any of their pleasure grounds. It passes over one of their drives which runs down a dingle to the coast: it passes under the other road without at all injuring the level and strange to say there is a high way, I mean a turnpike road betwixt the house and the intended Railway, and the same roads are crossed, one over the dingle and the other on the level, and the land the line passes over is tillage land. My senses are puzzled in judging how these people can set about making such paltry objections! It is compensation they want, nothing else. The line cannot be moved to the place Lord Howick alludes to, west of the house: it would require a tunnel a mile long, it would be very well for Lord Howick as it would pass through their Limestone Quarries. I understand from Mr. Grey that the line was to be put nearer the Sea, this might have been done well enough: This species of objection is a gentile way of picking subscribers' pockets there cannot be a doubt that it is meant to do so.

Although a line was eventually agreed, troubles with Lord Howick continued. As late as March 1845, Robert Stephenson was writing to Brunel:

Hudson has left town and I shall not see him until his return after Easter. I will do all I can but I fear that Howick and he have so misunderstood each other that reconciliation will be very difficult. Temper has in this instance like many others stepped in and to all appearances is riding roughshod over reason.

Meanwhile, as arguments continued over the route and work was progressing on the High Level Bridge, work on the other major feature on the route to Edinburgh was also under construction: the bridge across the Tweed near Berwick. Although this was another massive structure it presented no unusual problems. The river was not navigable, so a conventional masonry viaduct could be built. Having said that, it was still a challenging task. It consisted of twenty-eight semicircular arches, each with 61½ft span, thirteen of which crossed the river itself, while the remainder carried the approach line from the south. The total length was 2,160ft and the maximum height above the river 126ft. One problem the engineers faced was finding a firm foundation for the piers on the river section. Piles had to be driven through 40ft of gravel before bedrock was reached. As at Newcastle, the task was made easier by the use of steam-powered pile drivers. Even with the help of technology, a huge force was required for the job with at one time some 2,700 men at work. A temporary wooden bridge was built alongside the main bridge site, which helped with movement of material, and there was a lot to move: it was estimated that 8 million cu ft of stone was used and 2½ million bricks lined the arches. Work began in May 1847 and was completed in March 1850. It was originally known simply as the Tweed Bridge, but when Queen Victoria and Prince Albert arrived for the official opening ceremony in August of that year, she agreed to a new name: The Royal Border Bridge. It certainly was and is sufficiently grand to be officially described as majestic, but it is not actually on the border. The entire bridge lies on the English side. But with its opening, the east coast route from York to Edinburgh was completed.

By the end of the 1840s, Robert had been working with scarcely a break, apart from his enforced stay in the Lake District for his health. The old family friend, Edward Pease suggested that perhaps it was time to retire, and he replied in June 1850: 'Comparative retirement is however my intention and I trust that your prayer for the divine blessing to grant me happiness and quiet will be fulfilled'. But the name of 'Stephenson' still had a touch of magic for all would-be railway promoters, and following the death of George, anyone who wanted someone to plan a route for them or simply to confirm that the plans they already had were fit for purpose, now turned to Robert. It was not just British companies that wanted his advice and expertise: requests were coming in from around the world.

As described earlier, both George and Robert had been consulted about railway construction in Belgium, and the relationship continued to develop after George's retirement. Often, one or other of the Stephensons would be appointed as a consulting engineer, while all the actual construction was carried out under the supervision of a local man. The Belgian scene was complex. For example, when the line from Tournai to Jubise was proposed and opened for investment offers as a vital link in the growing system, it was coupled in the concession with another, quite independent route between Landen and Hassels. A London consortium took on the work, with Robert Stephenson and George Bidder as joint engineers. Overseas dealing was always bound to have more difficulties than the simpler relationship with British promoters. An unfortunate event happened in relation to the

The Royal Border Bridge across the Tweed.

Flanders Railway, with which George Stephenson had been closely involved. He had sent in an invoice for his work and several items were disputed. At this point George began legal proceedings. By now, it was Robert who was in charge of the line, which left him in an invidious position. However, he managed to resolve the situation by proposing that the dispute should be settled by arbitration 'instead of the tedious, expensive, and obscure proceedings of the Court of Chancery'. He was very wise. The Chancery proceedings were famously satirised in Dickens' novel, *Bleak House* which he was writing at about this time, and which features the interminable case of Jarndyce v Jarndyce, and that contains the memorable advice: 'suffer any wrong that can be done you rather than come here'.

The inaugural run of Norway's first steam railway.

Robert became far more actively involved in new European lines when he received a communication from the king and government of Norway asking for advice about building the country's very first railway. He and George Bidder visited the country to inspect the route. This was to run from the capital, Christiania, modern Oslo, for 40 miles to Eidsvoll at the southern end of Lake Mjosa. The lake itself was already used for transport, and at its northern end it lay right at the foot of the range of mountains that extends down the spine of Norway, so there was never any question at the time of extending the line northward beyond that point. In any case, Norway had only gained independence from Denmark in 1814 – though was still in a loose union with Sweden. As a result, money for construction was very limited. Robert was a practical man, who appreciated that his job was to make the best of the available resources. He later reported, with some pride, that this was 'the cheapest line of Railway that was ever made over a rough country'.

He certainly did everything he could to make the scheme work. Robert paid for the survey and preparation of plans and the total cost of £800 was put as a loan in his account. But in spite of approving the plans in 1847, nothing could be done because of a severe economic recession. It was not until 1850 that he put a deal together between a consortium of British contractors and financiers with the Norwegian government. The consortium contained the leading British contractors, Thomas Brassey, Samuel Peto and Edward Betts, together with the financier, John Ricardo. Even with finances assured, it was still a modest, single-track line, though locally it was known as the Trunk Railway, punningly appropriate as it carried more timber than passengers. Robert made two visits to supervise the operations and attended the opening ceremony in 1854. A grateful Norwegian government awarded him with the Grand Cross of Saint Olaf.

Norway may have been 'rough country', but Robert was also called on to advise on railways in Europe's most mountainous country, Switzerland. In other ways, the situation was also similar to Norway's in that the country had only recently become unified, following an attempt by the few Catholic cantons to form an independent alliance. There was a brief civil war, after which in 1848 a new federal constitution received an overwhelming vote of confidence. Certain matters such as defence and trade would be the responsibility of the national government, while the cantons were able to control their own local affairs. Before the federal system was set up, railway planning had been hampered by squabbling between the different cantons, to such an extent that between 1836 and 1848 the Swiss Northern Railway Company had only managed to complete 14½ miles of track from Zurich to Baden.

The new government was keen to modernise the transport system in the country and, in particular, consider developing an appropriate rail system. Almost inevitably, the consulate in London was given orders to approach Robert Stephenson to ask for his help in setting out the best routes. He suggested that the country needed international connections, and proposed investigating routes that would link Basle to the French border, a second route to the German network near Lake Constance and thirdly to consider a far more difficult route to Italy, crossing the Alps to Lugarno. He sent Henry Swinburne to Switzerland to carry out the initial surveys in 1850. Swinburne produced two reports, roughly based on Robert's original suggestions, featuring lines that largely kept to river valleys and served various important centres, including Basle, Lucerne, Berne, Thun and Zurich. The Alpine route was not even considered at that time. Stephenson and Swinburne looked over the proposed routes together and, after Robert had called in to meet the various Swiss ministers, he returned to write his report and make suggestions. It was a very practical affair, recommending railways more or less on the lines proposed by Swinburne, partly worked by locomotives and partly using inclines, linking in with the regular lake steamer services, and where necessary he proposed road improvements. What he did not recommend was a rail route across the Alps to Italy, which he regarded as impossible given current technology.

There is an interesting sidelight to the last decision on Alpine routes. The Austro-Hungarian Empire was keen to have a rail link from Vienna to the nearest port on the Adriatic coast at Trieste, which would involve constructing a railway that was to reach a summit level at 878 metres and, in spite of twists and turns, there would be sections with a ruling gradient of 1 in 40. This was the Semmering Railway, and inevitably there were questions as to whether or not it could be worked by locomotives. The suggestion was put forward in a journal: in Britain the question of whether locomotives could work a line was answered at the Rainhill Trials, so why not have Semmering Trials? The idea was adopted in 1851 and a number of locomotives were entered, the winner coming from the Maffei works in Munich. When Robert received the report from Swinburne, he had congratulated him on finding a better line than the local engineers, adding: 'I have often been astonished at the ignorance of some of the Continental Engineers in appreciating the features of a country'. Yet the Semmering was an indication that the days when British engineers could claim a near monopoly on railway expertise had come to an end. The continental engineers had done what Robert Stephenson had considered impossible: conquered the mountains with a railway worked by steam locomotives.

Following the developments in Norway, Denmark also began a period of further railway expansion. Once again, British interests were to the fore in proposing developments. This time it was Peto who took the lead, as he already had a financial interest in developing Lowestoft as a port with communications by steamer with Denmark. Peto's associates in the Norwegian line were once again prepared to put up some of the capital, so in 1851 Stephenson and Biddle set off for Copenhagen with Peto to discuss the issues with the Danish government. A proposal was put forward for an extension of the existing line from Copenhagen to Roskilde to the west coast of Zetland, and also to revive an earlier plan for a line from the west coast of Schleswig Holstein to the Baltic, in what would become known rather grandly as King Frederick VII's South Schleswig Railway. Beyond overseeing the planning, most of the work on the line was carried out under Bidder's control.

After Norway and Denmark, Sweden was next on the Stephenson list as he was asked to investigate the possibilities of building a major network. This time the man given the job of surveying the possible routes was William Lloyd, who had joined the Stephenson Company in 1848 after having had considerable experience as an assistant engineer in France. He was despatched to Sweden with the simplest instructions from Bidder: 'Don't go and make a fool of yourself'. He did not. His journeying began comfortably enough with a trip up the canal from Götenberg to Lake Vänern, which he crossed by steamer, but after that life became a great deal less comfortable. He travelled to Orebro in a vehicle that he described as an 'oblong box mounted without springs on four wheels'. The driver 'fortified with a good pint of fiery spirits' then set off, charging at high speed along rutted forest tracks; Stephenson's young assistants had to be made of stern stuff. For the main

The railway zigzagging up the steep escarpment of India's Western Ghats: the train seems almost like a model in this imposing landscape.

survey Lloyd had the assistance of a translator and thirty military engineers 'all of whom, with one exception, were either Barons or Counts'. Altogether Lloyd surveyed the land for some 700 miles of railway, the first section of which was opened in 1856.

Robert Stephenson's interests spread out beyond Europe. In the middle of the nineteenth century, large parts of India were in effect controlled by the East India Company, an organisation so large that its private army was actually bigger than the British army and the trade between the sub-continent and Britain was highly lucrative. Before the opening of the Suez Canal, this trade was mostly carried by ships making the long voyage round the tip of Africa, or trans-shipping between vessels in the Mediterranean and the Red Sea. The P & O Steamship Company transferred goods between these two points using some 3,000 camels, and passengers were carried over the rough roads in carriages It was obvious, however, that connections could be improved by building railways in Egypt and India. An obvious first step would have been a communication between Alexandria and Suez: Stephenson visited Egypt with other European engineers to consider the idea in 1848. But nothing was done at this time. In 1850 he was back in Egypt, and this time the viceroy suggested that he should consider the construction of a railway to connect Cairo with Alexandria. Robert was enthusiastic about the idea and fascinated by the country.

> The journey has been full of interests in many respects: in the first place the country and people offered an entirely new aspect of human society to me, in the second the natural scenery was totally different from anything I have seen in my extensive wanderings over the face of the globe, and in the third it is a district in which Engineering works are likely to form a conspicuous and an important feature in connection with our intercourse with India.
>
> The Viceroy has intimated his wish that I should undertake the construction of a Railway from Alexandria to Cairo, which I regard as an important instalment of the entire communication between the Mediterranean and Red Sea.'

He was, in fact, still thinking of an extension of this line down to Suez, the need for which was important for the British, but not necessarily so useful to the Egyptians. Michael Bothwick was the member of the team who this time was sent to survey the best route and prepare plans. The obvious route was straight down the Nile Valley, but the viceroy indicated that he wanted the line to reach Tanta in the heart of the Nile Delta. This involved crossing several waterways with substantial bridges across the Nile and over the Karrineen Canal. Robert decided to use the tubular form, already tested on the Holyhead route, though the bridges over navigable waterways had to be supplied with a swinging central section to allow boats through. The main Nile bridge proved the more difficult, and for a time passengers were ferried across the river. At first, this was by a conventional boat, but this was later replaced by a chain ferry, with rails on the deck to carry the trains.

In general, the work went ahead rapidly, largely due to the availability of a huge work force that numbered around 24,000. Most of the line had to be on embankments, to keep the tracks clear of the annual inundation of the Nile.

Robert had no doubt hoped that his company would also be required to complete the proposed route down to Suez, but the job went instead to M. Mouchelet. When Robert revisited Egypt in 1858, he also went to see work on the Suez line, which he described as 'a huge engineering blunder'. The station at Alexandria was designed by Edwin C. Barnes and was described in the *Illustrated London News* as 'the most substantially constructed edifice in the city, partaking more of a European or Anglican character than most civil structures in Alexandria'. The Cairo station was grander and rather less 'Anglican'. The Suez line was actually completed by 1858, but the opening of the Suez Canal made it largely redundant. Robert Stephenson had the last word after all: his Cairo to Alexandria line prospered, while the other withered and died.

India was rather slow in joining the railway world. Ambitious plans were put forward in the 1840s for two major rail networks: The Indian Peninsular Railway and the Madras Railway and, more or less inevitably, Robert Stephenson was called in to act as consultant. He gave his report in 1847 but there was still the economic recession that had hampered railway construction in Europe and it was not until the start of the 1850s that the ideas were resurrected, first for the Peninsular Railway. Investors could only be persuaded to put money into the scheme when the East India Company offered a guarantee of a decent return: the first offer of 3 per cent produced no response, but an increase to 5 per cent succeeded. It was to be a modest beginning, just 30 miles from Bombay (Mumbai) to Kalyan. At Robert Stephenson's suggestion, James Berkley was appointed as engineer, though Robert himself remained as consultant engineer. The first section as far as Thana was opened in April 1853.

Constructing the Victoria Bridge across the St Lawrence River at Montreal.

The real objective of the planners was to connect Bombay with the interior, but they faced a formidable obstacle. The central plateau stands around 2,500ft above the narrow coastal plain and falls away towards the coast as a steep escarpment – the Western Ghats. They represented the most formidable obstacles, but Berkley had planned to overcome them and his audacious ideas received overwhelming support from Stephenson.

The question of the ascent of the Ghats, is one of considerable difficulty, and demanding much knowledge, skill, and consideration Excellent designs of them have, however, been compared by Mr. Berkley and the explanations he has afforded me are so minute and interesting, that I assure you I should feel proud of being the author of the plans he has proposed.

Berkley's scheme took the line up the Thal and Bhore Ghats, with inclines at fierce gradients of between 1 in 48 and 1 in 37 over great lengths – the Bhore incline was 15 miles long. Both involved the construction of tunnels, bridges and massive embankments. The most distinctive feature was the zigzag route up the cliffs, that involved reversing stations, so that trains could creep up the face of the cliff, enter the reverser, then leave for the next slope travelling in the opposite direction. Even today, a century and a half later, the railway up the Ghats seems totally remarkable. It was built at a terrible cost of human life: at the peak of construction there were some 40,000 Indian labourers at work and conditions were so bad that almost a third of them died from diseases. Even the English contractors were not immune: Simon Tredwell arrived in India on 15 September 1855 and within two weeks he had died of fever. His wife Alice simply took over the contract and saw it through to completion.

Canada was also slow to join the railway world. The first line was to run from Ottawa to the American border at Prescott. The planning was obviously far from perfect. Rails were ordered from South Wales, but when they arrived on site there were not enough of them and no money to buy more, so the track was finished off using wooden rails with iron strapped to the top. There was a lonely outpost in Nova Scotia where Peter Crera created a short line and ordered a locomotive from Timothy Hackworth's Shildon works. By 1850, Canada still only had a paltry 68 miles of railway. That was about to change. In 1852, Robert Stephenson was approached by a consortium planning a much more extensive network centred on Montreal and stretching out to Portland, Maine, Quebec and Lake Huron. By far the greatest engineering problem was the crossing of the St Lawrence River at Montreal, which would require a bridge over 6,500ft long.

A Canadian, John Young, approached Alexander McKenzie Ross, who had worked with Stephenson at Conway, and asked him to come up with a proposal for bridging the river. He drew up plans for a tubular bridge then travelled to England in 1852 to discuss them with Stephenson, who not only approved them in principle but was sufficiently interested in the project to make the trip to Montreal to observe the site for himself. He approved everything he saw and recommended Ross's plans. The bridge was to be the largest of all the tubular bridges, to be built in twenty-five sections resting on twenty piers and standing 60ft above the high-water mark. The total length was 6,512ft and the approaches were via embankments faced with stone. Huge forces were employed in the construction. The workforce at its height consisted of over 3,000 men, helped by 144 horses and 4 locomotives. Out on the river, six steamers worked with seventy-five barges. The actual ironwork was manufactured back in England at Birkenhead under the supervision of Robert's cousin, George Robert Stephenson. Altogether 10,309 separate pieces of iron were manufactured, each drilled with holes for riveting on site – altogether a grand total of some half a million holes. It is a tribute to the Birkenhead workers that it all fitted together perfectly in Canada.

The good news for the engineers was that the riverbed was solid rock, well capable of supporting the piers, which was just as well as these needed to be substantial. In the long Canadian winter the river freezes, but the real problems occur in spring when the thaw begins and vast chunks of ice would be hurled against the piers. The winter also took its toll on the workmen who had come from Britain, quite unprepared for the freezing conditions, where in Montreal temperatures as low as -30°C have several times been recorded. In spite of all the difficulties, the work was completed in 1859 and officially named the Victoria Bridge. It was an engineering triumph for everyone involved, not least for Robert Stephenson, who was ultimately responsible for devising this form of construction.

Robert Stephenson was nearing the end of his career, but in the course of it he had been involved in railway construction on four continents. In many cases, he had been appointed as consultant engineer, consequently on some lines he had little to do with overseeing the actual construction. But he did take his responsibilities seriously, and usually the job of chief engineer went to one of his appointees, a man who would generally have learned his profession as one of the Stephenson team. That might seem enough for any man, but it did not represent quite all Robert Stephenson's interests and professional activities.

Chapter 18

THE END OF A CAREER

Following his wife's death, Robert felt her loss deeply and no longer felt comfortable living in the house where they had been so happy. Fanny had begged him to marry again, largely because she saw how he loved children, but Robert never considered the idea. Fanny was simply irreplaceable. It may have been this experience that made him so upset at his father's marrying again so soon after the death of his second wife. He moved to Cambridge Square, Westminster, conveniently close to the office. Robert had hardly settled in before the building was damaged by fire and he lived in temporary accommodation for ten months before settling in 1847 at 35 Gloucester Square, just north of Hyde Park, where he was to live for the rest of his life. He was to spend almost as much time in his office as in his house, and his quarters there contained a good part of his art collection. Not surprisingly, many of the pictures featured engineering works, especially those with which he and his father were personally associated. But there were other works, including a typical Landseer of sheep and lambs, two dramatic seascapes, a view of the River Avon at Bristol and a statue of a naked 'Fisher boy'. The seascapes are not too surprising. During these years Robert was in constant demand and if he was not in the office he would be chased down to his home. To escape these ever more pressing demands, he acquired 'The House that has no Knocker': he commissioned a yacht. Once at sea, he was safe from unwelcome visitors.

His sailing yacht *Titania* was a fine 100 ton vessel, built at the Thames shipyard of John Scott Russell. Launched in 1850, it provided an ideal home for him while engaged in Egypt, spending the winter of 1850-51 aboard her in Alexandria. The vessel also seems to have provided him with some stimulating if not necessarily very comfortable sails. In May 1850 he was out in rough weather.

She behaved very well, bearing everything we could find to sail with – she is certainly very fast, say 11 knots or 12½ miles an hour, and as a necessary consequence rather wet. I suppose it is in navigation as it is in Mechanics you cannot have both [word missing] and speed at the same time; we must therefore not expect velocity and dryness in a vessel in a boisterous sea and beating to windward.

The first *Titania* was destroyed when a fire started in a cabin when she was laid up at Cowes. It is a mark of Robert's enthusiasm for sailing that he promptly ordered a replacement from Scott Russell that was completed in 1852. She was larger than her predecessor at 184 ton, 92ft long and 22ft beam. She was slower – and presumably drier – than her predecessor, but fitted out luxuriously with a handsome, large saloon containing a library and plentiful supplies of wine and cigars for its owner's comfort and for entertaining friends who joined him for a sail. It brought him pleasure and relief from a hectic working life that never seemed to slacken its pace.

Robert Stephenson's reputation rests solidly on his work as a railway engineer, but he was also consulted on other projects that might seem to have little to do with his main interests. In particular, he was called on as a consultant for a number of dock development schemes. Looked at more closely, however, one soon finds that most of these schemes were being promoted by railway companies. Improved docks meant more trade for the port, and more trade meant more goods being moved in and out by rail. One scheme in which he took an early interest, working with Brunel, was the Bute dock development in Cardiff, promoted by the Taff Vale Railway. His role in this was marginal, but he took a more active role in Hull. Here three railway companies promoted the plans, including the Hull & Selby Railway that opened in 1840. Shortly afterwards, Robert produced his report and came down firmly in favour of a new dock being constructed on the 'west foreshore'. He saw the development as bringing a huge increase in trade along the Humber. It was eventually named the Victoria Dock.

Robert's next involvement was at Sunderland, where the main promoter of the scheme was the Railway King himself, George Hudson. Robert was appointed with John Murray as engineers to prepare the plans for the Act of Parliament. Once that was passed, he took no further part, and was rather critical of the way in which the work had been planned and executed. He was to go on to provide similar reports as a consultant engineer on other important schemes at Grimsby and Birkenhead. This was work that was at least tied in with the world of railways with which he was so familiar, but it is a little surprising to find him called in to offer opinion on matters of water supply. He was actually called on by a number of concerns. Including two schemes for London, neither of which was ever realised.

The advantage of the springs in the chalk around Watford had looked promising, and the idea was to sink a number of boreholes and pump up the pure water. One well sunk as a test was estimated to supply a million gallons a day. Robert was satisfied with the result, but an anonymous pamphlet

The Crystal Palace in Hyde Park: Robert Stephenson was on the committee formed to select a design.

decried it and pointed out, not unreasonably, that this was not an area where Robert had either experience or expertise. However, Robert went on to offer advice to major cities, who were faced with the same problem of coping with a rapidly increasing population. At Liverpool he was asked to give his opinion on different options, but came across a serious problem – infiltration of salt water. He reported the facts and added a disclaimer.

> I shall not, I am sure, be expected to pronounce an opinion on the effects that may be produced upon the human frame, by the presence of salts held in chemical solution by the water obtained from the public wells and employed by the inhabitants of Liverpool for all domestic purposes.

He also looked at schemes in Manchester and Glasgow. For the former the answer was to be found by building reservoirs in the hills. This was never a part of his main business, but it all took time and he undertook each report with his usual thoroughness. In spite of the huge workload, he still found time for other activities. Yet in 1847 he accepted an invitation from George Hudson to stand as Conservative candidate for Whitby. Being chosen for that party was virtually a guarantee of being elected, and so deeply Conservative was the town that the Liberals did not even field a candidate. Robert was duly elected and took his seat on the opposition benches.

It is difficult to understand why he accepted the offer. His home was in London, and in his speech to the electorate he more or less admitted that he might not be the ideal person to represent a port: 'I confess I am ignorant of maritime affairs'. He was, in fact, far from the ideal man for the job and seems to have spent very little time visiting his constituency and promoting its interests. He was, however, an active Parliamentarian and his various comments show him to have been a conservative as well as a Conservative. For example, he took a dim view of the Liberal plans for the education of the working classes. Robert argued that artisans needed to be taught exactly what they needed for their trade and nothing more. There were murmurs of dissatisfaction in Whitby and the previously unheard of event came about in the 1852 election: the Hon Edmund Phipps stood for the Liberals. He did not have an easy time of it. When he began his campaign and tried to book rooms for meetings, he found they had all been taken by the Conservatives, so was forced to hold open-air meetings. His argument was simple. Robert Stephenson was too busy with his engineering concerns to take a proper interest in the needs of Whitby and its citizens. This seems to be all too true, but it made no difference: Whitby was not going to change its allegiances, no matter what the shortcomings of their MP.

There was one piece of Parliamentary business in which Robert took a keen interest and played an active role. The story begins with another of Robert's new interests. In April 1842 he was elected to the Society of Arts. It might seem odd, given that Robert had never shown very great interest in the arts – even his paintings mostly had engineering subjects. But when the Society was founded in 1754 its full title was The Society for the Encouragement of Arts, Manufacture and Commerce. By 1847, he had been elected to the Committee of Mechanics and the following year he became one of the society's vice presidents. Unlike his role as Member of Parliament, he was an enthusiastic participant in a number of meetings. The Society was then an important forum for new ideas in science and manufacture, and it was to be the originator of one of the great, defining events of the nineteenth century.

In 1844, the French mounted an Exhibition of Manufacture in a specially designed building in the Champs Elysée in Paris. Britain at the time was the leading industrial nation in the world and for many people it was time to make a grand show of the country's achievements. That year, Francis Whishaw secretary of the society proposed that they should organise an exhibition that would be as grand as the French and preferably grander. A special committee was set up and Robert attended the first meeting, offering a personal loan of £1,000 to help get the process started. This was a great deal of money, roughly £60,000 at today's prices. Things did not go entirely smoothly and, as so often with large committees, differences of opinion emerged, as a result of which John Farey resigned from the executive committee and was replaced by Robert Stephenson. In the event it was of little consequence as a royal enthusiast began to make his presence felt. Prince Albert was always anxious to be something more than just the queen's consort and wanted to take a major role in promoting the country's industry. Thanks to his intervention, the whole project was taken from the Society of Arts and handed over to the government. And, of course, one member of the society's committee also happened to be an MP. Robert Stephenson continued to be involved in what was to become the Great Exhibition of 1851.

Robert was at once involved in the Parliamentary Commission, and though everything did not go smoothly at first, he was eventually appointed to the committee charged with finding an appropriate design. For the exhibition hall they came up first with a design by Brunel, which was a vast brick building, topped by a huge dome at one end. Once it was made public, there was, not surprisingly, a public outcry against this monstrous edifice. Edward Stanley Ellis was both an MP and chairman of the Midland Railway. One of the shareholders in that company was Joseph Paxton, who came to see Ellis in the Commons to discuss a new ventilation system he had devised. During lunch, Ellis suggested that Paxton might think about a design for the exhibition hall, at which point he sketched out a rough idea, based on his experiences with building huge glass houses. That sketch on a napkin was the basis for the Crystal Palace.

Ellis was impressed by the idea, and Paxton now approached Robert Stephenson to get his opinion of the practicality of a huge building consisting of glass panes held in an elaborate wrought-iron frame. Robert would, of course, have known Paxton through his friendship with his father, and would probably have visited the great glasshouse at Chatsworth. He became an immediate enthusiastic supporter of this revolutionary design. It was, as we know, adopted and erected in Hyde Park, where it attracted huge crowds when it opened in 1851. Among the most spectacular exhibits were the

Robert Stephenson, seated, and Brunel standing at the launch of the *Great Eastern*.

locomotives, particularly the *Lord of the Isles* doing the honours for the Great Western and the broad gauge. Even more impressive was the *Crampton*. This most unusual engine was notable for its immense driving wheels set at the rear of the engine – and it was built by Robert Stephenson and Co. Robert had every reason to be pleased with his work on the exhibition. But his pleasure was tempered by his deteriorating health. Never having had a very strong constitution, his years of incessant work were taking their toll. In spite of these problems, he accepted the position of president of the Institution of Civil Engineers in 1856. He clearly did not share his father's view of that body.

The Birmingham Society would eventually relocate to London to become the Institution of Mechanical Engineers,

Robert's one relief was, as always, to get away on *Titania*. In autumn 1857, he set off for a voyage round the British coast with friends including Bidder. He called in at many places he had known in earlier days, including the collieries and homes of his youth. A story has it that the strains of the years had so changed him that at first he went unrecognised, but when one old friend exclaimed that he was Robert Stephenson, he got the sad reply – 'all that's left of him'. He went on to Holyhead and revisited his great bridge across the Menai Straits, giving his guests a lively account of the problems involved in getting the giant tubes raised into place.

Brunel was at work on his last two great enterprises in the 1850s: the bridge over the Tamar that would take the Great Western into Cornwall and his ship the *Great Eastern*. This was an immense vessel, 692ft long, powered by paddles, screw propeller and sail. She was being built at John Scott Russell's yard on the Thames at Millwall, where Robert's yachts had been built. Getting a vessel of such unprecedented size into the river created immense problems, as the river was only wide enough to allow her to be launched sideways. Brunel who, like Robert, was feeling the strains of overwork and ill health, called on his old friend to come down to the launch site to offer support and advice. Robert, who had appreciated the same help with his own difficult task of creating the tubular bridges, responded at once. On a cold, wintry day at the end of 1857 he made an early morning visit to the site. Unfortunately, he caught his foot on a baulk of timber and found himself up to his waist in the muddy waters of the Thames. In spite of being urged to go home and change into dry clothes, he insisted on staying to help his old friend. After many problems had been overcome, the great ship was finally launched at the end of January 1858.

By the end of 1858, both Stephenson and Brunel were suffering from ill health. Robert decided to escape an English winter by taking *Titania* to Cairo. He was later joined by Brunel, and they dined together on Christmas Day. It was to be their last meeting. Both men had benefited from their stay in the sun, but it was only a temporary improvement. Brunel had been diagnosed with Bright's disease, a chronic kidney complaint, for which nineteenth century medicine recommended hot baths and bloodletting: today known as a form of nephritis the kidney complaint can be treated with antibiotics. Brunel was not lucky enough to have such treatment available. Unhappily, Robert was found to have the same condition.

Robert had been invited to Norway for the opening of the line from Christiania. He set off in his yacht accompanied by Bidder in his own yacht *Mayfly*, arriving in Norway in August 1859. It was a grand occasion and he was honoured with the award of the Order of St Olaf, which he wore to a banquet in his honour. It should have been a happy occasion, but Robert became ill during the speechmaking and toasts. He retired to his cabin, but was clearly in such a serious condition that it was decided to return at once to England, and it was arranged for a doctor to be on board for the voyage. They landed on the Suffolk coast on 13 September but had to spend an extra night at sea and could only tie up in Lowestoft harbour the following morning. The party hurried back to London, and only then heard the devastating news that Brunel had had a stroke and died aboard the *Great Eastern* the day they set sail from Norway. It seems that the effect on Robert was immediate. His friend was just 53, three years younger than Robert himself, had shared similar dreams and achieved many of them. Robert appeared simply to accept that his time too had come. He died 12 October 1859.

Robert Stephenson was revered at the time as the greatest engineer of the day, his reputation even higher than Brunel's. He was to be given the honour that had been given to Thomas Telford, his predecessor as president of the Institution of Civil Engineers: he was to be buried in Westminster Abbey. There was a huge funeral procession led by 1,500 employees from the Newcastle works through the crowded streets, and on the great rivers of England, ships flew their flags at half-mast. All the great names of British engineering were there to pay homage and it was a mark of the reconciliation that had taken place between two men who had been such close friends in youth, that Joseph Locke was one of the pall bearers. It was a great occasion befitting a great man.

Chapter 19

ASSESSMENT

George Stephenson has become known as 'The Father of Railways', which is not unreasonable, but Robert has never had any similar popular name. How much did each contribute to developing railways, not just in Britain but across the world? The first thing to be quite clear about is that neither invented the steam locomotive, but that does not mean that their role in development was not absolutely crucial.

George Stephenson is a complex character to analyse. His virtues are obvious. He was a man of great determination, integrity and bravery. Only the most determined could have started from such a background and risen to such eminence, entirely through his own efforts. He lacked even the most fundamental education, yet showed himself capable of quick understanding of complex problems. His honesty was never seriously questioned – though his judgement sometimes was. His bravery was first demonstrated when he insisted on testing his own design of a safety lamp in circumstances in which, had it failed, we would never have heard of him again. But this self-belief and awareness that he had only himself to thank for any success he gained also created the other side of his character. He mistrusted so-called experts, who were often theorists, well educated – and probably based in London. He had some justification. Sir Humphry Davy was clearly quite wrong to charge him with plagiarism over the safety lamp. On the other hand, when he received a humiliating cross-examination when giving evidence for the Liverpool & Manchester Bill, the criticism he received was quite fair, though that would not have made it any more palatable. But these experiences coloured his judgement and it is hard not to believe that his prejudices led him to deal unfairly with Vignoles, for example – though it is hard to see these two very different characters ever getting on and working well together.

So what was it that brought George Stephenson lasting fame and where did he fall short of perfection? His reputation does not depend on having made any great advances in locomotive design, indeed he scarcely improved on the work of his predecessors and contemporaries. But he alone kept faith with the whole idea that the age of the steam locomotive had arrived and that the future lay with railways as major transport routes. His advocacy of steam for the Stockton & Darlington was a turning point. No line of such a length had been worked by locomotives before and it was unlike other colliery lines in that it carried passengers, even if they only had horses to pull them along not engines. It was a foretaste of things to come. It was George Stephenson's passionate advocacy for using locomotives on the line that impressed the promoters and by the time the idea had been approved he was the one and only manufacturer of locomotives.

He was not, of course, the only advocate for railways – William James was equally enthusiastic, but George was the only one to carry schemes through to completion. It was this dogged persistence, often in the face of fierce opposition, that enabled him to see to completion both the first public railway to use locomotives and the first inter-city line that has won him a well-deserved place in history. He was also a man who was prepared to embrace the new, even when it was against his personal interest, as for example, when he advocated the new, rolled rails instead of the cast-iron system in which he had a financial interest. That is the mark of an honest man. But no one is without flaws, and his organisational skills were too often called into question, which resulted in work being parcelled out to others, who were not necessarily up to the job. The single-mindedness that was his greatest strength also tended to make him resentful of criticism and distrustful of 'experts'. But when it comes to advancing into the unknown, experts are often of little use, relying on precedents. George went his own way and in the final analysis achieved his goals. He was indeed the father of the rail system that now covers the world. But if that system was to grow and flourish, then progress had to be made in many directions. That was to be the work of the next generation.

Robert Stephenson was very different from his father, in almost every respect. Where, as a young man, George was strong and healthy with a reputation for throwing a hammer a long distance – Robert was always considered quite a delicate child. George never had any form of formal education, while Robert was able not only to attend school, but also to spend a short time at university. George never felt comfortable with 'London experts' and retained his strong North Country accent all his life. Robert had no such problems and lost his own accent at quite a young age. Where George often seemed to act impulsively and in a slightly haphazard fashion, Robert was far more methodical. They did, however, share some crucial characteristics: both were totally dedicated to developing railways and both had the personal drive and capacity for hard work to turn ideas into reality.

Both father and son tackled engineering problems that were so daunting that few thought they could be surmounted. For George the crossing of Chat Moss was probably his greatest challenge, while for Robert it was bridging the Menai Straits. Both triumphed as they did with many slightly lesser difficulties. Judged purely in terms of civil engineering, both were true pioneers, but Robert had the advantage of precedents set by his father, while George was breaking new ground. The greatest difference comes when one looks at mechanical engineering. Here Robert surpassed his father. In designing *Rocket* for the Rainhill Trials he transformed the locomotive from a slow, lumbering machine suitable only for moving coal from colliery to port, to a machine that was more powerful and far faster than any of its predecessors. For the railways to succeed as a transport system for both people and goods, it needed to have just this sort of machine. More importantly, *Rocket* had all the elements needed for future development, with the multi-tube boiler, exhaust blast pipe and cylinders no longer set vertically beside the boiler. And Stephenson would go on to make still further improvements. He was responsible for the most important development in locomotive design since Trevithick first put an engine on rails.

They had one other thing in common: both could have had their careers cut short at an early stage. George's humiliating experience when giving evidence for the Liverpool & Manchester Bill was so complete that he might never have been employed again. That he was brought back was as much due to his own qualities as anything else. Other engineers, such as the Rennie family, seem not to have grasped just what a revolutionary scheme the L & MR represented, but George most certainly did. It was part of his dream of building a great rail network in Britain that would eventually cover the world. Robert's downfall could have come with the collapse of the Dee Bridge. It was perhaps a mark of the respect with which he was held that so many eminent engineers came to his defence, leaving the jury convinced that the accident was not due to any fatal design fault. We now know the jury was wrong: the design was seriously flawed and it was structural collapse not derailment that caused the tragedy. It would have been deeply unfortunate if he had been found negligent. The science of materials had scarcely been developed at that time and it seemed that the bridge had been built using sound, well-tested ideas. Hindsight is a wonderful thing.

In finally assessing the importance of the two Stephensons in the history of technology, it is perhaps necessary to look at them in terms of their contemporary, Isambard Kingdom Brunel, now generally revered as the greatest engineer of the age. Looked at logically, purely in terms of railway development, there is no real contest. Brunel is famous for the broad gauge Great Western Railway. Ignoring for now any discussion of whether it was advisable to introduce a second gauge to the developing system, how successful was it in practice? Brunel, as always, went his own way designing a permanent way quite unlike any other, with longitudinal sleepers and the whole tied into a rigid grid. Experience has shown that it was, in fact, far too rigid and was never widely adopted. There is, of course, the other question: would a broad gauge system have given us all a better service down the years? That we can only conjecture, but it is to Brunel's credit that he at least thought about which system would be best for a national network, rather than arbitrarily accepting the gauge used on a humble colliery line. Undoubtedly, the GWR had some great engineering features that matched anything produced by the Stephenson's: Box tunnel and the Maidenhead and Tamar bridges, but civil engineering is only part of the story. When we look at mechanical engineering, Brunel's original ideas for locomotives proved so inferior that he had to turn to the Robert Stephenson works in Newcastle for engines to work the line, until he acquired an engineering genius of his own in the shape of Daniel Gooch. And the less said about the atmospheric railway the better. But Brunel is not only judged on his work on railways. He famously offered to extend his transport system from Bristol to New York: he designed ships. If *Rocket* is seen as the forerunner of generations of steam locomotives, then the SS *Great Britain* can claim a similar place in maritime history, with its size, its iron hull and a screw propeller powered by steam. Robert Stephenson and Isambard Brunel were both friends and rivals and though the Stephenson contribution to railways was the greater, when it comes to overall impact on the world of transport as a whole, they can happily share equal status in the engineering pantheon.

There is no need to try and distinguish between George and Robert Stephenson's status. It is sufficient to say that both were giants in their field whose names will always be revered whenever the history of railways is discussed.

SELECT BIBLIOGRAPHY

Anon, *A Chapter in the History of Railway Locomotives and a Memoir of Timothy Hackworth* 1875

Anon, *The Two James and the Two Stephensons* 1861

Bailey, Michael R., *Loco Motion: The World's Oldest Steam Engines* 2014

Bailey, Michael R., (ed) *Robert Stephenson, the Eminent Engineer* 2003

Booth, Henry. *An Account of the Liverpool and Manchester Railway* 1828

Burton, Anthony, *The Rainhill Story* 1980

Burton, Anthony, *Joseph Locke* 2017

Church, William Conant, *The Life of John Ericsson* 1890

Condor, F.R., *Personal Recollections of English Engineers* 1868

Francis, John, *History of the English Railway* 1852

Pease, Sir Alfred, *The Diaries of Edward Pease* 1907

Rolt, L.T.C., *George and Robert Stephenson*, 1960

Roscoe, Thomas, *The London and Birmingham Railway* 1855

Skeat, W.O., *George Stephenson, the Engineer and his Letters 1973*

Smiles, Samuel, *The Life of George Stephenson* 1857

Smiles, Samuel, *The Lives of George and Robert Stephenson* 1874

Stephenson, Robert Louis, *Records of a Family of Engineers* 1912

Summerside, T, *Anecdotes and Reminiscences and Conversations of and with the late George Stephenson*1878

Vignoles, Olinthus J., *Life of Charles Blacker Vignoles* 1889

Warren, J, G. H., *A Century of Locomotive Building by Robert Stephenson and Co,* 1923

Wood, Nicholas, *A Practical Treatise on Rail-Roads* 1825 and 1931

Young, Robert, *Timothy Hackworth and the Locomotive* 1923 (reprinted 1975)

INDEX

Railways, other: Avignon &
Marseilles, 149; Baltimore &
Susquehanna, 144; Bayerische
Ludwigbahn, 148-9;
Birmingham & Derby Junction,
156-7; Bolton & Leigh, 76;
Brussels & Ghent, 148; Camden &
Amboy, 147; Canadian, 205-6;
Canterbury & Whitstable, 60,
77-8; Chester & Holyhead, 181-92;
Danish, 200-1; Delaware &
Hudson, 146-7; Dublin &
Kingstown, 155; Durham
Junction, 162; Egyptian, 202-3;
Grand Junction, 120-3, 138, 169;
Great North of England, 163-4;
Great Western, 152-5, 169-72, 218;
Hartlepool, 162; Hull & Selby,
144, 208; Indian Peninsula,
203-5; Kenyon & Leigh, 120;
Leicester & Swannington, 116-7;
London, Brighton & South Coast,
136-7; London & Croydon, 155;
Madras, 203; Manchester &
Bolton, 66; Manchester &
Leeds, 124-6; Manchester &
Stockport, 87; Midland Counties,
156-7; Newcastle & Berwick, 123,
194-6; Newcastle & Carlisle, 126;
New Orleans, 153; Northern &
Eastern, 184; North Midland,
124, 156; North Yorkshire
Moors, 118; Norwegian, 198-200;
Orleans & Tour, 173; Pontop &
South Shields, 162; Preston &
Wyre; St. Etienne & Lyon, 145-6;
Sheffield & Manchester, 116;
Sheffield & Rotherham, 158;
Shrewsbury & Chester, 190-2;
Stanhope & Tyne, 159-63;
Stratford & Moreton, 81, 85;
Swedish, 201-2; Taff Vale, 208;
Tsarokoe Selo & St. Petersburg,
150-1; Warrington & Newton,
116, 121; Whitby & Pickering, 118;
York & North Midland, 138,
159-60
Rainhill, 88-103
Rastrick, John Urpeth, 68, 88
Rainsbeck, Leonard, 38
Redcar, 172
Rennie, John, 67-8, 120
Rennie, Sir John, 38
Rennie, George, 67-8
Richardson, Thomas, 51
Robertson, Andrew, 10-11
Ross, Alexander McKenzie, 205
Royal Mint, 69

St. Lawrence bridge, 215-6
Sandar, Joseph, 59, 117
Sankey viaduct, 78-9
Santa Ana mines, 71-3
Satow, Mike, 54, 102
Seguin, Marc, 145
Semming trial, 200
Shildon, 102
Shrewsbury, 168-9
Smeaton, John, 18
Smiles, Samuel, 8
Smith, Lt. Col. J. M. F., 170-1
Society of Arts, 210-1
Stephenson, Eleanor, 17
Stephenson, Ellen, 179-80
Stephenson, Elizabeth, 25, 71
Stephenson, Frances, 13-15